W9-CEL-804

# Country Inn Cooking
## with GAIL GRECO

For you,
Mom,
The artist
& the angel
on my
Shoulder.

A. G.

# Country Inn Cooking

## with GAIL GRECO

Companion to the Public Television Series

Gail Greco

ILLUSTRATED BY *Trish Crowe*

RUTLEDGE HILL PRESS

NASHVILLE, TENNESSEE

Copyright © 1995 by Gail Greco

Companion to the Public Television series *Country Inn Cooking with Gail Greco,* a co-production of Maryland Public Television and Country Inn Partners.

All rights reserved. Written permission must be secured from the publisher to use or reproduce any part of this book, except for brief quotations in critical reviews or articles.

Published in Nashville, Tennessee, by Rutledge Hill Press, Inc., 211 Seventh Avenue North, Nashville, Tennessee 37219. Distributed in Canada by H. B. Fenn & Company, Ltd., 1090 Lorimar Drive, Mississauga, Ontario L5S 1R7. Distributed in Australia by Millennium Books, 13/3 Maddox Street, Alexandria NSW 2015. Distributed in New Zealand by Tandem Press, 2 Rugby Road, Birkenhead, Auckland 10. Distributed in the United Kingdom by Verulam Publishing, Ltd., 152a Park Street Lane, Park Street, St. Albans, Hertfordshire AL2 2AU.

Illustrated by Trish Crowe

Book design by Harriette Bateman

Typesetting by D&T/Bailey Typesetting, Inc., Nashville, TN 37203

Front and back cover photography by Tom Bagley
Photo of Gingerbread Mansion Inn by Bob von Normann
All recipes selected and edited for the home kitchen by Gail Greco
Assistant recipe editor Dottie Greco

Recipes featured on the front cover: From left, Medallions of Pork with Cider Cream and Glazed Apples from Rowell's Inn; Warm Cranberry Napoleon from Antrim 1844; White Chocolate Ravioli with Raspberry Sauce from Checkerberry Inn; Gingered Scallops with Capers and Bell Peppers from Heritage Park B&B Inn. Food preparation by Chef Sharon K. Ashburn of Antrim 1844.

Cover Photo: Gail Greco in the Smokehouse Restaurant at Antrim 1844 Inn, Taneytown, MD

**Library of Congress Cataloging-in-Publication Data**

Greco, Gail
    Country inn cooking with Gail Greco / [illustrated by Trish Crowe],
        p.   cm.
    "Companion to the Public Television Series."
    Includes index.
    ISBN 1-55853-361-3 (pbk.)
    1. Cookery   2. Bed and breakfast accommodations—United States.   I, Country inn cooking with Gail Greco (Television program)   II. Title.
TX714.G748   1995
641.5—dc20                                                                                                          95-33241
                                                                                                                              CIP

Printed in the United States of America

1 2 3 4 5 6 7 8 9 — 99 98 97 96 95

# Innteriors

# Other Books by Gail Greco

*Great Cooking with Country Inn Chefs*

*The Romance of Country Inns*

*Tea-Time at the Inn*

*Secrets of Entertaining from America's Best Innkeepers*

*A Country Inn Breakfast*

*Bridal Shower Handbook*

*World Class Cuisine Companion Books for 1993, 1994, and 1995*

# About This Book

M arvelous entertaining takes place every day at bed-and-breakfast and country inns all over America. Traditions such as
afternoon tea as well as old-fashioned methods such as cooking in an eighteenth-century hearth or over a blazing campfire live on
at the inns. And new traditions are coming to life through their trend-
setting cuisine and up-to-date entertaining ideas. You can apply these
creative touches in your own home to make for a more peaceful, pampering environment when you cannot be at the inns themselves. And
these are the ideas that have been the basis for all of the books I have
written about these wonderful little hostelries.

My motivation has been to try to make dreams come true. So
many times, I hear guests moan longingly about how much they
would like to live in the inn environment. You can if you take home
the inns' tips, their cooking, and thus their essence. It is foolish to
long for anything, especially something that is within one's grasp. Inns
nurture inventiveness and creativity. They offer us templates from
which to model great things in our environments.

*Country Inn Cooking with Gail Greco* is another attempt to remind
all of us that the romantic life does exist and is being lived out every
day all over at small inns. This time, I am offering you the companion
book to the television series that shows you in action what I have
been talking about in print all these years.

Most of the recipes in this book were either demonstrated on camera or, when time did not permit, were merely shown on camera. I
compiled the recipes categorically so that you can locate something
easily. The tagline at the end of each recipe tells you the inn of origin.
Look up the location and other information about the inn in the directory in the back. By the way, most of these places are country inns, so
they are full-service facilities that serve dinner. Some bed-and-break-
fasts have been included, so the term "country inn" is used here a bit
loosely to indicate a pervasive spirit of hospitality in an intimate environment.

*Country Inn Cooking with Gail Greco* is first a cookbook, so you
will find more than two-hundred recipes, plus lots of kitchen tips,
many of which you see me demonstrate after I learn them from the

chefs. Included in the tips are innkeepers' ideas on setting up a guest room in your own home and some tips on traveling and staying at the inns.

The culinary crafts that you see in the book are projects we show you on camera. Having these instructions in the book also will make it easier for you to remember how to make the crafts yourself.

*Inn the Cupboard* contains basic recipes that can be incorporated with other recipes.

A few quotes from innkeepers are sprinkled throughout the book to remind you every day to live the sensitive, artful life they live at country inns.

Be sure to look to the back of the book in the "Inn Directory" for a listing of the chefs who gave us these recipes and some information on the inns when you want to go for dinner or an overnight stay.

Meanwhile, may your home always be filled with the innkeeping spirit—laughter, good friends, bountiful feasts, and heirloom memories.

# Inn Appreciation

*For not only the longevity of PBS and the Corporation for Public
Broadcasting but for its enhancement. . . .*

*As I have said so many times to those country inn chefs and cooks I have
spent so much time with in the kitchen, "I'm innspired—with a double n."
And I truly am, as usual when I visit the inns. . . .*

### CHEFS, INNKEEPERS, STAFFS

So, my first thanks go to you, the chefs and innkeepers who
opened your doors, making it possible to do the series and put this
book together with fine recipes—tested time and again in your
kitchens and mine. I know my deadlines for submission were brutal
for all of you. Please extend another big thank you to all those individuals on your staff who made our stay a pleasant one and supported
our efforts with helping hands as well as caring hearts.

### DOTTIE GRECO

You are a special sister. And on a business level, once again I thank
you for your tenacity in working with me so expertly. You have that
rare devotion and indomitable spirit for your work. As you know, the
recipes can be "bears to wrestle with" when it comes to perfecting
them for the book, and you certainly handled them marvelously.

### TRICIA CONATY

I just wanted to thank you for spending your weekends volun-
teering your services to do some of the laborious administrative work
on this book, even though I know you would rather be writing. You,
too, are dedicated and exceptional.

### TRISH CROWE

Your illustrations brought the food at the inn and the inns themselves to life with such style and grace. Thank you for wielding your
pen and ink to reflect exactly what was in my mind and heart. And
thank you, Trish, for sharing the garden period of your life with me.

## TOM BAGLEY

Once again, your photographic style has captured warmth and character in another one of my books. The covers of this book would have been missing something without your impressive touch. And Tom, thank you for the expert way you supported the TV show in preproduction—lining up the inns and spearheading early publicity. I know when you do a job, it will be done nearly flawlessly. You are the best, and as someone from DuPont once said, "You are awesome."

## LARRY STONE

As always, Rutledge Hill Press was there to work *with* me, not for me or against me. The team spirit that you have fostered as publisher, Larry, has enabled me to blossom in the way I have always hoped to. Thank you for never sitting in an ivory tower, but always being available and involved.

## THE TELEVISION CREW

The TV crew made my job on camera so free of stress that I could devote the time I needed to write. So, I'll conclude my appreciation with them:

## JOHN POTTHAST

In your role as executive producer for Maryland Public Television, you have been like a rock. From coming up with ideas to cheering and supporting all of mine, you enhanced *Country Inn Cooking* as no one else could have. Your attitude was remarkable—always willing to listen to other possibilities, lend a hand, and offer good humor. Your laugh is intoxicating. The way you worked with us on the road and especially the intensity and interest you employed in postproduction gave a new meaning to the words *professional* and *friend*. I can't say enough thank yous to you.

## RICHARD SCHREIER

Thank you, Richard, for your role as senior producer and director. You are a genius in the kitchen, working with food and the chefs as though you are a real *cuisinière*. (After all these inn kitchens and the others throughout the world, where you have directed, you should be given an honorary culinary degree!) It's not hard to see how your sensitivity, passion, and focus make you the success you are.

### PRODUCTION AND POSTPRODUCTION

A big thank you to Coordinating Producer Joe Martin; Editor Nichole Lewis; Post-Production Producer Melissa Forster Martin; and Publicist Dorothy Fuchs. Thank you to cameramen Mike Zeitzmann and especially Tony Cunningham, and other crew members especially, sound engineer John Woods (Woody) and a real professional and hard worker, grip Jonathan Zurer.

### ARNA VODENOS

I thank you, my co-executive producer on the television show for helping make it a reality. The illustration on page 146 is for you.

### THE SPONSORS

DuPont's No-Stick Systems cookware is the primary sponsor of *Country Inn Cooking.* I want to thank the corporation as a whole for helping to fund public broadcasting and keeping educational television alive, teaching millions of viewers. *Country Inn Cooking* is not a travel show but a how-to series meant to enhance the culinary experiences of people everywhere. In addition to the corporation, I want to thank the individuals with whom I have worked many years on past country inn chefs projects.

First, I want to thank Christa Kaiser, No-Stick Systems Worldwide Communications Manager, who has been both a dependable businesswoman and a friend with a shoulder to lean on. I value our relationship far beyond the desk.

The entire No-Stick systems team at DuPont is like a family to me. I want to thank all of you for your friendship and support, especially Jim Forte, Rosanne Miller, Deb Goodge, Kristin Finio, Chris Mohan, and Natalie Sharbaugh.

I want to thank DuPont for bringing country inn chefs together. For the first time in history, country inn chefs were recognized for their culinary contributions as a group by DuPont, who chose fifty of them nationwide to be on an ongoing cookware test panel. I am proud to be a part of that panel.

### BUDGET RENT A CAR

A big thank you to Garry Bricker for being such a wonderful human being.

# Inntroduction

## The Soul of an Inn and the Sensations of the Table

I am repeatedly asked, "Gail, what is your favorite inn?" The question comes with a dreamy expression painted on the face of the questioner, already anticipating what my answer will be, preparing to go there—if not in person, at least with me vicariously. The query is accompanied by a look of expectation as though my reply will have the impact of telling someone where to find the fountain of youth. My answer, however, although enjoyed by the questioning party, turns out to be very different from what was expected.

"Inns are like snowflakes," I respond metaphorically. "Each is created individually with its own personality, style, and atmosphere. So, a favorite inn? Well . . ."

I choose an inn depending on the mood I am in and what I want to get out of the visit. Sometimes I just want a place where I can leave my silks and chiffons at home and take only my jeans and flannel shirts. It doesn't matter how many diamonds or stars glitter there on a sign or how many plaques hang on its walls. (However, my criteria often bring me to the front door of a much-heralded facility, because those with awards usually espouse the philosophies that make for a good inn.) I tend to choose an inn based on the dedication of the people who own or run the inn. Oh, and one more thing—perhaps the most important of all—I choose an inn based on the food it serves.

In fact, the sensations of the table are one of the primary attractions of inns, for we are all beginning to recognize that the cooking at small inns is special and alluring. Country inn cooking is coming into its own and finally being recognized as a style that imparts the best products a region has to offer, combined with the freshest ingredients in an environment that stimulates passion, peace, and simple pleasures. Even bed-and-breakfast inns that only serve the morning meal always offer a sensual experience, leaving the taste buds longing in memory. To me, this is what eating is all about.

At Le Manoir aux Quat' Saisons, a country house hotel I visited in Oxford, England, in 1994, the chef has defined his style of dining this way. "The table is a very strong symbol of togetherness, friendship, of the celebration of life, and of course, sensuality," says chef and owner Raymond Blanc. Food is cooked at small inns with this same romance and attention to detail. "Truly, whether it is gourmet or simpler foods, it is cooked with the tender loving care we have always given it at home," describes Chef Yvonne Martin of White Oak Inn in Ohio.

Country inn chefs are not confined in their culinary pursuits but are allowed to be artists, dictating the inn's menus, often based on what is growing in the garden or swimming in a nearby stream. An inn's culinary hallmark is almost always founded on its regional food basket. The result of all this personal foraging is a table set with love—pure and simple.

Eating at a small country inn or country home here or abroad is a pampering experience. I have seen something as simple as fruit or homemade breads and cookies in my room upon arrival, welcoming me with elegance and certainly good taste. I have walked into my guest room and there on the dresser found a set of crystal glasses with a small box of chocolates and a fresh red rose on top of a lace doily or a pot of hot tea wrapped in a quilted cozy beside freshly baked scones and inn-made preserves.

At dinner, I have sampled hearty soups, freshly caught trout, and hickory-smoked pork chops, even a vegetable stew cooked in an antique caldron over an open fire. I have dined in rooms lit by the reflection of elegant gilded tapers and enjoyed the finest ingredients served on resplendent golden chargers crowned with the likes of roasted pheasant or grilled duck with plum sauce or angel hair pasta threaded with sun-drenched tomatoes and a tabletop shake of freshly snipped oregano from an antique crystal muffinière.

At breakfast I have witnessed the first meal of the day turn into a celebration with hand-kneaded breads, coffeecakes, unusual egg casseroles, waffles, and fruit soups. And again, all are served with an air of royalty and the guests are the courted recipients. Inns have reminded me of the genteel charms of taking tea served with tassies of nut-filled chocolate, creamy pastries, fruity tarts, buttery cookies, and dainty savories.

From inns where donning ski pants and a tunic in a casual setting is appropriate to inns where a black tie in a more luxurious setting is preferred, there is no one that stands out to me as a favorite, because they are all so different and must be taken on their own individual merit and character. The beauty of an inn is in the eye and spirit of the visiting beholder. No one can decide for someone else which is the best inn. For me, I seek food served with high quality, fresh ingredients and interesting, inventive cuisine—down-home or gourmet. The setting is only dictated by my plans.

So, the question to me should be, "Gail, what are some inns you have really enjoyed and why?" You will find the answer in the pages that follow. The wonderful country inn mix is all here—the glorious breakfasts, the sumptuous dinners, the ranch styles, the tasty teas, and even the historic fireside fare. I cannot live without any of them— from the primitive to the luxurious.

In my ongoing quest to bring the soul of the inns home to you, as I have done for more than a dozen years, this book is particularly special to me because I have been able to show you—almost in person— how to do it, through the magic of television.

I learned a great deal by working once again with the chefs in the kitchen while actually cooking with them on TV. I'm sure you have seen me trying to master the dough-making behind the sweetly puffed cinnamon rolls served at Canyon Villa or perfecting the technique of torching a crème brulée. You have seen me at times *all thumbs* and at other times passing with flying colors while shaping pasta or creating edible objects out of fruit. The point is that I did it and so can you now that you have the cookbook that reflects the Public Television series. I hope this book helps you have as much fun as I have had and that you remember to get out to the inns and treat yourself as well.

My hope is that you embrace the nature of country inn cooking at home—cooking with passion and pleasure and serving it up with romance and good taste. I think we all would agree when all is said and done, if there is an answer to the question, "What is your favorite place?" it has to be your home, where the country inn spirit is alive every day.

# Country Inn Cooking
### *with* GAIL GRECO

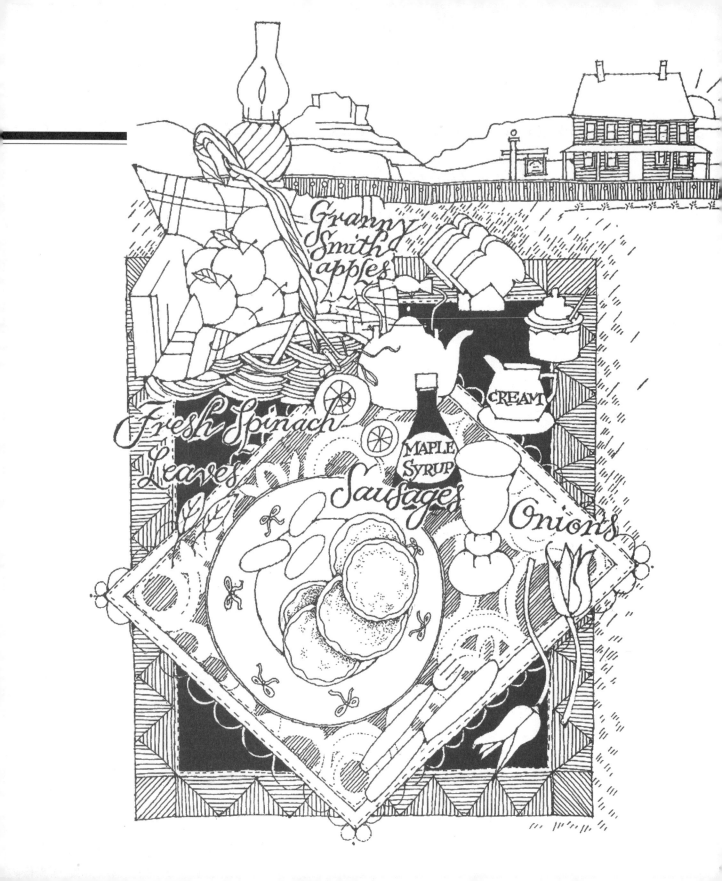

# BREAKFAST

## Chalet Suzanne's Famous Cinnamon Grapefruit

*The chalet has been serving this grapefruit with cinnamon and chicken livers for so long that it has become a trademark of the inn.*

1 white or pink grapefruit
3 tablespoons butter
1 teaspoon sugar
¼ cup cinnamon-sugar mixture
  (1 part cinnamon to 4 parts
  sugar)

2 chicken livers, rolled in
  seasoned flour and cooked,
  optional
Fresh mint for garnish

Slice the grapefruit in half and remove the center membrane. Section the grapefruit so that the fruit is completely loosened from its shell. Fill the center of each half with 1½ tablespoons butter. Sprinkle ½ teaspoon sugar over each half, followed by 2 tablespoons of the cinnamon mixture.

Place the grapefruit halves in a shallow baking pan and broil just long enough to brown the tops and to heat to just bubbling. Watch the fruit carefully while it broils. Remove from the heat and, if desired, top with a chicken liver in the center of each grapefruit half or garnish with mint.

Yield: 2 servings

*CHALET SUZANNE*

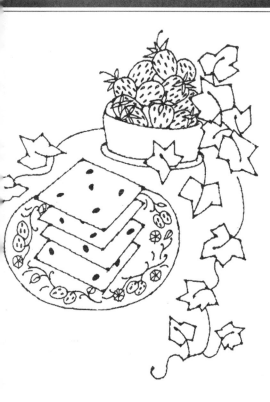

## Rise 'n Shine Fruit 'n Bread Custard

*Use raspberries, blueberries, peaches, strawberries, blackberries, or a combination of these fruits for a topping. You will be preparing a bain marie or a water bath, in which to bake the custard. During the baking process, the layers of bread will rise to the top. Be sure to cover the pan well with the bread so that the custard can form underneath and not come up through any cracks.*

⅓ cup butter, melted
12 slices raisin bread, crust
   removed
6 eggs, 2 separated (reserve
   whites for another recipe)
¾ cup sugar

1 cup whipping cream
2 cups milk
1 teaspoon vanilla extract
   Confectioners' sugar
   Fresh or frozen fruit, slightly
   sweetened

Preheat the oven to 350°. Place a 7x11-inch baking dish near your work area. With a pastry brush, spread melted butter on both sides of the bread slices. Place the bread in the baking dish (filling all cracks) in 2 layers.

In a medium bowl, beat together the 4 whole eggs and 2 egg yolks with a wire whisk. Continue to beat, gradually adding the sugar. Add the cream, milk, and vanilla. Mix well. Pour the custard over the raisin bread.

Place the baking dish in a larger pan and pour warm water into the larger pan halfway up its sides. Bake 45 minutes or until puffy and brown and a knife inserted in the center comes out clean. Dust with confectioners' sugar. Top with fruit.

Yield: 6 to 8 servings

*CANYON VILLA*

## Hawaiian Potato Bread

*This is a great bread, with a hint of sweetness, to have with a cup of macadamia nut coffee in the morning and a slathering of mango preserves or other tropical sweet spread.*

BREAD
- 5 to 6 cups all-purpose flour, divided
- 2 teaspoons salt
- 2 packages active dry yeast
- 1 cup pineapple juice
- 1½ cups water
- ¼ cup butter
- 2 eggs
- 2 cups Hungry Jack brand potato flakes

TOPPING
- ¼ cup sugar
- 3 tablespoons all-purpose flour
- ¼ teaspoon ground nutmeg
- 1 tablespoon butter

In the large bowl of an electric mixer, combine 1½ cups of the flour, the salt, and the yeast. Combine the pineapple juice, water, and butter in a saucepan, and heat until very warm. Add the liquid to the flour mixture. Add the eggs and beat for 4 minutes at medium speed. Add the potato flakes and beat until just moistened. Stir in enough of the remaining flour to make a stiff dough. Knead the dough for 10 minutes, then place it in a greased bowl. Cover and let it rise for 1 hour. Punch the dough down and divide it into 2 round loaves. Place the loaves into 2 greased 9-inch cake pans and let rise for 45 minutes. Preheat the oven to 350°. Combine the ingredients for the topping and crumble the mixture over the dough. Bake for 40 minutes or until golden brown. Remove from the pans, let cool, and serve.

Yield: 2 loaves

*SETTLERS INN*

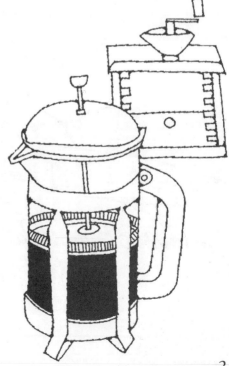

## Carrot-and-Walnut Muffins

4 eggs
¾ cup vegetable oil
1½ cups sugar
½ teaspoon salt
1½ cups bread flour
1 tablespoon cinnamon

1 teaspoon baking soda
¼ teaspoon baking powder
1 pound carrots, peeled and
    finely grated
¼ cup chopped walnuts

Preheat the oven to 375°. In the bowl of an electric mixer, whip the eggs until tripled in volume and until a ribbon forms when you pour them off of a spoon. Beat in the oil gradually. Adjust the mixer speed to low and mix in the sugar and salt. Sift together the flour, cinnamon, baking soda, and baking powder and add them to the egg mixture; blend only until fully mixed. Fold in the carrots and walnuts. (Do not overmix.) Pour the batter into a nonstick muffin pan. Bake for 15 to 20 minutes or until golden brown.

Yield: 12 muffins

*CLIFTON COUNTRY INN*

## Rum Raisin Bread

5 cups all-purpose flour
1 cup sugar
1 cup loosely packed brown
    sugar
2 tablespoons plus 1 teaspoon
    baking powder

2 teaspoons salt
6 tablespoons vegetable oil
2½ cups milk
2 eggs, lightly beaten
1½ teaspoons rum extract
1 cup raisins

Preheat the oven to 350°. In a large bowl, mix the flour, sugars, baking powder, and salt. Add the remaining ingredients and mix gently until well combined. Pour the mixture into 2 greased or nonstick 5x9-inch loaf pans. Bake for 1 hour or until a knife inserted in the center comes out clean.

Yield: 2 loaves

*SETTLERS INN*

## Gingerbread Mansion Granola

*Homemade granola is served at country inns all across America every day, and just as every inn is individual, so, too, is this ubiquitous delicious morning favorite.*

1 cup honey
2 tablespoons molasses
1 cup corn oil
5 to 7 cups quick rolled oats
1 cup unsalted sunflower seeds
1 cup unsalted sesame seeds
1 cup dry milk (not instant)

1 cup wheat germ
1 cup raisins or chopped dates
1 cup grated coconut
1 cup chopped nuts (such as pecans or walnuts)
2 tablespoons cinnamon

Preheat the oven to 300°. In a medium nonstick saucepan, warm together the honey, molasses, and oil. Combine the remaining dry ingredients in a large mixing bowl. Pour the honey mixture over the dry ingredients and mix well. Spread the mixture evenly on 2 cookie sheets and bake for 25 to 35 minutes or until lightly browned. Cool and store in the refrigerator.

Yield: 4 quarts

*GINGERBREAD MANSION INN*

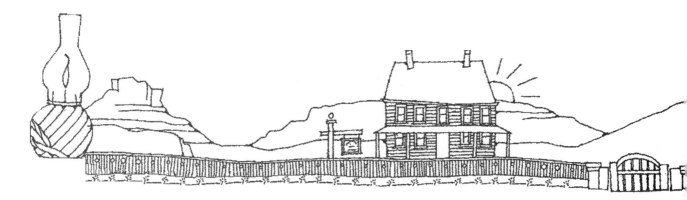

## Light-on-the-Eggs Breakfast Pie

*Only three eggs go into this sumptuous morning casserole. You may vary the recipe by omitting the sausage and substituting crumbled cooked bacon (about ⅓ cup). For vegetarian preferences, you may use fresh mushrooms as a substitute for the sausage.*

2 large onions, thinly sliced
2 tablespoons butter
1 9-inch unbaked pie shell (commercially prepared or see Page 221 for Marion's pie crust recipe)
½ pound Swiss cheese, grated
1 tablespoon all-purpose flour
10 sausage links (small breakfast size), cooked until brown, drained, and cut into ¼-inch pieces

6 fresh spinach leaves, finely chopped
3 eggs
1 cup heavy cream
¼ teaspoon salt
⅛ teaspoon pepper
1 sweet red bell pepper ring for garnish (¼-inch slice)

Preheat the oven to 400°. In a small skillet, sauté the onions in the butter until tender. Turn the onions into the pie shell. Toss the grated cheese with the flour and sprinkle it over the onions. Add the sausage and chopped spinach.

In a separate bowl, beat the eggs well. Stir in the cream, salt, and pepper, and pour the mixture over the pie filling. Place the red pepper ring in the center. Bake for 20 minutes. Reduce the temperature to 300° and bake 35 minutes more or until a knife inserted in the center comes out clean. Serve hot, cut into wedges.

Yield: 6 to 8 servings

*CANYON VILLA*

7

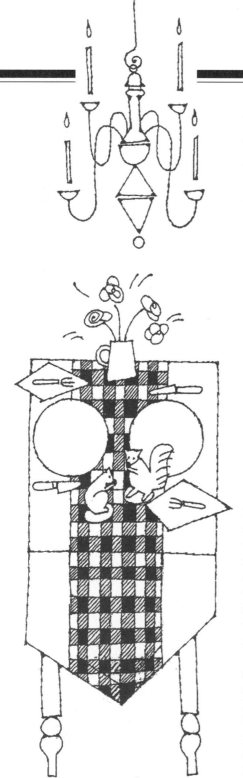

## Eggs-and-Black-Bean Cakes with Roasted-Red-Pepper Sauce

*They serve this at Highland Lake Inn with poached eggs.*

**SAUCE**
- 1 tablespoon olive oil
- 1 cup chopped onion
- 3 large cloves garlic, minced
- 6 ripe plum tomatoes, chopped
- 4 medium sweet red bell peppers, roasted and seeded, or 1 cup canned roasted peppers
- ¼ cup chicken broth
- ¾ teaspoon dried oregano, crushed
- ½ teaspoon cumin
- ½ teaspoon vinegar, any type
- ¼ teaspoon salt
- ¼ teaspoon ground red pepper

**CAKES**
- 3 cups cooked and drained black beans (or drained canned beans)
- 2 tablespoons plus 2 teaspoons olive oil, divided
- ½ cup chopped onion
- 2 scallions, chopped
- 4 cloves garlic, minced
- 2 eggs, well beaten
- ⅛ teaspoon chili powder
- ⅛ teaspoon ground red pepper
- ½ teaspoon salt
- ¼ teaspoon white pepper
- 1 cup blue cornmeal, divided
- 2 tablespoons butter

**EGGS**
- 8 eggs

Make the sauce. In a medium saucepan, heat the olive oil. Add the onion, garlic, and tomatoes, and cook for 6 to 8 minutes, until the tomatoes are tender. Place the roasted peppers and the tomato mixture in a food processor or blender. Add the chicken broth, oregano, cumin, vinegar, salt, and red pepper. Purée until well blended. Strain the sauce by pressing it through a food mill or strainer to remove any solids. Transfer the liquid back to the saucepan. Boil the sauce gently until it reaches desired thickness (about 5 to 7 minutes). Set aside and make the bean cakes.

Using a food processor or blender, finely chop the black beans, about 1 cup at a time. Remove to a large mixing bowl; set aside. In a small skillet, heat 2 teaspoons of the olive oil. Cook the onion, scallions, and garlic about 5 minutes, until tender. Add this mixture to the beans. Blend in the eggs, chili powder, red pepper, salt, and white pepper. Stir in ½ cup of the blue cornmeal. Divide the mixture into 8 equal portions and shape each into a ball. Roll each ball in the remaining cornmeal. Flatten the balls into ¾-inch patties (about 3 to 3½

inches across). In a large skillet, heat the butter and the remaining olive oil. Cook the patties over medium-low heat for 4 to 5 minutes on each side. Drain on a paper towel. Place a bean cake on each of 8 individual serving plates. Keep warm.

Poach the eggs. Lightly grease a 10-inch frying pan to cook up to 4 eggs at a time. Half-fill the pan with water; bring the water to boiling. Reduce the heat to simmer. Break 1 egg into a small dish. Slide the egg into the water, holding the lip of the dish as close to the water as possible. Repeat with the remaining eggs. Simmer, uncovered, 3 to 5 minutes. Remove with a slotted spoon. Place 1 egg on each bean cake. Ladle the sauce overtop and serve immediately.

Yield: 8 servings

*HIGHLAND LAKE INN*

## Eggs Florentine with Creamy Cheese Sauce

EGGS
- 6 eggs
- 1 cup cottage cheese
- 4 ounces Swiss cheese, grated
- 4 ounces Feta cheese, cubed
- 2 tablespoons butter, softened
- 1 10-ounce package frozen chopped spinach, thawed and drained
- ½ teaspoon ground nutmeg

SAUCE
- 1 tablespoon butter
- 1½ teaspoons all-purpose flour
- 1 cup milk
- 1 cup grated Monterey Jack cheese
- ¼ teaspoon salt
- ⅛ teaspoon dry mustard
- ⅛ teaspoon cayenne pepper

Preheat the oven to 350°. Prepare the eggs by beating them slightly. Add the cheeses and the butter, and mix well. Stir in the spinach and the nutmeg and mix until combined. Pour into 6 greased, 8-ounce ramekins. Bake for 30 to 45 minutes or until a toothpick inserted in the center comes out clean.

Prepare the sauce. In a small saucepan, melt the butter over medium heat, then stir in the flour. Cook until bubbly, about 1 minute. Remove from the heat. Gradually add the milk and stir until combined. Return the mixture to the heat. Cook until the sauce thickens and is bubbly, stirring constantly. Stir in the cheese and seasonings. Cook until the cheese is melted. Serve the sauce with the eggs.

Yield: 6 servings

*GINGERBREAD MANSION INN*

# Eggs Jerusalem with Puréed Carrots and Orange-Champagne Sauce

*Although we didn't make this on camera, I've been preparing and enjoying this recipe from Carter House for years. I felt I had to include it in the cookbook!*

ARTICHOKES
2 large artichokes
1 lemon, halved
2 small carrots, peeled

EGGS
2 eggs
1 teaspoon fresh chives, chopped
Salt and pepper

SAUCE
½ cup freshly squeezed orange juice
½ cup champagne
½ cup unsalted butter, melted

Prepare the artichokes. Bring a large pot of water to a boil. Cut off and discard the stems of the artichokes. Rub the artichokes with the halved lemon. Cut off the top leaves just above the choke and discard them. Rub the tops of the artichoke with lemon. Squeeze the remaining lemon juice into the boiling water and add the artichokes. Boil the artichokes for about 25 minutes or until the bottoms can be pierced easily with a knife. Cook the carrots in lightly salted water until tender.

While the artichokes and carrots are cooking, prepare the sauce. In a heavy saucepan, over medium-high heat, combine the orange juice and champagne. Reduce the liquid until it becomes a glaze (about ¾ its original volume). Remove the pan from the heat and whisk the butter into the liquid, 2 tablespoons at a time. Return the pan to the heat each time you add the butter, and whisk until all the butter is incorporated. The sauce should have the consistency of Hollandaise when finished. Set the sauce aside in a warm place.

Cut the carrots into chunks and purée in a food processor. Set aside. Cool the cooked artichokes by running them under cool water. Remove the remaining leaves and chokes, and trim the hearts flat. Arrange the artichokes in a plate. Spoon the carrot purée onto the hearts. Place into a slightly warm oven.

Prepare the eggs. Bring another pan of water to a boil. Remove the pan of water from the heat and poach the eggs in the water for 3 to 4 minutes. Remove the artichoke hearts from the oven. Using a slotted spoon, remove the eggs from the water and place them onto the artichoke hearts and carrot purée. Spoon champagne sauce over the eggs and artichokes, and garnish with chives.

Yield: 2 servings

*CARTER HOUSE*

## Poached Eggs with Asiago Cheese Sauce and Pansies

*CHEESE SAUCE*
- 2 tablespoons unsalted butter
- 2 tablespoons all-purpose flour
- ½ cup chicken broth
- ½ cup heavy cream
- 2 ounces Asiago cheese, grated

*EGGS*
- 4 slices sweet Virginia ham
- 2 English muffins, split and buttered
- 4 eggs
  Freshly ground pepper
  Fresh herb sprigs and pansies, for garnish

Prepare the sauce. In a small saucepan, melt the butter. Blend in the flour. Stir over medium-high heat for 1 minute. Whisk in the chicken broth and the cream. Cook, whisking constantly, until thickened and bubbly. Whisk in the cheese until melted. Cover the sauce and set aside in a warm place.

Prepare the eggs. On a baking sheet, arrange the ham slices on the English muffin halves. Broil 3 inches from the heat for 2 minutes. Keep warm. In a large skillet, bring ½ inch of water to a boil. Reduce the heat. Crack open the eggs, slip them into the water, and simmer for 4 to 6 minutes. Baste the yolks with the simmering water. Remove the eggs from the water with a slotted spoon and arrange them over the ham and muffins. Pour sauce over each egg. Sprinkle with pepper. Garnish with herb sprigs and edible pansies.

Yield: 4 servings

*CARTER HOUSE*

## Poached Eggs and Shrimp with Asparagus in a Brandied Gruyère Sauce

*As a brunch dish, this recipe is ideal served on a platter, but it may also be made in individual ramekins for a gourmet sit-down breakfast. Serve with the inn's famous grapefruit, page 1, and the rum raisin bread on page 5.*

ASPARAGUS
1½ pounds fresh asparagus
  spears, woody ends snapped
  and discarded
½ cup butter, melted and divided
1 tablespoon lemon juice

SAUCE
½ cup sour cream
2 tablespoons brandy
⅔ cup shredded Gruyère cheese
½ teaspoon tarragon
  Salt and pepper

EGGS
6 large eggs
1 pound medium-size shrimp,
  peeled and cooked
1 tablespoon finely chopped
  parsley

Cook the asparagus in boiling salted water until crisp tender, about 3 to 4 minutes. Transfer the vegetables to a shallow baking dish. Sprinkle with ¼ cup of the melted butter and the lemon juice. Keep the asparagus warm.

Prepare the sauce. In a bowl, combine the sour cream, brandy, cheese, tarragon, the remaining butter, and salt and pepper. Set aside.

Heat ½ inch of water in a large skillet to boiling. Crack the eggs and slip them into the water. Simmer 4 to 6 minutes. Drain with a slotted spoon and place the eggs on top of the asparagus. Arrange the shrimp overtop. Pour the brandy-and-cheese sauce overtop and place under a broiler, heating through until the cheese is melted. Sprinkle parsley over all.

Yield: 4 to 6 servings

*CHALET SUZANNE*

---

*Break things down to the simplest they can be. That way you will have the courage to try.*

JOHN SCHUMACHER,
Schumacher's New Prague Hotel

## Panettone French Toast with Cinnamon Raisin Sauce

*Panettone is a slightly sweet, light-textured yeast bread made in Italy and widely available in the United States. Raisins, citron, and anise are baked in 6- to 8-inch tall rounds. Chef Larry Martin's use of the bread in French toast is a treat. At holiday time, replace the half-and-half and cream with eggnog for a Christmas breakfast.*

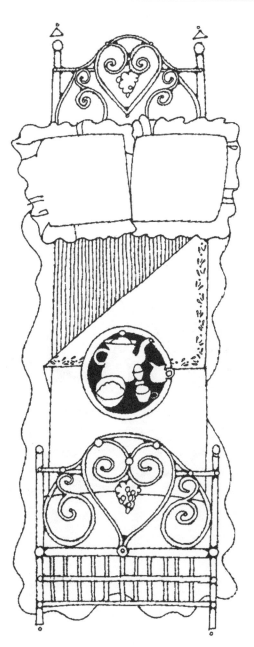

FRENCH TOAST
- 6 eggs
- 1½ cups half-and-half
- ¾ cup heavy cream
- ½ cup sugar
- ¼ cup dark rum
- 1½ teaspoons grated orange peel
- 3 teaspoons vanilla extract
- ¼ teaspoon cinnamon
- ¼ teaspoon ground nutmeg
  Butter for frying
- 8 slices day-old panettone
- 2 cups cornflakes, crushed
  Confectioners' sugar, for garnish

SAUCE
- 2 tablespoons butter
- 1 tablespoon all-purpose flour
- 1 cup water
- 1 cup sugar
- 1 teaspoon vanilla extract
- 1 teaspoon cinnamon
- ½ cup raisins

Prepare the French toast. In a large bowl, beat the eggs slightly. Add the creams, sugar, rum, orange peel, vanilla, cinnamon, and nutmeg, beating well. Melt a tablespoon or so of butter in a medium-hot skillet. Dip the bread slices in the egg mixture, then dip them in the crushed cornflakes, turning to coat both sides. Fry the bread slices in the butter until golden brown. Turn and brown the other side. When done, remove to a serving platter, sprinkle with confectioners' sugar, and serve with sauce.

To make the sauce, melt the butter in a saucepan over medium heat. Blend in the flour, stirring constantly for 1 to 2 minutes, until the mixture bubbles. Remove the pan from the heat and gradually whisk in the water, then the sugar. Return to the heat and cook until thick and just beginning to boil. Add the vanilla, cinnamon, and raisins, mixing well. Serve warm over the French toast.

Yield: 8 servings

*GINGERBREAD MANSION INN*

## Puffed Apple-and-Cinnamon-Baked Pancakes with Red Rock Syrup

*I just couldn't help renaming this syrup for Chef Marion Yadon. The syrup that accompanies the pancake is actually made with mulled apple cider. Marion uses cider made locally in Sedona at Oak Creek Orchards, which we visit on the show to watch the cider being pressed. Apples played a major role in Sedona's original settlement. I call it Red Rock Syrup because the apples are grown in trees planted in Sedona's rich red rock soil. The syrup will yield 1½ cups. As for the pancake, it bakes up into a luscious golden brown puff, and the nice thing is that you can start the preparations the day before.*

PANCAKE
6 tablespoons butter
6 large Granny Smith apples, peeled, cored, and sliced into ¼-inch thick slices
1 cup sugar
3 tablespoons cinnamon
9 eggs
1½ cups all-purpose flour
1½ cups milk

SYRUP
1 cup sugar
3 tablespoons cornstarch
1 teaspoon cinnamon
½ teaspoon nutmeg
1½ cups mulled or plain cider

In a large skillet, melt the butter. Sauté the apples until tender. Combine the sugar and cinnamon. Pour ¾ cup of the mixture over the apples and stir until thoroughly mixed in. (Reserve ¼ cup of the mixture for later.)

Coat a 10x15-inch glass baking dish with a nonstick cooking spray. Spread the apple mixture in the bottom of the dish. Cover and refrigerate overnight.

In the morning, preheat the oven to 400°. Place the apples, uncovered, in the oven for 10 minutes. Meanwhile, beat the eggs well. Add the flour and beat until smooth, scraping the side and bottom of the bowl. Add the milk and stir.

Pour the batter over the heated apples and return the pancake to the oven for 12 to 15 minutes until the edges begin to cook and puff.

Meanwhile, cook the syrup. In a heavy medium saucepan, combine the cider, sugar, cornstarch, cinnamon, and nutmeg. Place the pan over medium heat and cook, stirring constantly until the mixture thickens and comes to a boil. Stir while boiling, for about 1 minute. Set aside and keep warm.

Remove the pancake from the oven and sprinkle with the reserved cinnamon mixture. Dot with additional butter. Return to the oven for another 12 to 15 minutes or until the pancake is puffed and peaked. Cut into squares and serve with the apple cider syrup.

Yield: 10 to 12 servings

*CANYON VILLA*

## Fresh Corn-on-the-Cob Waffles with Cilantro Butter

*WAFFLE BATTER*
- 1 cup all-purpose flour
- ½ cup yellow cornmeal
- 2 tablespoons sugar
- 2 teaspoons baking powder
- ¼ teaspoon salt
- 1 large egg
- 2 tablespoons unsalted butter, melted
- ½ cup water
- 1 cup fresh corn, cut off the cob
- 1 teaspoon vanilla extract
  Vegetable oil

*CILANTRO BUTTER*
- ¼ pound unsalted butter, softened
- ¼ cup freshly chopped cilantro
  Pure maple syrup

Prepare the waffles. In a large bowl, combine the flour, cornmeal, sugar, baking powder, and salt. In a separate large bowl, whip together the egg, melted butter, water, corn, and vanilla. Add the egg mixture to the flour mixture and mix just until combined. Oil and heat a waffle iron. Ladle the mixture into the iron and cook the waffles according to the manufacturer's specifications.

Prepare the butter. Whip together the butter and the cilantro until smooth and creamy. Top each waffle with cilantro butter and serve with pure maple syrup.

Yield: 6 servings

*CARTER HOUSE*

# Scotch Waffles with Dried-Mango Syrup and Orange Cream

*While the waffles cook, you have time to make the syrup and cream. The waffles, with the sour cream and whiskey, offer a nutty flavor. Enjoy this as a dessert, too.*

MANGO SYRUP
- ¼ cup honey
- 2 cups pure maple syrup
- 1 whole vanilla bean scraped (with seeds)
- 1 cup dried mangos, diced
- 1 tablespoon freshly chopped mint leaves
- 2 tablespoons butter

ORANGE CREAM
- 2 cups heavy cream
- Juice and zest of 1 orange
- 2 tablespoons confectioners' sugar

WAFFLE BATTER
- 1 cup cake flour
- ¼ teaspoon baking powder
- 1 teaspoon sugar
- ⅛ teaspoon salt
- ½ cup cornmeal
- 1 egg, separated
- ⅛ teaspoon lemon extract
- 2 tablespoons butter, melted
- ¼ cup buttermilk
- 1 tablespoon sour cream
- 1 tablespoon Scotch whiskey

GARNISH
- Confectioners' sugar
- Orange zest
- Roasted pecans

Prepare the mango syrup. Combine all of the ingredients in a small saucepan. Heat and simmer the syrup for 5 minutes. Set aside and keep warm.

Prepare the orange cream. Combine all of the ingredients in a mixing bowl and whip until the mixture is stiff. Set aside.

Prepare the waffles. Combine the flour, baking powder, sugar, salt, and cornmeal. In the bowl of an electric mixer, combine the egg yolk and the remaining ingredients except for the egg white; then add the dry mixture. Mix just until combined. In a clean mixing bowl, beat the egg white until stiff peaks form, then lightly fold it into the waffle mixture. Heat and oil a waffle iron. Ladle the mixture into the waffle iron and cook until the steam no longer comes out of the side. Serve with hot mango syrup and orange cream. Garnish with butter, confectioners' sugar, orange zest, and roasted pecans.

Yield: 4 to 6 servings

*INN OF THE ANASAZI*

## Morning Saffron Potatoes and Bacon

*The pleasure of this recipe is that you may start it a day ahead.*

6 medium red new potatoes
3 green onions
½ red bell pepper
6 slices bacon

½ teaspoon ground cumin
½ teaspoon saffron or turmeric
Salt and pepper

Parboil the potatoes, with skins on, until just barely done, 8 to 10 minutes (do not overcook). Cover and refrigerate for several hours or overnight.

Next morning, preheat the oven to 300°. Cube the potatoes and set aside. Chop the onion and bell pepper coarsely and set aside. In a large skillet, sauté the bacon until crisp; drain on a paper towel. Sauté the onion and the bell pepper in the bacon drippings until they are tender. Add the potatoes, cumin, and saffron. Salt and pepper to taste, tossing the potatoes to coat. Cook for several minutes while continuing to toss. Crumble the bacon and add it to the potatoes. Pour the potatoes into a 9x13-inch baking dish. Cover with aluminum foil and bake for 30 minutes or until tender.

Yield: 6 to 8 servings

*GINGERBREAD MANSION INN*

## Highland Lake Inn's Yellow Grits

4 cups water
1 cup fresh corn, removed from the cob (or frozen corn)
½ teaspoon salt
½ teaspoon freshly ground black pepper

1 cup yellow or quick white grits
¼ cup heavy cream
¼ cup butter, cut up

In a large saucepan, combine the water, corn, salt, and pepper; bring to a boil. Add the grits slowly, stirring constantly. Reduce the heat to medium low. Cover and cook for 5 to 7 minutes until thickened, stirring occasionally. Add the cream and the butter, stirring until combined. Serve hot.

Yield: 6 to 8 servings

*HIGHLAND LAKE INN*

## Canyon Villa's Cinnamon Rolls

*I have been to Marion and Chuck Yadon's luxurious villa many times. By now they know when I come, they must roll out the cinnamon buns to make me completely happy. The rolls remind me of when I was a young girl and my father would go to the neighborhood bakery on a Sunday morning and come back with hard rolls and sweet buns. He always made sure cinnamon rolls were in the bundle for me.*

*Marion's rolls may be prepared and refrigerated overnight. The next morning, before baking, cover and let them rise in a warm place for 1 hour or until doubled in size. Bake as directed.*

ROLLS
- 1 cup milk
- 1 cup water
- ½ cup butter
- 1 egg, slightly beaten
- 6 cups all-purpose flour (or more), divided
- ½ cup sugar
- 1 package active dry yeast
- 2 teaspoons salt

FILLING
- ½ cup brown sugar
- 1½ tablespoons cinnamon
- ⅓ cup butter, melted

GLAZE
- 2 tablespoons butter
- 1 tablespoon milk
- 1 teaspoon vanilla extract
- 2 to 3 cups sifted confectioners' sugar

In a small saucepan, combine the milk, water, and butter; heat until very warm (about 120°) and the butter melts. Remove from heat. Cool slightly. Add the egg.

In the large bowl of an electric mixer, combine 2 cups of the flour with the sugar, yeast, and salt. Stir well. Add milk-egg mixture to the flour mixture. Beat at medium speed until batter is smooth and elastic, about 5 to 8 minutes. Add enough remaining flour to make a soft dough. Place in a greased bowl, turning once to grease the top of the dough. Cover with a damp tea towel and let rise in a warm place for 1 hour until doubled in size.

Meanwhile, prepare the filling. Combine the brown sugar and cinnamon in a small bowl and melt the butter. Set aside.

Punch the dough down. Cover again and let rest 10 minutes more. Divide the dough in half and set half aside. Roll the other half out onto a floured surface to form a 12x18-inch rectangle; brush with half of the melted butter, leaving a ½-inch border. Sprinkle with half of the brown sugar and cinnamon mixture. Beginning at the long side, roll up jelly-roll fashion; moisten the edges with water and press together to seal. Cut the jellyroll into 1½-inch slices; place cut sides of slices (rolls) down in a greased 9x13-inch baking pan (12 rolls to a pan). Cover with a damp tea towel and let rise in a warm place for 45 minutes to an hour or until doubled in size. Repeat with remaining half of the dough.

When the rolls have risen, bake them in a preheated 375° oven for 20 minutes or until golden brown. While the rolls are baking, prepare the glaze.

In a small saucepan, heat the butter and milk until the butter is melted. (You can use a glass measuring cup in the microwave to do this.) Add the vanilla and enough of the powdered sugar for desired spreading consistency. Apply the glaze when rolls have cooled slightly.

Yield: 2 dozen rolls

*CANYON VILLA*

## Green Onion and Apple Sausage

1½ pounds ground pork
½ teaspoon salt
½ teaspoon black pepper
⅛ teaspoon ground red pepper
⅛ teaspoon ground white pepper
1½ teaspoons dried sage

4 green onions, thinly sliced
1 cooking apple (such as Granny Smith), cored, peeled, and finely chopped
1 tablespoon butter

In a large bowl, combine the pork, salt, peppers, sage, green onions, and apple pieces. Mix thoroughly and form into ¾-inch-thick patties. In a large, heavy skillet, melt the butter over medium-high heat. Cook the patties in the butter until the sausages are brown on both sides and the centers are no longer pink (10 to 12 minutes total).

Yield: 6 servings

*HIGHLAND LAKE INN*

Birdseed
Multi-Grain
Bread

# BREADS, SOUPS, SALADS

## Birdseed Multigrain Bread

*The various textures from the assortment of grains used in this recipe suggested the avian name for this popular Settlers Inn bread. You need at least 5 hours to prepare the bread ahead of time. Better yet, start the day before (see method).*

*SEED MIX*
2 tablespoons sesame seeds
2 tablespoons flax seeds
2 tablespoons poppy seeds
2 tablespoons sunflower seeds

*DOUGH*
1 cup milk
1 cup water
⅔ cup steel-cut oats
⅔ cup quick (not instant) rolled oats

¼ cup bulgur wheat (or substitute cracked wheat)
1 tablespoon salt
⅓ cup brown sugar, firmly-packed
¼ cup vegetable oil
1 tablespoon active dry yeast, dissolved in ¼ cup water
3½ to 4 cups bread flour, divided
1 egg white

Prepare the seed mix. In a small bowl, combine all of the ingredients. Set aside.

Prepare the dough. In a medium bowl, combine the milk, water, steel-cut and rolled oats, bulgur, salt, brown sugar, and oil. Let soak overnight. (To speed this part of the process, simply heat the milk and water, and soak the grains for about 3 hours.)

Add the yeast and 3 cups of the bread flour to a bread mixer, or, if doing by hand, to a bowl. Add ¼ cup of the seed mix and any additional flour to make a firm but slightly sticky dough. Knead for 5 to 8 minutes until the dough is pliable and has some elasticity.

Place the dough in a large, greased bowl and let it rise for 1½ to 2 hours in a warm place until it doubles in size. (On a cold day this rising may take longer.) Punch the dough down and divide it in half. Form each half into a loaf and place each in a lightly greased 5x9-inch loaf pan. Let rise, covered, in a draft-free place, until almost doubled in size (about 1½ hours).

Preheat the oven to 350°. Mix the egg white with ¼ cup of water, then lightly brush the loaves with this mixture. Sprinkle the remaining seed mix over the loaves. Bake until the loaves sound hollow when rapped lightly with your knuckles (about 40 to 50 minutes).

Yield: 2 loaves

*SETTLERS INN*

*Return to a time when life was art, & art was gracious living.*

Erna Rubin-Clanin, Château du Sureau

## Coffee-Can Bread

*The sight of round bread on the table, especially at a party, makes everyone want to dig in. You will need to use two 1-pound coffee cans with plastic lids; the lighter-weight cans are too small.*

4 cups all-purpose flour, divided
1 ¼-ounce package active dry yeast
½ cup water
½ cup milk
½ cup vegetable oil
¼ cup sugar
1 teaspoon salt
2 eggs, beaten

Combine 1½ cups of the flour and the yeast in a large bowl. Mix well and set aside.

In a medium saucepan, combine the water, milk, oil, sugar, and salt. Place over medium heat and cook until the mixture reaches 105° to 115°. Remove from the heat and pour the heated mixture into the flour and yeast mixture.

Preheat the oven to 375°. Beat the mixture with an electric mixer until smooth. Add the eggs, mixing well to incorporate. Slowly add the remaining flour, beating with the mixer until a smooth, elastic, very stiff batter is formed.

Spoon the batter into 2 well-greased 1-pound coffee cans. Cover with the coffee can lids. Allow to rise in a warm place for 35 to 45 minutes or until the batter rises to within 1½ to 2 inches from the top of the can. Uncover the cans and bake for 30 to 35 minutes or until the bread is golden brown. The loaf should sound hollow when tapped. Cool the bread in the cans for 10 minutes. Remove from the cans and cool on wire racks.

Yield: 2 loaves

*Y. O. RANCH*

# Jalapeño Cornbread

*Hot chilies and cheese are what separate this cornbread from the rest, making it truly Texan. The creamed corn keeps the bread moist and tasty.*

2 jalapeño chilies, finely chopped (seeds and ribs included)
1 17-ounce can creamed corn
½ teaspoon baking soda
½ teaspoon salt
1 tablespoon sugar
2 eggs
¾ cup buttermilk
⅓ cup vegetable or canola oil
1 cup grated Longhorn cheese
2 cups yellow cornmeal

Preheat the oven to 350°. Grease a 17½x12-inch baking pan.

In a large bowl, mix the jalapeños with the creamed corn. Beat in the baking soda, salt, and sugar. Add the eggs, one at a time, beating well after each addition. Add the buttermilk and oil, then whisk in the cheese and cornmeal.

Pour the batter into the prepared pan, distributing it evenly, and bake in the center of the oven for 30 to 40 minutes or until the top is brown and a tester inserted in the center comes out clean. Cool in the pan and cut into squares to serve.

Yield: 24 servings

*Y. O. RANCH*

## Focaccia Bread with Rosemary

*Whatever the ethnic menu at the inn, the chef always prepares a complementary bread. The focaccia or flat bread, made here with herbs, makes a pleasing accompaniment to spicy soups and entrées, and is particularly suited to many of the Italian meals in this cookbook. Focaccia bread is made with thumb-size indentations that are great for catching sauce, especially when dipping.*

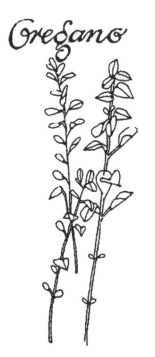

1 tablespoon active dry yeast
¼ cup warm water and 2¼ cups plus 1 to 2 tablespoons water at room temperature
3 tablespoons olive oil, divided
7½ cups all purpose flour, divided

1 tablespoon coarse salt, plus more for sprinkling
2 tablespoons freshly chopped rosemary or herb of choice, divided

In a bowl with the ¼ cup warm water, proof the yeast for 10 minutes.

In the large bowl of an electric mixer, combine the 2¼ cups warm water with 1 tablespoon of the olive oil. Add 2 cups of flour and the salt and beat until smooth. Gradually stir in the rest of the flour, 1 cup at a time, until the dough pulls away from the sides of the bowl. Knead for 8 to 10 minutes until velvety and soft. As you wind down on the kneading, add 1 tablespoon of the rosemary. Place the dough in an oiled bowl and cover tightly with plastic wrap for 1½ hours or until doubled in bulk. Punch down and divide into 3 equal pieces. Press the dough into 3 greased 9-inch cake pans. Cover the pans with tea towels and allow to rise for 30 minutes. Dimple the dough with your fingertips, leaving ½-inch indentations. Cover again and allow to rise until doubled, about 1½ hours.

Preheat the oven to 400°. Brush the dough with the remaining olive oil. Sprinkle 1 to 2 teaspoons salt and the remaining rosemary overtop. Cover the tops of the dough with a light spray of water. Bake in the oven 20 to 25 minutes, spraying with water at least 3 times during the first 5 to 10 minutes of baking. Bake until golden and the bread sounds hollow when tapped. Remove the bread from the pans immediately and return it to the oven for 1 to 2 minutes to crisp the bottoms. Serve warm.

Yield: 3 loaves

*OCTOBER COUNTRY INN*

## Baked Polenta and Cheese

*Polenta is a traditional northern Italian bread that is served at any meal including breakfast. Since it is such a basic dish, you can use your imagination in seasoning it with herbs or adding a savory sauce such as a spaghetti sauce.*

2 cups chicken broth
1 clove garlic, minced
½ cup cornmeal
¼ cup butter
¼ cup grated Cheddar cheese
¼ cup grated Parmesan cheese, plus more for sprinkling

In a large saucepan, bring the broth and the garlic to a boil on high heat. Gradually add the cornmeal while stirring the broth. Reduce the heat and boil gently, stirring constantly until the cornmeal becomes thick and pulls away from the sides of the pan (about 20 to 30 minutes). Add the butter and the cheeses and stir well to combine. Pour the mixture into a greased 5x9-inch loaf pan and set aside. When cool, cover and refrigerate overnight.

Next day, preheat the oven to 350°. Remove the polenta from the pan and cut ¾-inch thick slices. Place the slices into a greased 9x13-inch casserole dish or other shallow pan that will allow the pieces to overlap. Pour the melted butter overtop and sprinkle with Parmesan cheese. Bake uncovered for 30 minutes. Serve hot.

Yield: 8 to 10 servings

*GINGERBREAD MANSION INN*

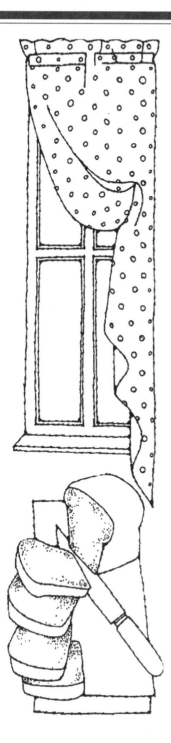

## Brown Bread with Raisins

*At Randall's, they know when a loaf of bread is finished baking just by looking at it, without using a thermostat, because the breads are cooked in an old-fashioned beehive oven. This recipe is adapted for the home kitchen. The bread will have a medium to hard consistency.*

2 teaspoons vinegar, any type
2¼ cups milk
1¾ cups yellow cornmeal
1¾ cups rye flour
2 teaspoons baking soda

1 teaspoon salt
1 cup molasses
1 cup golden raisins, dusted
  with flour

Preheat the oven to 350°. In a small bowl, combine the vinegar and milk; set aside. In another bowl, combine the yellow cornmeal, rye flour, baking soda, and salt. Stir the molasses into the milk mixture. Combine the wet and dry ingredients and mix well. Add the raisins and mix well.

Pour the batter into a greased 5x9-inch loaf pan. Bake for 35 to 40 minutes (check for doneness at 35 minutes by testing with a toothpick). Remove the bread from the pan and let cool before serving.

Yield: 1 loaf

*RANDALL'S ORDINARY*

## Tattie Scones
## (Potato Biscuits)

*Scones are a favorite food in Scotland. They can be savory or sweet; and, in keeping with the thrift for which Scottish people are famed, they often incorporate leftover ingredients. In Scotland you will hear the name pronounced "Scawn" (rhymes with lawn) rather than the better known American pronunciation that rhymes with stone. The Scottish slang word for potatoes is tattie, and this recipe uses up leftover mashed potatoes. Serve these savory scones any time of day.*

2 cups all-purpose flour
2 teaspoons baking powder
½ teaspoon salt
3 tablespoons butter or margarine

1 cup cold mashed potatoes
1 egg, beaten
  Milk to moisten (about 3
  tablespoons)

Preheat the oven to 425°. Combine the flour, baking powder, and salt. Cut in the butter or margarine with a pastry blender or in the food processor. With a fork, mix in the mashed potatoes and the egg. Gradually mix in enough milk to form a dough.

Turn the dough out onto a floured pastry board and knead lightly (about 16 times). Then roll it out to ¾-inch thickness. Cut the dough into 2- or 3-inch rounds using a cookie cutter. (If you don't have a cookie cutter, the lip of a drinking glass dipped in flour works just fine.) Place the rounds on an ungreased cookie sheet and bake for 10 to 15 minutes until light brown on top.

Yield: 16 scones

*WHITE OAK INN*

## Cheddar-Dill Scones

2½ cups all-purpose flour
1 tablespoon dried parsley flakes or 2 tablespoons freshly chopped parsley
1 tablespoon baking powder
1 teaspoon dried dill or 2 teaspoons freshly chopped dill
½ teaspoon salt
¾ cup butter
1 cup shredded sharp Cheddar cheese
2 eggs
½ cup half-and-half

Preheat the oven to 400°. Place the flour, parsley, baking powder, dill, salt, and butter in a food processor. Using on/off pulses, cut in the butter until the mixture resembles uncooked rolled oats. Then mix in the cheese.

In a separate bowl, beat the eggs with the half-and-half. Stir the mixture into the flour mixture. When the mixture becomes a dough, turn it onto a lightly floured surface and knead the dough until smooth, about 1 minute.

Divide the dough in half and pat each half into an 8-inch circle. Cut the circles into 8 wedges each, using a sharp knife. Place the wedges onto ungreased cookie sheets and bake 15 to 20 minutes or until lightly browned. Serve with butter.

Yield: 16 scones

*WHITE OAK INN*

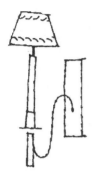

## Reuben Strudel

*By using basically the same method used to prepare an apple strudel, you can make a savory corned beef, cabbage, and cheese strudel, and it's scrumptious. You will also be adding Chef John Schumacher's version of a Thousand Island dressing. Prepare the dressing (see page 222) before starting the strudel.*

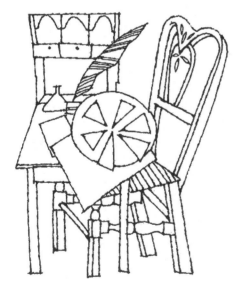

**DOUGH**
- 3 cups all-purpose flour
- ⅛ teaspoon salt
- ¼ cup butter, melted
- ¼ cup warm water
- 2 eggs, beaten

**FILLING**
- 1 cup Schumacher's Thousand Island dressing (page 222)
- 2 cups shredded Swiss cheese
- 3 cups sauerkraut, drained well
- 4 cups coarsely ground corned beef

**ASSEMBLY**
- Egg wash or water
- Mustard, optional

Combine the flour and salt in a large bowl and set aside. In another bowl, mix the butter, water, and eggs. Add the flour mixture to make a soft, but not sticky, dough. Knead for about 150 strokes. Place in a greased and covered bowl in a warm place for 1 hour. Roll out on a floured cloth, and stretch very thin, making an 18x24-inch rectangle.

Preheat the oven to 400°. To make the strudel, layer the dressing over the dough and add the remaining filling ingredients in the order listed, making sure ingredients are evenly distributed. Dampen the edge of the crust with egg wash or water. Roll strudel up jellyroll-style, beginning at the shorter end. Place on a greased baking sheet, seam side down. Brush with egg wash. Bake 40 to 45 minutes or until golden brown. Serve with mustard on the side, if desired.

Yield: 6 to 8 servings

*SCHUMACHER'S NEW PRAGUE HOTEL*

## Blue-Corn Pizza with Chilies, Cheese, and Prosciutto

*Cachiota Marigold cheese is a type of farmer's cheese that includes freshly chopped marigold mint. If the cheese is not available in your area, then substitute with a peppered Monterey Jack cheese and mix in a little chopped tarragon.*

PIZZA CRUST
2½ cups warm water
 2 ¼-ounce packages active dry
     yeast
 4 ears corn, cut off the cob
1½ cups bread flour
 1 cup blue cornmeal, plus more
     for pressing out the dough
1½ teaspoons salt
 ¼ cup olive oil, plus more for
     brushing
 ¼ cup honey

PIZZA TOPPING
 1 tablespoon extra virgin olive
     oil
 1 teaspoon red chili flakes
 ½ pound Cachiota Marigold
     cheese, grated
 ¼ pound prosciutto ham, thinly
     sliced
 3 Sandia chilies (or substitute
     with whole green canned
     chilies) sliced in ¼-inch strips
12 fresh basil leaves

Preheat the oven to 350°. Prepare the crust. Place the water in a medium-size bowl. Sprinkle the yeast over the top, and mix gently until it is fully dissolved. Let the mixture stand for 10 minutes. In a large bowl, combine the remaining crust ingredients, then add the yeast mixture. Once combined, knead the dough until smooth, approximately 5 to 7 minutes. Form into 6 equal balls and brush each with olive oil. Cover the dough with plastic wrap and let it stand for 25 minutes at room temperature. On a cornmeal-covered surface, hand form each ball of dough into an 8-inch circle by pressing down and flattening the dough to about ¼-inch thick. Pre-grill (on stovetop or barbecue grill) each circle of dough on medium heat (about 1 minute for each side). Set aside.

   Prepare the topping. Brush the pizza shells with olive oil, then sprinkle them with the chili flakes and the cheese. Arrange the sliced chilies and prosciutto neatly on top. Gently tear the fresh basil and arrange it on top. Bake pizzas directly on the oven rack for 5 to 7 minutes.

   Yield: 6  8-inch pizzas

   *INN OF THE ANASAZI*

## Herbed Minestrone Soup New England Style

*Chef Patrick Runkel adds a heartier twist to this traditional favorite by cutting the vegetables a bit chunkier—the way they like to make soups in this part of the country.*

2 tablespoons olive oil
1 leek (mainly white part with a little green)
1 rib celery, cut into ½-inch chunks
1 carrot, peeled, cut into 1-inch chunks
1 clove garlic, minced
1 green bell pepper, seeded and chopped
6 fresh plum tomatoes, seeded and diced
6 cups chicken stock
¼ pound green beans, cut into 1-inch pieces

1 zucchini, cut into 1-inch chunks
1 yellow squash, cut into 1-inch chunks
1 tablespoon chopped fresh marjoram, or 1 teaspoon dried
1 teaspoon chopped fresh thyme, or ½ teaspoon dried
Salt and pepper
Grated Parmesan cheese

In a large saucepan, heat the olive oil and sauté the leek, celery, and carrot for 5 minutes. Add the garlic and green pepper, and sauté all for 2 minutes more. Next, add the tomatoes and cook until they release their juices. Add the stock and bring to a boil. Reduce the heat and simmer for 10 minutes. (The soup may be prepared ahead of time at this point.)

About 30 minutes before serving, return the soup to a boil. Add the green beans, squashes, herbs, and seasonings. Lower the heat to a simmer and cook the vegetables until crisp tender. Serve garnished with freshly grated Parmesan cheese.

Yield: 6 to 8 servings

*OCTOBER COUNTRY INN*

## Shaker Tomato Soup

*Get out your pottery crocks and serve this hearty soup any time of year. The flavor is magnificent and if you get courageous, cook it over an open fire in a black kettle as they do at Randall's.*

4 to 5 ribs celery
1 green bell pepper, seeded
4 quarts crushed tomatoes
   (fresh or canned)
4 quarts water
1 teaspoon fresh basil

1 to 2 bay leaves
⅛ teaspoon cayenne pepper
1 teaspoon chopped parsley
1 teaspoon minced onion
1 teaspoon lemon juice
   Salt and pepper

Purée the celery and green pepper in a food processor. Add to a large saucepan with the tomatoes, water, basil, and bay leaves. Cook until the mixture is reduced by ⅓. Remove the bay leaves. Stir in the cayenne, parsley, onion, and lemon juice, and season with salt and pepper.

Yield: 8 servings

*RANDALL'S ORDINARY*

Cook over an open fire

# Corn Chowder

*Besides being a very pretty soup with colorful pieces of red pepper and yellow corn, this is lower in fat and has a lighter consistency than most chowders. Although the recipe is particularly good when made with fresh corn in season, it can be made with canned or frozen corn kernels instead.*

1 tablespoon olive oil
1 cup chopped onion
¼ teaspoon hot red pepper flakes
2 cups peeled and diced white
   potatoes
1 cup chopped celery
½ cup chopped sweet red bell
   pepper

3 cups chicken stock
2 cups fresh corn kernels
16 ounces cream-style corn
1 cup milk
2 tablespoons freshly chopped
   parsley or fresh cilantro
   Salt and pepper

In a large pot, heat the oil. Add the onion and red pepper flakes, and cook for about 1 minute. Add the potatoes, celery, and red bell pepper. Cook for 2 minutes. Pour in the chicken stock, cover and simmer for 5 to 10 minutes until the vegetables are cooked. Add the fresh and cream-style corn, milk, and parsley. Heat through. Season with salt and pepper to taste.

   Yield: 4 to 6 servings

*WHITE OAK INN*

# Sweet-Potato-and-Chili Chowder

*Ancho chilies are large and mild and offer the dish a sweet but earthy taste. The salsa is optional as the chowder tastes great even without the salsa garnish.*

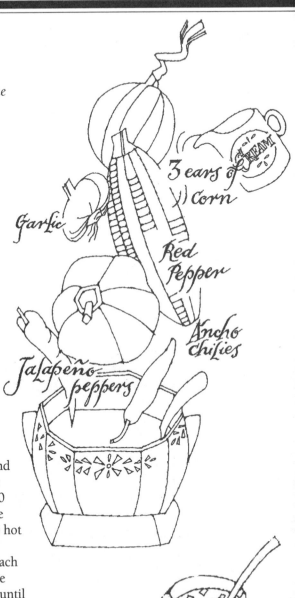

CHOWDER
- 3 tablespoons olive oil
- 4 red onions, 3 sliced, 1 diced
- 1 stalk celery, sliced
- 4 cloves garlic
- 10 ancho chilies, seeded and julienned; keep 1 diced pepper separated from the rest
- 2 jalapeño peppers with seeds, halved
- 3 quarts chicken stock
- 10 medium sweet potatoes, baked, 8 peeled, 2 peeled and diced
- 1 quart heavy cream or milk
- 1 red bell pepper, diced
- 3 ears corn, cooked and cut off the cob
- Salt and cayenne pepper

SALSA
- 1 4- to 5-ounce duck breast
- 1 papaya, diced
- ¼ cup finely chopped fresh cilantro
- 1 red onion, diced
- Juice and zest of 1 lime
- 1 red bell pepper, diced
- 1 poblano pepper, seeded and diced
- 1 tablespoon honey
- 1 whole vanilla bean, scraped
- Salt and cayenne pepper

Prepare the chowder. In a large stock pot, heat the olive oil until smoking. Sauté the sliced onions, celery, garlic, 9 of the anchos, and the jalapeños until tender. Add the chicken stock and the 8 whole potatoes, and boil for 5 minutes. Add the cream and simmer for 30 minutes. Purée the soup in a blender until it is smooth. Return the soup to the pot; add all of the diced vegetables and the corn. Keep hot until serving time. Serve with salsa.

Prepare the salsa. Grill the duck breast for 2 to 3 minutes on each side. Dice the breast finely. In a small mixing bowl, combine all the ingredients and season to taste with the salt and pepper. Set aside until serving time.

To serve, ladle the chowder into individual bowls. Add a dollop of the salsa in the center. Garnish with the reserved ancho, sliced.

Yield: 24 servings

*INN OF THE ANASAZI*

# Black-Bean Chili

## Chill(i)-Out

Red chili stains such kitchen utensils as rubber spatulas and some enamelware. To remove the stains, soak the affected area in a solution of 2 parts water to 1 part chlorine bleach.

*Begin preparing this recipe the night before in order to soak the beans.*

2 cups dry black beans
1 bay leaf
4 teaspoons each: cumin, oregano, and paprika
½ teaspoon cayenne pepper
1 dried green or ancho chili, or 2 to 3 tablespoons chili powder
3 tablespoons corn or peanut oil
3 medium yellow onions, coarsely chopped
4 cloves garlic, coarsely chopped

½ teaspoon salt
1½ pounds ripe or canned tomatoes, peeled, seeded, and chopped, juice reserved
1 to 2 tablespoons chopped chipotle chili (canned or dried), optional (adds a smoky flavor)
1 tablespoon rice wine vinegar
Grated Cheddar cheese, cilantro, and chopped chilies for garnish

Sort through the beans, remove the stones, and rinse. Cover well with water and soak overnight in a bowl. Next day, drain the beans and place them in a 4-quart saucepan along with the bay leaf. Cover with fresh water by 2 inches and bring to a boil over high heat. Lower the heat and allow the beans to simmer about 1 hour while you prepare the rest of the ingredients.

Heat a small nonstick skillet over medium heat and add the cumin. When the cumin begins to color, add the oregano, shaking the pan frequently so that the herbs don't scorch. When the fragrance is strong, remove the pan from the heat and quickly stir in the paprika and cayenne. Then remove the herbs from the pan and cool. Grind the seasonings in a mortar or spice mill to make a coarse powder.

Preheat the oven to 375°. To make a chili powder, place the dried chili in the oven for 3 to 5 minutes to make it crispy. Cool the chili briefly, then remove the stem, seeds, and veins. Tear the pod into small pieces and grind it into a powder in a mortar or spice mill.

In a large skillet, heat the oil and sauté the onions over medium heat until they soften. Add the garlic, the salt, the ground herbs, and the chili powder, and cook another 5 minutes, stirring frequently. Add the tomatoes, their juices, and the chipotle chili. Simmer for 15 minutes, then add this mixture to the beans. If necessary, add enough water so that the beans are covered by at least 1 inch. Continue cooking the beans slowly until they are soft, an hour or so longer. If necessary, add just enough water to prevent the beans from scorching.

When the beans are cooked, taste and correct the seasonings. Just before serving, add the vinegar and additional salt to bring out the flavors. Remove and discard the bay leaf. Serve garnished with cheese, cilantro, and chilies.

Yield: 8 to 10 servings

*OCTOBER COUNTRY INN*

## Portuguese Soup

*The area of North Stonington was heavily settled by the Portuguese, and this soup has been an inn favorite. Chorizo is a highly seasoned sausage, heavy on the garlic and used extensively in soups, casseroles, and stews in Portugal, Spain, and Mexico. At Randall's this soup hangs from a crane in a black cauldron, simmering over an open fire.*

| | |
|---|---|
| 1 cup small white dry pea beans | 1 tablespoon vinegar, any type |
| 1 large onion, diced | 2 quarts water |
| 1 pound chorizo or other spicy pork sausage, thinly sliced | 2 cups diced new white potatoes |
| 1 pound fresh kale, finely chopped | |

Soak the pea beans overnight in cold water. Combine the drained pea beans, onions, chorizo, and kale in a kettle or large saucepan. Add the vinegar and the water. Bring to a boil and simmer for 2 to 3 hours. Add the potatoes and continue cooking until the potatoes are tender (at least another half hour). Add more water, if necessary.

Yield: 8 to 10 servings

*RANDALL'S ORDINARY*

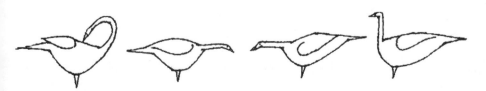

## Chicken-and-Tortilla Soup

*South-of-the-Border nights are only some of the many ethnic dinner themes the inn prepares for guests. This soup is a favorite and easy to make.*

1½ tablespoons peanut oil
1 large clove garlic, minced
4 scallions (including green tops), finely chopped
7 cups chicken stock or broth
2 small boned and skinless chicken breasts, cut in half
1 teaspoon Tabasco sauce
1½ teaspoons oregano
1½ teaspoons marjoram
½ teaspoon freshly ground black pepper

2 cups or more vegetable oil for frying
8 6-inch corn tortillas, halved and cut crosswise into ¼-inch-thick strips
1 cup drained and chopped fresh plum tomatoes
Finely chopped fresh parsley, for garnish
Grated Cheddar cheese, for garnish

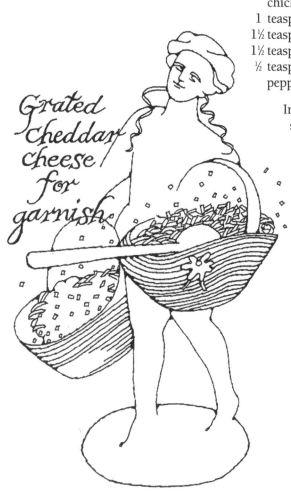

*Grated Cheddar cheese for garnish*

In a 3- to 4-quart soup pot, combine the peanut oil, garlic, and scallions over medium-high heat. Cook, stirring for 4 to 5 minutes or until the scallions are limp. Add the chicken stock, chicken, Tabasco, herbs, and pepper and bring the mixture to a boil. Lower the heat. Cover the pot and simmer for 12 to 15 minutes or until the chicken breasts are cooked through.

Meanwhile, in a large, nonstick frying pan, heat 1 to 2 inches of vegetable oil to hot but not smoking. Add the tortilla strips and fry, stirring constantly, for 3 to 4 minutes until crisped and lightly browned. With a slotted spoon, transfer the strips to paper towels, spreading them out in an even layer. Sprinkle lightly with salt.

When the chicken is cooked through, remove from the pot and set aside until cool enough to handle. Add the tomatoes to the soup stock and return the soup to a simmer. Cut the chicken meat into bite-size pieces and return it to the pot. Continue cooking until the chicken is just heated through, 2 to 3 minutes longer. Stir in the parsley.

Ladle the soup into individual serving bowls. Sprinkle some of the tortilla strips and the grated cheese into each serving. Serve immediately.

Yield: 6 to 8 servings

*OCTOBER COUNTRY INN*

## Mediterranean Onion Soup

*This soup is best when prepared a day ahead and reheated. The soup may be served with a side bowl of freshly grated Parmesan cheese.*

| | |
|---|---|
| 2 tablespoons olive oil | 2 tablespoons all-purpose flour |
| 4 to 5 cups thinly sliced onions | 1 tablespoon tomato paste |
| Salt and freshly ground pepper to taste | 8 large ripe tomatoes, peeled, seeded, and chopped, or 1 35-ounce can Italian plum tomatoes, drained and chopped |
| 1 teaspoon sugar | |
| 1 teaspoon thyme | |
| 3 cloves garlic, peeled and crushed | 6 to 8 cups chicken stock or broth |
| 1 bay leaf | Minced fresh parsley |
| ½ teaspoon oregano | for garnish |
| 1 large sprig fresh parsley | |

In a heavy-bottomed casserole, heat the olive oil and add the onions. Season with salt and pepper and add the sugar. Cook the onions over medium heat for 15 minutes or until lightly browned. Add the thyme, garlic, bay leaf, oregano, and parsley sprig. Partially cover the casserole and continue cooking the onions over low heat for 30 to 40 minutes or until they are soft and nicely browned. Stir the mixture occasionally to prevent onions from burning. Add the flour and stir to blend thoroughly with the onion mixture.

Add the tomato paste, tomatoes, and stock, and bring to a boil. Reduce the heat and simmer the soup, partially covered, for 30 to 40 minutes. Taste the soup and correct seasonings. Remove and discard the bay leaf.

Garnish the soup with the minced parsley and serve.

Yield: 6 to 8 servings

*OCTOBER COUNTRY INN*

## Sausage-and-Beer Soup with Potato Dumplings

**SOUP**

¾ pound garlic sausage, or
  Italian sweet sausage
4 ribs celery, diced
1 large onion, diced
2 carrots, diced
2 cloves garlic, minced
1 cup chopped, peeled tomatoes
  with juice
8 cups beef stock
1 cup amber beer
2 teaspoons granulated brown
  sugar
1 bay leaf
¼ teaspoon thyme
2 sprigs parsley, chopped
1 tablespoon arrowroot
1 tablespoon red wine vinegar
Salt and pepper

**DUMPLINGS**

2 medium baking potatoes,
  peeled and cubed
1 tablespoon butter
1 tablespoon minced onion
  Zest of ½ lemon
⅛ teaspoon freshly grated nutmeg
1 tablespoon chopped parsley or
  watercress
  Salt
1 egg yolk
2 tablespoons all-purpose flour

Prepare the soup. In a 3-quart nonstick saucepan, brown the sausage. Add the celery, onion, carrots, and garlic, and cook until soft. Add the tomatoes, stock, beer, brown sugar, bay leaf, thyme, and parsley. Bring to a boil, then reduce heat and simmer about 20 minutes. In a separate bowl, blend the arrowroot and the red wine vinegar; mix into the soup. Add the salt and pepper to taste and simmer to blend the flavors. When ready to serve, add the potato dumplings to the soup and simmer for 5 to 10 minutes. Do not stir. Remove the bay leaf.

Prepare the dumplings. Boil the potatoes in salted water until soft. Drain and mash the potatoes, mixing in the butter, onion, lemon zest, nutmeg, parsley, and salt. Blend in the egg yolk and the flour. Take 1 teaspoon of the dumpling mix at a time and add it to the hot soup by gently pushing it off the spoon with another teaspoon and dropping it into the soup. Repeat until all of the mix is used. Serve the soup hot.

Yield: 6 to 8 servings

*SETTLERS INN*

## Cream of Onion Soup with Tawny Port

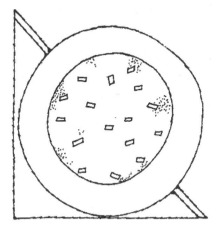

2 tablespoons extra virgin olive
  oil
5 Spanish onions, sliced
5 red onions, sliced
5 Vidalia onions, sliced

2 cups tawny port
4 cups chicken stock
1 cup heavy cream
  Salt and pepper

Heat the oil in a medium skillet, add the onions, and sauté until they are caramelized about 3 to 4 minutes. Deglaze the pan with ½ of the port. Add the chicken stock and simmer for 30 to 40 minutes. Purée the soup mixture in a food processor, then strain it through a chinois or a fine mesh strainer. Return the mixture to the pan and bring it to a simmer. Then add the remainder of the port and all of the heavy cream. Add salt and pepper to taste. Serve hot.

Yield: 6 servings

*SIGN OF THE SORREL HORSE*

## Roasted-Eggplant-and-Garlic Soup

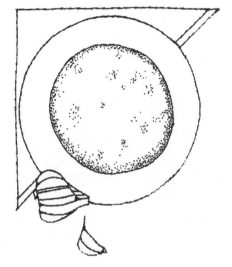

*Chef Sharon Ashburn is a creative cook who offers this unusual combination for garlic lovers. The taste is superb.*

2 small to medium eggplants
4 whole heads garlic
1 cup chopped onion
1 tablespoon olive oil

2 cups chicken stock or broth
½ cup white wine
1 cup heavy or light cream
  Salt and pepper

Prick the eggplants with a fork and roast them on a grill or in a 500° oven for 20 minutes or until tender, turning occasionally. Roast the garlic in the same manner for 10 minutes or until tender.

Let the vegetables cool. Remove the skins from the eggplants and squeeze the garlic from their bulbs. Set aside.

In a small skillet, sauté the onion in the olive oil until soft. Then place the eggplant, garlic, and onion in a food processor and purée until smooth, adding stock if necessary. Turn out into a medium saucepan with the remaining stock, wine, and cream. Heat to boiling and simmer briefly until slightly thickened. Add salt and pepper to taste.

Yield: 6 servings

*ANTRIM 1844*

# Tomato-Mushroom Soup

¼ cup dried boletus or any other dried mushrooms
1 cup hot water
2 tablespoons olive oil
1 small onion, peeled and finely diced
¾ pound button mushrooms, thinly sliced
¼ cup dry white wine
2 cups chicken broth
½ cup fresh tomatoes, chopped and seeded
½ cup each: coarsely chopped parsley and celery leaves
Coarse salt
Freshly ground pepper

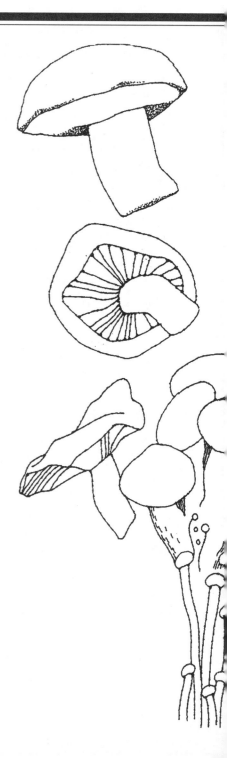

Place the dried mushrooms in a small heatproof bowl. Pour the hot water over them and allow to stand until softened, about 10 minutes. Line a sieve with a double thickness of cheesecloth and place the sieve over a bowl. Turn the soaked mushrooms and liquid into the sieve. Reserve the liquid. Remove the cheesecloth and rinse the mushrooms thoroughly under cold running water to remove all of the sand and grit. Finely chop the mushrooms.

Heat the olive oil in a heavy, 4-quart saucepan over medium heat. Add the onions and sauté, stirring until just golden, about 10 minutes. Stir in the button mushrooms and chopped mushrooms. Reduce the heat to low. Cover the saucepan and cook, stirring occasionally, until the mushrooms have rendered their liquid, about 10 minutes.

Stir in the wine. Simmer 2 minutes. Stir in the broth, tomatoes, parsley, celery leaves, and salt and pepper to taste. Simmer for 5 minutes and serve.

Yield: 6 servings

*CHECKERBERRY INN*

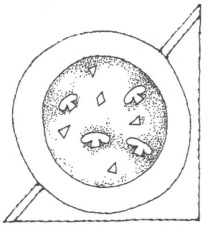

## Wild-Rice-and-Mushroom Soup

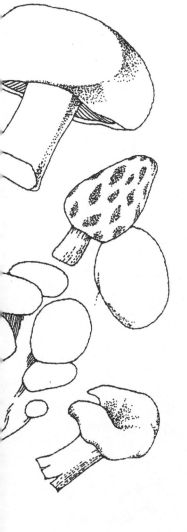

¼ teaspoon salt
⅓ cup wild rice
¼ cup butter
½ cup diced onion
½ cup diced carrot
¼ cup diced celery
4 cups coarsely chopped wild
   mushrooms such as portobello, shiitake, or crimini

¼ cup all-purpose flour
4 cups beef stock
½ cup heavy cream
   Salt and pepper

Bring 3 cups of water to a boil in a saucepan. Add the ¼ teaspoon salt
and the wild rice. Cover and simmer for 45 minutes or until the rice
has opened up. Drain and set aside.

In a 3-quart stockpot, melt the butter and sauté the onions, carrots, and celery until soft. Add the mushrooms and cook for about 3
minutes. Add the flour and cook on low heat, stirring occasionally, for
about 10 to 15 minutes. Add the stock and simmer for 10 minutes.
Season to taste. Stir in the rice and the cream. Heat to blend flavors.

Yield: 6 to 8 servings

*SETTLERS INN*

## Carrot-and-Chestnut Soup

*When selecting chestnuts, choose firm, plump nuts without blemishes on the shells.*

6 tablespoons unsalted butter
1 large onion, chopped
3 cups minced carrots
1 pound shelled chestnuts, chopped
5 cups chicken stock

¼ cup brandy
½ cup heavy cream
Freshly ground pepper
Crème fraîche (optional), (see page 220)

Melt the butter in a large saucepan. Add the chopped onion and sauté until soft, about 5 minutes. Add the carrots, and sauté 5 minutes more. Add the chestnuts, and sauté for an additional 5 minutes.

Add the chicken stock and brandy, and bring to a boil. Reduce the heat, cover, and simmer for 30 minutes, stirring occasionally.

Purée the soup, in batches, in a food processor or blender, and return it to the saucepan. Add the heavy cream and pepper, and heat the soup over low heat (do not let it boil).

Serve the soup garnished with crème fraîche, if desired.

Yield: 6 servings

*NEWCASTLE INN*

# Yukon Gold Potato and Vidalia Onion Soup

*I have been with Chef Craig Hartman a few times when he has served this soup at cooking demonstrations. Everyone is wild about the taste and they scramble for the recipe. Here it is, and it is, in itself, like gold. Yukon Gold potatoes are just becoming available, and what is so special about them is that they emit a slightly sweet flavor, thus they are a potato of choice for many recipes and are great for mashed potatoes.*

| | |
|---|---|
| ¼ cup extra virgin olive oil | 4 cups chicken or vegetable stock |
| 3 cups peeled and sliced Yukon Gold potatoes (2–3 potatoes) | 2 cups sour cream |
| 3 cups sliced Vidalia onions (2–3 onions) | 1 cup freshly chopped herbs of choice |
| Salt, pepper, and sugar | Garlic croutons |

Place the olive oil in a nonstick saucepan and heat over low heat. Add the potatoes, onions, and seasonings. Stir and cover. Cook over medium-low heat, stirring frequently. After about 10 minutes, add the stock, bring to a boil, and reduce to a simmer. Simmer until the vegetables are soft.

Purée in a food processor until smooth. Add the sour cream and herbs, reserving some of the herbs for garnish. Adjust the seasonings as needed. Garnish with chopped herbs and croutons.

Yield: 10 to 12 servings

*CLIFTON COUNTRY INN*

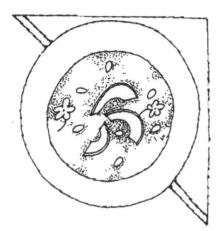

# Spicy Southern California Avocado Soup

*Southern California is the nation's avocado capital, so it is most fitting that we have this soup from Chef Ralph Randau's repertoire, which includes the unusual addition of chutney for a hint of sweetness. The soup is served cold, so it may be made a day in advance of serving. When purchasing avocados, look for those that are blemish free. If they yield to pressure when squeezed, then they are ripe. Otherwise, to hasten ripening, store the avocados in a paper bag at room temperature.*

| | |
|---|---|
| 1 large or 2 small very ripe, green-skinned avocados, peeled and stones removed | ¼ teaspoon lemon zest |
| | ¼ teaspoon finely chopped garlic |
| | ¼ teaspoon chutney of choice |
| 2 cups concentrated chicken stock or chicken broth | ¼ teaspoon curry powder |
| | Salt |
| ½ cup half-and-half | ½ teaspoon fresh lime juice |
| 1 tablespoon tomato salsa, mild or spicy | Edible flowers and almonds for garnish |

### How to Cut an Avocado

Using a chef's knife, cut the avocado in half lengthwise. Place the half of the avocado that contains the stone in the palm of your hand. Using the heel of the chef's knife, gently tap the stone so that the heel of the chef's knife will remain in the stone. (Be careful not to tap the stone too hard, as the knife may slip and create an injurious situation.) Then, twist the seed and remove it by lifting the stone upward.

Cut the avocado into chunks and place in a blender. Add 1 cup of the chicken stock. At medium speed, blend until the avocado is puréed. Scrape the bottom and sides of the blender with a rubber spatula, pouring the soup into a medium bowl. Add all of the remaining ingredients except the lime juice and garnishes, and blend well, adding salt to taste. Add the lime juice slowly so that the half-and-half does not curdle. Chill the soup in the refrigerator. Serve in chilled soup plates and garnish with edible flowers and almonds.

Yield: 2 to 4 servings

*HERITAGE PARK B&B INN*

## Tangy Tropical Floridian Salad

MARINADE
¾ cup oil
¼ cup red wine vinegar
1 tablespoon sugar
⅓ cup ketchup
¼ cup snipped Italian parsley

SALAD
4 oranges, skinned, sectioned, and seeded
2 medium onions, thinly sliced
1 7.8-ounce can small hearts of palm, sliced into 1-inch bits
1 large, ripe green-skinned avocado, peeled, sliced, and stone removed
Lettuce

In a large bowl, combine the marinade ingredients and add the orange sections, onions, and hearts of palm. Marinate for 2 hours in the refrigerator, turning occasionally.

Arrange the avocado slices in a medium serving bowl on a bed of lettuce. Using a slotted spoon, place the oranges, onions, and hearts of palm in the bowl. Dress the salad by drizzling the marinade overtop.

Yield: 4 to 6 servings

CHALET SUZANNE

# Cherimoya Fruit Salad with Lime Dressing

*The cherimoya is a fairly new fruit in many areas of the United States. It is selling wildly in California, and it has been likened to a baby cactus or a small artichoke.*

Limes

SALAD
- 1 ¼-ounce envelope unflavored gelatin
- 1 cup cold ginger ale
- 1 cup boiling water
- 1 tablespoon sugar
- 2 tablespoons lemon juice
- ½ cup bite-size chunks cherimoya, skin removed
- ½ cup bite-size chunks avocado, skin removed
- ½ cup bite-size chunks unpeeled apple

DRESSING
- ¼ cup sour cream
- ¼ cup mayonnaise
- ½ teaspoon sugar
- 1 teaspoon lime juice
- ¼ teaspoon lime zest

Prepare the salad. In a medium bowl, mix the gelatin and the ginger ale; let stand for 1 minute. Add the boiling water and the sugar, and stir until the sugar and gelatin are completely dissolved. Stir in the lemon juice. Chill, stirring occasionally, until the mixture is the consistency of unbeaten egg whites. Fold in the fruit and turn the mixture into individual 1-cup molds or a single 4-cup mold. Chill until firm. Unmold and serve with the Lime Dressing.

Prepare the dressing by combining all ingredients; beat until smooth.

Yield: 4 servings

*HERITAGE PARK B&B INN*

## Dried Cherries and Pecan Salad with Red Raspberry Vinaigrette

*In the state that produces red cherries, Victorian Villa Inn developed this salad as a salute to the past, as cherries have long been a mainstay here. The dressing, which makes eight cups, can be made ahead and refrigerated for up to one week.*

DRESSING

- 4 cups cold-pressed soybean oil
- 1 cup light corn syrup
- ¾ cup red wine vinegar
- ¾ cup sugar
- 12 ounces frozen red raspberry concentrate, thawed
- 12 ounces frozen red raspberries, thawed
- 1½ teaspoons salt
- 1 teaspoon lemon zest
- 1 tablespoon fresh lemon juice

SALAD

- 2 small heads romaine lettuce, cleaned and hand-torn into salad-size pieces
- 2 small heads red leaf lettuce, cleaned and hand-torn into salad-size pieces
- 1 head fresh endive, cleaned and hand-torn into salad-size pieces
- 1 cup coarsely chopped pecans
- 1 cup dried tart cherries

Prepare the dressing by combining all of the dressing ingredients in a blender or food processor. Whirl until completely combined. Refrigerate immediately.

Prepare the salad by tossing all the lettuce together, mixing well. Divide the salad evenly among individual salad plates. Sprinkle the pecans evenly overtop of each salad. Do the same with the cherries. Top with the dressing as desired.

Yield: 8 to 10 servings

*VICTORIAN VILLA*

## Poppy-Seed Vegetable Slaw

*This elegant vegetable salad couldn't be easier to make or its sweet-and-sour flavor more inviting.*

**MARINADE**
1½ cups cider vinegar
¾ cup vegetable oil
½ cup sugar
1½ cups honey
2 teaspoons dry mustard
2 tablespoons salt

**VEGETABLES**
2 pounds cabbage, shredded
½ cup chopped onion
2 cups julienned carrots
2 cups julienned zucchini
2 cups small broccoli florets
2 cups small cauliflower florets
1 cup julienned red bell pepper
½ cup mayonnaise
2 tablespoons poppy seeds
Salt and pepper

Prepare the marinade, the cabbage, and the onion the day before serving. Make the marinade by whisking together all the marinade ingredients. Place the shredded cabbage and the chopped onion in a large, deep bowl, then pour the marinade mixture overtop and refrigerate overnight.

Using a colander, strain the cabbage-and-onion mixture well. Place the mixture in a large mixing bowl and add the remaining vegetables. Stir in the mayonnaise and the poppy seeds until well combined. Season with salt and pepper to taste.

Yield: 12 servings

*ANTRIM 1844*

# Bacon in Beer Potato Salad

*Chef John Schumacher likes to say, "This dish will transport you to Grinzing, the playground of Vienna, on a summer day." But I'm not sure he means the potato salad because his footnote to this recipe says, ". . . and don't forget to drink the beer you didn't use in the recipe."*

| | |
|---|---|
| 6 medium white potatoes | 1 cup German beer of choice |
| 4 slices bacon | ¼ teaspoon Tabasco sauce |
| 1 rib celery, peeled and cut into ¼-inch dice | 1 teaspoon salt |
| 2 tablespoons butter | ½ teaspoon black pepper |
| 2 tablespoons chopped onions | ½ teaspoon celery seeds |
| 2 tablespoons all-purpose flour | 2 tablespoons chopped parsley |
| ½ teaspoon dry mustard | 2 hard-boiled eggs, peeled and diced |
| 1 tablespoon sugar | |

Boil the potatoes until tender; then peel and cut each potato in half. Slice the potatoes into ½-inch-thick slices. Place the slices in a large bowl and set aside. Fry the bacon until crisp, then break into small pieces in a bowl and mix with the celery.

In a small saucepan, melt the butter and sauté the onions until clear. Mix in the flour until blended thoroughly. Add the mustard and the sugar. Add the beer slowly and stir. Add the Tabasco sauce and stir. Bring the mixture to a boil, stirring constantly. Pour the sauce over the potatoes; add the salt, pepper, and celery seeds. Sprinkle with the parsley, then toss lightly and let stand for 1 hour. Add the bacon mixture and toss gently. Garnish with chopped egg.

Yield: 6 to 8 servings

*SCHUMACHER'S NEW PRAGUE HOTEL*

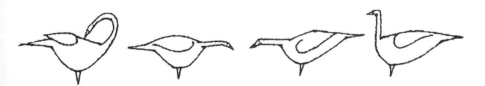

49

# Sauté of Spinach, Escarole, and Radicchio with Hot-Sherried-Bacon Dressing

*The dressing will yield 2 cups.*

DRESSING
- 2 ounces bacon, diced
- 1 tablespoon all-purpose flour
- 2 tablespoons honey
- 2 tablespoons sugar
- 1 large egg, beaten
- ¼ cup cider vinegar
- 1 cup water
- ¼ cup olive oil
- ¼ cup rice vinegar
- 5 tablespoons dry sherry
- ½ teaspoon oregano
- ¼ teaspoon tarragon
- Salt and pepper

SALAD
- 1 to 2 tablespoons olive oil
- 1 very small head radicchio lettuce, julienned
- 1 10-ounce package fresh spinach, washed and stemmed
- 1 large head escarole, coarsely chopped

To make the dressing, sauté the bacon until crisp. Remove the bacon with a slotted spoon and set aside. Reserve the bacon fat in the pan.

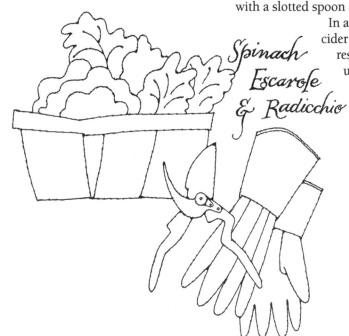

Spinach Escarole & Radicchio

In a bowl, beat together the flour, honey, sugar, egg, cider vinegar, and water. Stir the egg mixture into the reserved bacon drippings and cook 3 to 4 minutes until thick, stirring occasionally. In a separate bowl, mix the olive oil, rice vinegar, sherry, herbs, salt, and pepper; add to the bacon-egg mixture. Stir while heating, blending the dressing thoroughly. Keep warm.

Prepare the salad. Add the olive oil to a large skillet, and sauté the radicchio and the greens in small to medium batches. The vegetables should just be nicely wilted. Serve the greens immediately in individual portions with 1 ounce or so of dressing per portion. Chop the bacon and add to the salad if desired.

Yield: 8 servings

*HIGHLAND LAKE INN*

## Green Beans Balsamic with Garden-Ripe Tomatoes

1½ pounds green beans, trimmed
1 teaspoon salt
2 large ripe tomatoes, peeled
1 red onion, finely chopped
1 large clove garlic, finely chopped
1 small fresh hot pepper (such as jalapeño), seeded and chopped

3 tablespoons extra virgin olive oil
2 tablespoons balsamic or red wine vinegar
½ to 1 teaspoon sugar
Salt and freshly ground black pepper

Fill a large saucepan with water and bring to a boil. Add the beans and salt. Cook on high for 6 to 8 minutes or until the beans have lost their raw taste, but are still crisp. Transfer the beans immediately to a colander and run cold water over them. Set aside.

Cut the tomatoes in half and squeeze gently to remove the seeds and excess juice. Chop them coarsely. In a nonstick skillet, sauté the onion, garlic, hot pepper, and tomatoes in the olive oil until soft, about 5 minutes. Set aside.

Just before serving, reheat the tomato mixture. Add the beans and vinegar and toss. Taste and add the sugar, salt, and pepper as needed.

Yield: 6 to 8 servings

*GLEN-ELLA SPRINGS INN*

## Apple Salad with Lemon-Poppy-Seed Dressing

SALAD
5 red or Golden Delicious apples, peeled, cored and cut into bite-size pieces
1½ cups raisins
1 cup chopped pecans
1½ cups chopped celery

DRESSING
6 tablespoons salad oil
¾ cup honey
2 teaspoons poppy seeds
½ cup frozen lemonade concentrate

In a large bowl, mix the apples, raisins, pecans, and celery. In a separate bowl, whisk the oil, honey, poppy seeds, and lemonade concentrate. Add the dressing to the apple mixture and mix thoroughly.

Yield: 6 to 8 servings

*HIGHLAND LAKE INN*

## Black-Eyed-Pea-and-Corn Salad

*Any time of year this salad may be served separately with bread and cheese or as an aside to fish or poultry.*

DRESSING
- ⅓ cup balsamic vinegar
- 1 tablespoon Dijon-style mustard
- 2 tablespoons finely chopped fresh cilantro
- 2 tablespoons finely chopped fresh Italian parsley
- ¼ teaspoon dried red pepper flakes
- ¼ cup extra virgin olive oil
- ½ teaspoon salt

SALAD
- ½ pound fresh black-eyed peas, shelled (or 1 10-ounce box premium quality frozen)
- 1½ cups fresh corn kernels (or premium quality frozen)
- 1 cup chopped red bell pepper
- 1 cup chopped red or Vidalia onion
- 1 cup chopped celery

Prepare the dressing by mixing together all of the ingredients. Then set aside.

Prepare the salad. Cook the peas in a small amount of lightly salted boiling water until barely tender, about 20 minutes. Drain. In a separate saucepan, cook the fresh corn the same way. (If using frozen corn, just thaw the corn under running water.) One hour before serving, combine the peas and the corn with the other vegetables and toss with the dressing. Taste and correct seasonings.

Yield: 6 servings

*GLEN-ELLA SPRINGS INN*

# Salad of Warm Goat Cheese in Squash Blossoms

*Squash blossoms are the flowers from summer or winter squash. They can be found in specialty produce markets from late spring through early fall.*

**MUSTARD DRESSING**
- 1 large clove garlic
- ½ teaspoon salt
- ¼ cup red wine vinegar
- 1 tablespoon Dijon-style mustard
- Freshly ground pepper
- ½ cup quality olive oil

**STUFFING**
- 2 cups fresh Goat cheese
- 1 tablespoon freshly chopped thyme
- 1 teaspoon freshly ground black pepper

- ⅓ cup olive oil
- 16 squash blossoms, stems removed

**GREENS**
- 2 cups torn greens per person, incorporating 4 or 5 types of lettuce: romaine and endive for crunch, red and green lettuces, Boston and Bibb for softer buttery texture, and radicchio and arugula for color and strong flavor

Squash Blossoms

With a knife or a mortar and pestle, mash the garlic with the salt. Blend in the vinegar, mustard, and black pepper. Whisk in the oil. Set aside briefly.

In a medium bowl, mix the cheese, thyme, and pepper well. Let the mixture stand at room temperature at least 1 hour to blend the flavors. Preheat the broiler. Open the squash blossoms gently. Put a spoonful of goat cheese in each open blossom. Gently roll the flower closed. Oil a baking sheet and place the flowers on the sheet. Broil for 5 minutes or until the cheese begins to melt and the flowers begin to become crisp.

Toss the greens with the dressing. Divide and pile the greens in the center of luncheon plates. Place the warm squash blossoms around the greens. Serve immediately.

Yield: 4 servings

*SETTLERS INN*

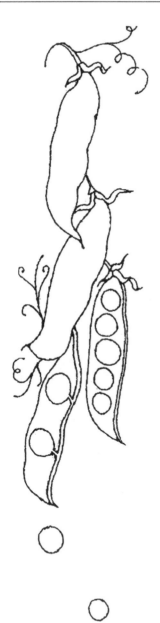

## Luncheon Salad with Green Peas and Water Chestnuts

*You can make this a day in advance of serving time. The salad serves a lot of people, or cut the recipe in half or in thirds.*

1 medium head iceberg lettuce, rinsed and dried
½ cup thinly sliced green onion
1 cup thinly sliced celery
1 8-ounce can water chestnuts, drained and sliced
1 10-ounce package frozen peas
2 cups mayonnaise
2 teaspoons sugar
½ cup grated Parmesan cheese
1 teaspoon seasoned salt
¼ teaspoon garlic powder
3 hard-boiled eggs, chopped
¾ pound bacon, crisply fried, well drained, and crumbled
2 ripe medium tomatoes, cut into wedges

Shred the lettuce and place the greens in a shallow 4-quart serving dish. Top with green onion, celery, and water chestnuts. Break apart frozen peas and sprinkle them over the salad. Spread mayonnaise evenly overtop. Sprinkle with sugar, cheese, salt, and garlic powder. Cover and chill salad in the refrigerator for up to 24 hours.

Just before serving, sprinkle the salad with the hard-boiled eggs and the bacon. Arrange the tomatoes around the salad. To serve, use a spoon and fork to lift complete layered sections.

Yield: 12 to 14 servings

*CANYON VILLA*

## Couscous Salad

2 cups orange juice
1 cup couscous
¼ cup vegetable oil
½ cup raisins
½ cup cashews
½ cup thinly sliced spring onion
½ cup thinly sliced red bell pepper
½ cup thinly sliced green bell pepper
Salt and pepper

In a nonreactive saucepan, bring the orange juice to a boil. Stir in the couscous and remove the pan from the heat. Cover and let it stand for 10 minutes. Then stir in the oil. Turn the mixture out onto a cookie sheet to cool, stirring occasionally. Place mixture in a bowl. Stir in the remaining ingredients, and season to taste with salt and pepper.

Yield: 6 servings

*ANTRIM 1844*

~Menu~

Duck in
Puff Pastry
with
Fig Sauce

# APPETIZERS

## Garlic Bread Bathed in Curried Crab

*You may also serve this spread with melba toast rounds or an assortment of crackers and skip the making of the garlic toast. The spread will yield 2 cups.*

SPREAD
- 1 8-ounce package cream cheese, softened
- ½ cup mayonnaise or sour cream, or ¼ cup each
- 2 tablespoons chopped chives
- ½ teaspoon curry powder
- 1 tablespoon Worcestershire sauce
  Salt and pepper
- 6 ounces fresh lump crabmeat, flaked

GARLIC TOAST
- 1 medium-size French bread baguette, sliced in ¼- to ½-inch-thick slices
- ½ cup butter, melted
- 4 cloves garlic, minced
- 2 teaspoons dried parsley

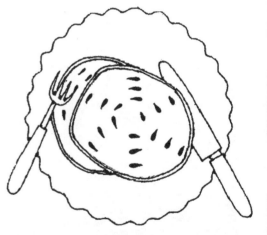

Allow the cream cheese to soften to room temperature. Add the mayonnaise, chives, curry powder, Worcestershire sauce, salt, and pepper. Blend well. Fold in the crabmeat. Set aside.

Preheat the oven to 375°. Brush only the tops of the bread slices with the butter. Combine the garlic and the parsley and sprinkle over the butter. Bake in the oven 5 to 6 minutes or until golden. Cool the slices on a rack over paper grocery bags to absorb excess butter. Spread the toasted slices with the crab mixture. (Note: You may store the toasted bread in a plastic container or a bag.)

Yield: 4 to 6 servings

*CANYON VILLA*

## Radicchio Cups of Crabmeat with Roasted-Red-Pepper-Mayonnaise and Garlic Phyllo Crisps

### RED PEPPER MAYONNAISE

3 red bell peppers, cored, seeded, and cut into quarters
6 shallots, peeled and cut in half
1 cup olive oil, divided
Salt, pepper, and sugar
2 egg yolks
2 tablespoons champagne vinegar
2 tablespoons chopped chives
Warm water

### PHYLLO CRISPS

3 sheets phyllo dough
¼ cup clarified butter (see recipe page 220)
Salt and pepper
2 cloves garlic, minced

### ASSEMBLY

1 pound jumbo lump crabmeat
2 small heads radicchio lettuce
Chives for garnish

Preheat the oven to 350° and roast the peppers and shallots in 2 tablespoons of the olive oil with some salt, pepper, and sugar to taste. Roast until soft, about 15 minutes. (Keep checking your oven; you do not want the vegetables to blacken, just soften.) Remove from the oven and purée in a food processor until creamy. Turn oven up to 400°. Place about 3 tablespoons of the purée aside for garnish later. Let the rest of the purée cool down. Once the purée has cooled, place it back into the food processor and add the egg yolks, vinegar, and chives. Add the remaining olive oil slowly, with the processor running. Whirl until the mixture thickens. Add warm water to thin if desired.

Prepare the phyllo crisps. Place the first sheet of phyllo onto the work surface. Add the salt, pepper, and garlic to the clarified butter. Brush the phyllo layer with the garlic butter. Top with another sheet of dough, brushing again with the garlic butter. Repeat again with the third and final layer. Cut the phyllo into 2- to 3-inch triangles as desired, cutting at least 8 or so triangles. Bake for 5 minutes or until crisp.

To assemble, carefully pick through the crabmeat to remove any pieces of shell. Try not to break up the lumps. Carefully remove radicchio leaves from the head to form 8 palm-size cups. Place each leaf in the center of each individual serving plate. Add about 2 ounces of crabmeat into each radicchio cup and drizzle some of the mayonnaise around the outside. Top with a dollop of the reserved red pepper

purée. Place a phyllo crisp in the center of the crab so that it elevates like a sail in the wind. Sprinkle chives around the outside.

Yield: 8 servings

*CLIFTON COUNTRY INN*

## Marsala Melon Medley

4 cups mixed cantaloupe and
   honeydew cubes
1 cup Marsala wine

⅛ to ¼ teaspoon black pepper
⅛ teaspoon cayenne pepper

In a large bowl, toss the melon with ½ cup of the Marsala. Cover and chill for 1 hour. Drain, reserving the wine. Sprinkle the melon with the peppers. Toss to coat. To serve, spoon some of the reserved Marsala over the melon.

Yield: 4 to 6 servings

*HIGHLAND LAKE INN*

## Baked Shrimp Curry

⅓ cup butter
3 tablespoons all-purpose flour
1 or 2 tablespoons curry powder
½ teaspoon salt
¼ teaspoon paprika
¼ teaspoon grated nutmeg
2 cups half-and-half
1½ pounds large cleaned and
   cooked shrimp

1 tablespoon finely chopped
   candied ginger or grated fresh
   ginger
1 tablespoon fresh lemon juice
1 teaspoon onion juice
¼ teaspoon Worcestershire sauce

Preheat the oven to 400°. In a medium nonstick saucepan, melt the butter. Blend in the flour, curry powder, salt, paprika, and nutmeg. Gradually stir in the half-and-half. Cook over medium-high heat until the mixture thickens, stirring constantly. Add the remaining ingredients and heat through. Pour into individual 2- to 4-cup baking dishes and bake for 10 minutes or until the tops are lightly browned.

Yield: 4 servings

*CHALET SUZANNE*

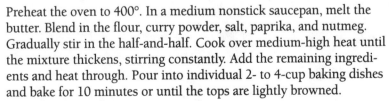

# Parchment Hearts of Shrimp and Vegetables

*You will need kitchen parchment paper to complete this recipe.*

¼ cup plus 1 tablespoon olive oil
18 large shrimp, cleaned
½ cup each: julienned carrots,
  celery, leeks, parsnips
2 tablespoons minced shallots

Salt and pepper
¼ cup plus 1 tablespoon white
  wine
¾ cup shrimp or fish stock

Preheat the oven to 400°. Cut 6  8-inch-diameter hearts out of parchment paper. Brush the hearts with olive oil to seal the paper later. Place 3 shrimp in the center of each heart. Add the julienned vegetables and shallots, portioning the mixture out evenly among the hearts. Season overall with salt and pepper.

Fold the paper over in half to cover, and seal the edges together by folding over the edges a few times, leaving a 1-inch opening. The idea here is to fully seal in the fish except for a steam hole. Add ½ ounce wine to each pouch, followed by 1 ounce of the shrimp stock. Place on a cookie sheet and bake for 10 minutes or until the parchment pouch is puffed and the shrimp are just cooked.

Yield: 6 servings

*BEE & THISTLE INN*

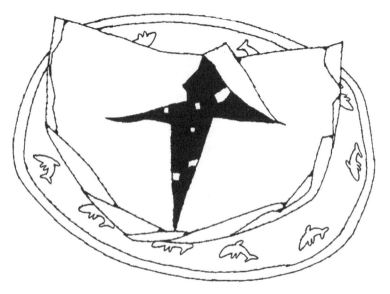

# Potato Crêpes with Smoked Salmon and Caviar

*Chef François de Melogue was born in Chicago of French parents, so he spoke only their native language until the age of five. He is a chef with a gentle but powerful hand in the kitchen. Delicate but intense foods, such as this superb appetizer, are his hallmark.*

### CRÊPES
- ¾ cup potato purée (1 large potato, cubed and boiled in salted water until soft, then puréed)
- 2 tablespoons milk
- 1 tablespoon all-purpose flour
- 1 egg, separated (egg white, beaten)
- Sea salt and white pepper
- 2 tablespoons clarified butter (see recipe page 220)

### SAUCE
- 1 shallot, finely chopped
- ½ cup fish stock
- ½ cup white wine
- 2 tablespoons heavy cream
- 2 tablespoons unsalted butter
- 1 teaspoon white wine vinegar
- 1 tablespoon chopped fresh chives
- 1 tablespoon chopped fresh chervil
- 2 teaspoons chopped fresh thyme

### ASSEMBLY
- 1 ounce bowfin caviar
- ¾ pound sliced smoked salmon
- ¼ cup crème fraîche (see recipe page 220)

Combine the puréed potatoes with the milk, flour, egg yolk, and beaten egg white. Season with the sea salt and white pepper. Let the crêpe batter rest for 30 minutes at room temperature.

Prepare the sauce. In a small saucepan, combine the shallot, fish stock, and wine and cook over medium-high heat, reducing by half. Add the cream and reduce until the mixture coats the back of a spoon. Whisk in the butter and the vinegar. Stir in the chopped herbs. Remove from heat. Cook the crêpes in a round pan in the clarified butter. Flip the crêpes so that they brown evenly on both sides and the edges become crisp.

To assemble the dish, place ¼ of the caviar in the center of each individual serving plate. Add a tablespoon of crème fraîche on top. Arrange the salmon on top and then cover with the crêpe. Spoon the sauce overtop and around the crêpe.

Yield: 4 servings

*OLD DROVERS INN*

## Marinated Salmon with Black Bread and Capers

### Chocolate-Dipped Nuts

This recipe is a cinch to prepare and is delicious. Melt 1 square (1-ounce) of semisweet chocolate in a cup, set into hot, not boiling water. Into the chocolate, dip 12 hazelnuts or whole almonds. Remove with a fork to waxed paper. Refrigerate until chocolate has hardened. Serve on a doily or in a special candy dish.

*The salmon marinates for three days, so start this easy recipe ahead of time.*

MARINADE
¼ cup sugar
1 cup kosher salt
2 cups minced onion
1 cup minced carrot
1 cup minced celery
2 tablespoons crumbled, dried bay leaf
2 cups freshly chopped garden herbs, such as basil, dill, marjoram, tarragon
1 teaspoon ground pepper
1 teaspoon cayenne pepper
1 teaspoon crushed juniper berries or dried cranberries
2 teaspoons crushed coriander seed
1 teaspoon crushed mustard seed
1 2- to 3-pound gravlax salmon filet, skin on and pin bones removed

GARNISH
Black bread
Capers
Red onion
Dill

Prepare the marinade. Combine all ingredients, except the salmon, in a bowl. Spread out a piece of plastic wrap (3 times the length of the fish) in a glass baking pan, draping the excess over the sides. Place the fish in the pan, skin-side down. Spread the marinade mixture over the fish and wrap the plastic around it. Place a second baking pan on top of the fish and weigh it down with abut 10 pounds of canned goods, dinner plates, or such.

Marinate for three days in the refrigerator, draining off accumulated liquid daily. Remove the fish from the marinade and rinse it in cold water. Cut into paper-thin slices and serve it on pieces of black bread, garnishing with the capers, red onion, and dill.

Yield: 30 to 40 hors d'oeuvres

*ANTRIM 1844*

## Hot Artichoke Dip

*Quick and easy, this is a great appetizer or snack.*

1 cup mayonnaise
1 cup grated Parmesan cheese
1 14-ounce can artichoke hearts,
  coarsely chopped
1 clove garlic, minced
Juice of 1 small lemon

Preheat the oven to 350°. Combine all of the above ingredients and place in a greased 1-quart glass dish or casserole. Bake for 30 minutes or until lightly browned. Serve hot with crackers.

   Yield: 3 cups

   *CANYON VILLA*

## Bleu-Cheese-and-Poppy-Seed Mousse

*A nice make-ahead hors d'oeuvre, serve the mousse with crackers or toast points.*

6 egg yolks
3 egg whites, stiffly beaten
6 tablespoons light cream
1½ tablespoons unflavored gelatin
¼ cup cold water
¾ pound Roquefort or bleu
  cheese
1½ cups heavy cream, whipped
2 tablespoons poppy seeds
  Endive or watercress for garnish

In a nonstick saucepan over low heat, beat the egg yolks with the light cream until the mixture is creamy and stiff. Remove from heat.

   Soften the gelatin in the water and dissolve it over hot water in a double boiler. Add it to the egg yolks.

   Force the cheese through a sieve or whirl it in a blender, and add it to the eggs-and-gelatin mixture. Place the mixture in the refrigerator and cool for 15 minutes or so.

   Fold the whipped cream, stiffly beaten egg whites, and poppy seeds into the cheese mixture. Pour the mousse into a greased 4- to 6-cup mold and chill in the refrigerator for at least 2 hours.

   Unmold the mousse onto a platter and garnish with either endive or watercress.

   Yield: 4 to 6 cups

   *CHALET SUZANNE*

*Artichokes*

### Baby Artichokes How-To

   Baby artichokes make a delightful item for an appetizer tray or for use as a side dish or garnish. To prepare them with ease and taste, we learned at Carter House to cut the stems and tops from the artichokes and then trim off the tip from every leaf. Rub the artichokes with fresh lemon and place them in a pot of boiling water. Reduce the heat and simmer the artichokes for 20 to 30 minutes or until tender. Before serving, brush the artichokes with a mixture of olive oil, melted butter, and lemon juice.

63

## Venison Pâté

*Chef Sharon Ashburn suggests making this three days ahead of time. A local butcher or supermarket can get you the venison and pork butt.*

2 tablespoons butter
6 large (about 6 ounces) mushrooms, sliced
1 McIntosh apple, peeled, cored, and cut into eighths
1 celery root (about ½ pound), peeled and cut into ¼-inch cubes
1 pound venison, 10 ounces cut into chunks, 6 ounces cut into ¼-inch cubes
14 ounces pork fat, 12 ounces cut into chunks, 2 ounces cut into ¼-inch cubes
½ pound pork butt (half lean, half fat), cut into chunks
1½ cups dry red wine

1 tablespoon green peppercorns packed in saltwater, drained and crushed
4 bay leaves
2 cloves garlic, minced
6 shallots, minced
¼ teaspoon celery seed
½ cup Calvados brandy
2 eggs
⅓ cup shelled, blanched, and peeled pistachio nuts
¼ pound boiled ham, cut into ¼-inch cubes
2 tablespoons kosher salt
½ teaspoon freshly ground black pepper
6 to 8 slices bacon

In a 10-inch skillet, melt the butter. Add the mushrooms, the apple pieces, and the celery root. Cook until softened but not brown. Remove from the heat and let cool. Stir in the chunks of venison, pork fat, and pork butt (reserve all ¼-inch cubes for later). Put the mixture through the fine blade of a meat grinder.

In a saucepan, mix the red wine, green peppercorns, 1 bay leaf, garlic, shallots, and celery seed; heat through. In another small saucepan, heat the brandy. Ignite the brandy by touching a lit match to the edge of the saucepan. While the brandy flames, pour it over the wine mixture. Shake the pan until the flames die down. Cook the mixture over high heat until only 2 tablespoons of liquid remain. Remove and discard the bay leaf. Let the liquid cool, then stir the contents of the saucepan into the ground-meat mixture. Stir in the remaining ¼-inch cubes of venison and pork fat, the eggs, the pistachio nuts, and the ham. Season with salt and pepper. Mix until well blended.

Heat the oven to 350°. Line a 2-quart terrine or pâté mold with the bacon, bacon edges slightly overlapping. Spoon the mixture into the terrine. Smooth out the top. Bang the terrine against the counter a

few times to eliminate any air bubbles. Place the 3 remaining
bay leaves across the top. Cover the terrine with a double
thickness of aluminum foil. Place the terrine in a large pan
with high sides. Add hot water to a point halfway up the
sides of the terrine. Place the pan and terrine in the
oven and bake for 1 hour and 15 minutes.

Remove the terrine from the pan. Let it stand
until cool, then chill. For full flavor to
develop, wait 2 or 3 days before
serving. Serve sliced, directly
from the terrine.

Yield: 30 slices

_ANTRIM 1844_

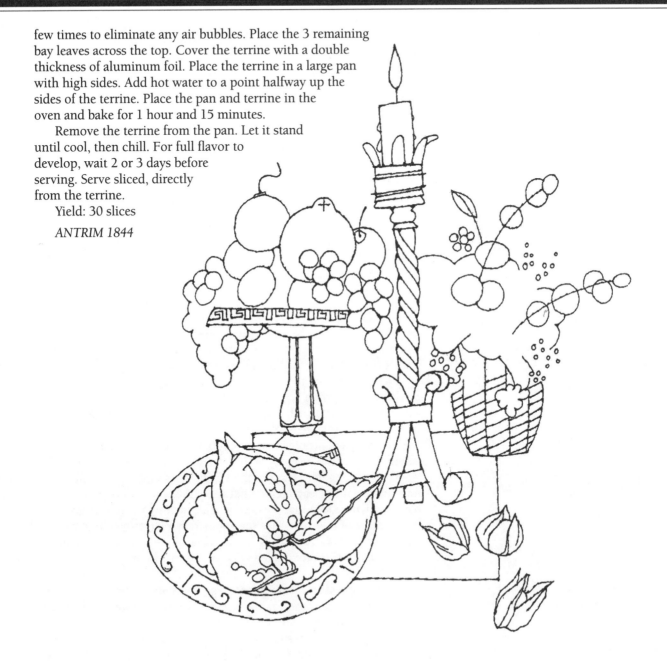

## Asparagus Pâté with Fresh-Chive Hollandaise

*Make this unusual appetizer a day ahead of time.*

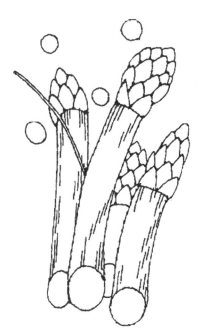

**TERRINE**

5 medium mushrooms
  Juice and zest of 1 lemon
8 asparagus spears, woody ends
  snapped and discarded
4 eggs
1 cup grated Mozzarella cheese
1 cup heavy cream
1 teaspoon salt
1 teaspoon white pepper
  Olive oil
1 small bunch mustard greens
  or spinach leaves

**SAUCE**

4 egg yolks
2 tablespoons water
1½ cups clarified butter (see
  recipe page 220)
2 tablespoons finely chopped
  fresh chives
  Salt and white pepper
⅛ teaspoon cayenne pepper
½ teaspoon freshly squeezed
  lemon juice

Prepare the terrine. Blanch the mushrooms in water and the lemon juice for approximately 5 minutes. In another pan filled with slightly salted water, blanch the asparagus spears for approximately 2 minutes. Immediately cool the blanched mushrooms and asparagus over ice.

Preheat the oven to 350°. In a mixing bowl, blend the eggs, Mozzarella, cream, lemon zest, salt, and white pepper until the mixture is smooth. Set aside. Brush a 5x9-inch loaf pan with olive oil, and line it with the mustard greens. Next, pour half of the egg-cream mixture into the pan, and arrange the mushrooms, caps down, in a line lengthwise down the center of the pan. Place the asparagus spears lengthwise along both sides of the mushrooms (4 spears per side). Add the remaining egg-cream mixture to the pan, covering the vegetables. Top with additional mustard greens, tucking them in along the inside edges of the pan. Place the loaf pan in a larger pan, filling the larger pan with water halfway up the sides of the loaf pan. Bake until the pâté has set, approximately 45 minutes to 1 hour. Let cool overnight.

Prepare the sauce. Combine the egg yolks and water in the top of a double boiler, and beat for about 1 minute with a wire whisk. Then place the mixture over simmering water. (The bottom of the pan should not touch the water.) Whip vigorously with the whisk for 8 to 10 minutes or until the mixture is thick and creamy. Take care not to curdle the eggs, and do not allow the mixture to become so hot that you cannot dip your finger into it. When the mixture is perfectly

combined, you will be able to see the bottom of the pan between strokes and the sauce will be slow to cover the lines made by the whisk.

Remove the pan from the heat and place it on a towel (to prevent slipping). Add the hot butter very slowly, whipping constantly. When the butter is thoroughly incorporated, mix in the chives until they are evenly distributed throughout the sauce. Season to taste with the salt, pepper, and cayenne pepper, and then stir in the lemon juice.

If not served right away, keep the sauce warm in a pan of tepid water. If the sauce becomes too thick, beat in 1 or 2 tablespoons of water to achieve the desired consistency. To serve, slice the pâté into ¾- to 1-inch pieces. Place on individual serving plates and top with sauce.

Yield: 8 servings

*CARTER HOUSE*

## Venison-and-Jalapeño Roll-Ups

*Game meat is becoming as popular on Texas ranches as chicken and beef have been. This hors d'oeuvre recipe, with no set amounts, allows you to serve as few or as many as you wish.*

| | |
|---|---|
| Tenderized venison cutlets | Whole pickled Jalapeños, cut |
| Fajita seasoning | into strips |
| Vinaigrette dressing | Sliced bacon |

Cut the venison into 2x3-inch medallions. Sprinkle with fajita seasoning and marinate in a vinaigrette dressing. Place a venison medallion on top of a bacon strip. Place a jalapeño strip on top of the venison. Roll the meat up and fasten with a toothpick. Cook over a mesquite grill until the bacon is crispy and the meat is medium rare to medium. Serve immediately.

*Y. O. RANCH*

*Never do anything in your business that you wouldn't want to tell your spouse, parents, or children about.*

John Schumacher, Schumacher's New Prague Hotel

## Cheese-Filled Phyllo Pillows
## with Olive Vinaigrette

*FILLING*
½ pound fresh Mozzarella, such as Buffalo
½ pound smoked Mozzarella
2 tablespoons grated Romano cheese
2 tablespoons Monterey Jack cheese
1 tablespoon finely chopped garlic
¼ cup fresh chopped basil

*PHYLLO*
4 sheets phyllo dough
Olive oil

*VINAIGRETTE*
1 teaspoon chopped garlic
1 tablespoon chopped shallots
1 tablespoon capers
1 cup peeled and seeded tomatoes
1 cup fresh tomato juice
¼ cup extra virgin olive oil
¼ cup fresh lemon juice
¼ cup pitted, chopped kalamata olives
¼ cup chopped fresh basil
½ cup chopped sun-dried tomatoes
½ cup olive paste

*ASSEMBLY*
Salad greens

Dice the Mozzarella cheeses. In a large bowl, toss the cheeses with the remaining ingredients.

Place 1 sheet of the phyllo dough on a flat surface and brush with olive oil. Place another sheet on top and brush with olive oil. Repeat until all 4 sheets are used. Carefully cut the phyllo into 8 equal squares. Shape the cheese mixture into 8 equal round balls. Place 1 ball in the middle of each piece of phyllo. Grab the edges of the phyllo and shape into a small pouch. Brush with olive oil and refrigerate for 1 hour.

Preheat the oven to 350°. Bake the phyllo pillows for 10 to 12 minutes or until golden brown. While the phyllo bakes, prepare the olive vinaigrette.

In a small bowl, mix together all of the vinaigrette ingredients and let stand at room temperature for 1 hour before serving.

To assemble, spoon about 6 tablespoons of the vinaigrette onto each plate. Add salad greens and top each with a warm cheese phyllo pillow.

Yield: 8 servings

*SAN YSIDRO RANCH*

## Goat Cheese Soufflé

*Goat cheese has a light and airy taste and, in this soufflé, makes for a very impressive appetizer. It is best served as soon as it comes out of the oven.*

| | |
|---|---|
| 1 cup walnuts | 1½ cups crumbled mild goat cheese |
| 1½ cups milk | |
| ¼ cup unsalted butter | 2 tablespoons cognac |
| ¼ cup all-purpose flour | 1½ teaspoons *herbes de Provence* |
| 1 teaspoon cornstarch | Freshly ground black pepper |
| 6 eggs, separated | ⅛ teaspoon cream of tartar |

Preheat the oven to 350°. Toast the walnuts by spreading them in a single layer on a baking sheet. Place the baking sheet in the oven, and toast the walnuts for 10 minutes. Remove the pan from the oven. Raise the temperature to 400°. Let the nuts cool, then finely chop.

Grease well the bottoms and sides of eight 3½-ounce soufflé cups, then coat the bottoms and sides with chopped walnuts. Reserve the remaining walnuts.

Heat the milk in a heavy saucepan, but do not let it boil.

Melt the butter over low heat in another heavy saucepan. Whisk in the flour and cornstarch and cook, whisking constantly, for 3 minutes. Still whisking, slowly add the milk to the flour mixture. Bring to a boil, stirring constantly, then remove the pan from the heat. Transfer the mixture to a bowl and let it cool slightly.

Whisk the egg yolks into the cooled mixture, one at a time. Then add the goat cheese, cognac, *herbes de Provence,* and pepper, and whisk until all are combined.

Beat the egg whites with the cream of tartar just until they form stiff peaks. Stir ¼ of the whites into the cheese mixture to lighten it. Gently fold in the remaining whites.

Divide the soufflé mixture among the soufflé cups and sprinkle each with about 1 tablespoon of the remaining walnuts. Bake the soufflés for 20 minutes or until they are puffed and golden brown. Serve immediately.

Yield: 8 servings

Note: *Herbes de Provence,* which can be found in the spice section of large supermarkets, is a blend of dried herbs commonly used in southern France. Herbs usually combined in the mixture are basil, fennel seed, lavender, marjoram, rosemary, sage, and thyme.

*NEWCASTLE INN*

# Goat Cheese Toasts with Tomato-and-Egg Vinaigrette

*Everyone clamors for this when they sit down to dinner at Stonehedge. "It has become a signature of the inn," remarks Chef Jim Overbaugh. Try this recipe at home and you'll see why its bright taste and pleasing texture are so inviting.*

SAUCE
½ hard-boiled egg, finely chopped
1 teaspoon capers
1½ teaspoons finely chopped Gherkins
1 medium ripe tomato, peeled, seeded, and finely diced
¼ teaspoon Dijon-style mustard
1 tablespoon fresh lemon juice
⅛ teaspoon sugar
⅓ cup extra virgin olive oil

CHEESE
7 ounces goat cheese
2 tablespoons extra virgin olive oil
½ tablespoon fresh lemon juice

ASSEMBLY
12 slices rye bread, toasted
12 large pieces thinly sliced smoked salmon
1 small bunch watercress or other baby lettuce for garnish

In a medium bowl, mix together all of the sauce ingredients. Set aside. In another bowl, mix together all of the cheese ingredients and set aside.

Spread the goat cheese on top of each piece of toast. Place 1 slice of the salmon overtop the cheese, taking care not to hang any excess salmon over the edge. Trim the crusts and then cut each piece into 2 large triangles.

Plate the dish by stacking 4 triangles alternately with the sauce on each plate. Pour a little more sauce overtop so that it spills out onto the plate. Garnish with watercress or small pieces of baby lettuce.

Yield: 6 servings

*STONEHEDGE INN*

# Vermont Cheddar Cheese Pie

⅓ cup fine, plain, dry bread crumbs

¼ cup Parmesan cheese

4 8-ounce packages cream cheese

5 eggs

3 egg yolks

⅓ cup heavy cream

¼ cup all purpose flour

2 cloves garlic, minced

1 yellow onion, grated

2 to 3 cups grated Cheddar cheese

1 tablespoon minced parsley

1 teaspoon chopped fresh basil leaves or ½ teaspoon dried

½ teaspoon chopped fresh tarragon or ¼ teaspoon dried

1 teaspoon chopped fresh dill or 1 teaspoon dried

½ cup beer

Preheat the oven to 250°. Wrap the outside of a 10-inch springform pan in aluminum foil. Butter the bottom and sides of the pan, and sprinkle with bread crumbs and Parmesan cheese.

In a large bowl, beat together the cream cheese, eggs, yolks, cream, and flour until well mixed. Fold in the garlic, onion, Cheddar cheese, and herbs. Add the beer, mixing just until blended. Pour the filling into the springform pan.

Prepare a *bain marie* by placing the springform pan in a larger pan. Add enough boiling water to come halfway up the sides of the springform pan. Bake the pie for 1 hour and 40 minutes. Turn the oven off and leave the pie for 1 hour. The pie is done when the top is light brown and the center is firm, determined by shaking it from side to side.

Remove the pie from the oven and let it cool for 2 hours. Remove the foil from the pan and discard it. Cut the pie into wedges and serve.

Yield: 12 pieces

*ROWELL'S INN*

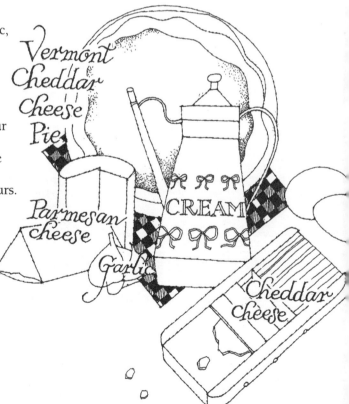

# Duck in Puff Pastry with Fig Sauce

*When Chef Sharon Ashburn serves this dish at Antrim 1844, she shapes
the pastry into a duck form. This is simple to do and looks attractive on
the plate.*

### FIG SAUCE
8 fresh figs, sliced ¼-inch thick
1 teaspoon sugar
½ cup Sauternes
1 cup duck or chicken stock
¼ cup butter

### DUCK
1 tablespoon clarified butter
  (see recipe page 220)
4 duck breasts, skins removed,
  seasoned with salt and pepper
1 tablespoon butter
6 ounces mushrooms, finely
  chopped

### DUCK LIVER MOUSSE
4 duck or chicken livers (about
  6 ounces)
1 shallot, diced
1 apple, peeled, cored and sliced
½ cup plus 1 tablespoon butter,
  divided
2 tablespoons Calvados brandy
  Salt and pepper

### PASTRY
1 8x10-inch puff pastry sheet
1 egg, beaten with 2 tablespoons
  water

Poach the fig slices in the sugar and Sauternes for about 2 minutes
over medium-high heat. Carefully remove the figs with a slotted
spoon and keep them warm. Reduce the poaching liquid slightly by
cooking for a few minutes more. Add the duck stock and reduce
again, this time by ⅓. Reduce the heat and slowly whisk in the ¼ cup
butter. Set the sauce aside until serving time.

Prepare the duck. Heat a heavy sauté pan over high heat. Add the
clarified butter and sear each duck breast 1 minute per side. Remove
the breasts from the pan and let cool.

In a nonstick sauté pan, heat the 1 tablespoon of butter and sauté
the mushrooms for about 5 to 7 minutes or until the mushrooms
begin to dry out. Remove the mushrooms from the heat and cool.
Preheat the oven to 450°.

Prepare the duck liver mousse. In a medium skillet, sauté the
liver, shallot, and apple in 1 tablespoon of the butter over high heat
until the livers are just pink inside. Add the Calvados and cook until
the flames subside. Let cool completely. Transfer to a food processor
and purée the liver mixture until smooth. While puréeing, add the
remaining butter, 1 tablespoon at a time. Season with salt and pepper.
Set aside.

Prepare the pastry. Cut the dough into 4 equal parts and roll each part out to twice the original size. Place 1 duck breast in the middle of each piece of dough; spread with 2 tablespoons of the duck liver mousse and about 2 tablespoons of the mushrooms. Fold the pastry overtop and pinch the dough together on either side of each duck breast. Turn the whole package over and form one side of the pastry into the shape of a duck head and neck and the other side into a tail. (Shaping into a duck form is optional.)

Brush the pastry with the egg wash and bake in the oven for 10 to 12 minutes or until golden brown. Reheat the fig sauce and serve over the pastry.

Yield: 4 servings

*ANTRIM 1844*

## Belgian Endive Stuffed with Montrachet and Alfalfa Sprouts

4 ounces Montrachet or other goat cheese, at room temperature

4 ounces cream cheese, at room temperature

⅛ teaspoon dried thyme

⅛ teaspoon dried basil

⅛ teaspoon dried oregano

3 heads Belgian endive, with bases cut off and leaves separated and cleaned

Alfalfa sprouts for garnish

In the bowl of an electric mixer, beat the cheeses until smooth and light in texture. Stir in the dried herbs. Fill a pastry bag fitted with a star tip, then pipe about ¾ of a tablespoon of the cheese mixture into each endive leaf. Garnish with a small bunch of alfalfa sprouts.

Yield: 24 hors d'oeuvres

*ANTRIM 1844*

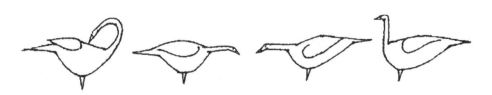

## Bedtime Stories

• Have extra pillows (one set of soft feathery pillows and another harder, even foam pillows).

• Keep an extra blanket at the foot of the bed.

• Turn comforter or bed dressing down for your guests if you are afraid something will happen to a delicate fabric, etc.

• If you have lots of decorative pillows and/or shams and a small guest room, store those pillows away for your guests at bedtime.

• If you do not have a bed stand on each side of the bed, hang one of those fabric compartments that rests between the mattresses. These can hold your guest's reading glasses, pencil, book, etc.

• You may scent the mattresses by placing only a handful of potpourri underneath the mattress pad. Guests who are allergic to perfumery, however, will not appreciate this gesture.

• If your sheets are not permanent press, be sure to iron them. There is nothing like hopping into a strange bed with wrinkled sheets. Eeek!

## Hickory-Smoked Duck Breast with Apple-Corn Relish and Sally Lunn Toast

*Sally Lunn is a historic batter bread that is a cinch to make because it requires no yeast. Created by early American cooks, the bread was originally named for the Latin soleil et luna, or sun and moon, because it apparently reminded the Colonists of the two heavenly bodies. Note that the duck requires four hours to marinate in maple syrup.*

BREAD
4 large eggs, separated and at room temperature
1 cup sugar
1½ cups milk
3 cups all-purpose flour
2 tablespoons baking powder
1 teaspoon salt
¼ cup butter, melted

RELISH
1 cup finely diced Golden Delicious apple
1 cup freshly cooked corn, preferably from the cob
1 cup mixture of finely diced yellow, green, and red bell peppers

¾ cup finely diced red onion
1 tablespoon freshly chopped sage
2 tablespoons freshly chopped parsley
½ cup (generous) raspberry vinegar
Coarse salt and pepper
⅛ teaspoon sugar

DUCK
2 10-ounce boneless duck breasts, trimmed and cut in half
Salt, pepper, and sugar
1 cup pure maple syrup

Begin by preparing the bread. Preheat the oven to 350°. In a large mixing bowl, beat the 4 egg yolks until incorporated and whisk in the sugar and then the milk. In a separate bowl, mix together the flour, baking powder, and salt. Add to the egg mixture, mixing just until incorporated. Mix in the melted butter and set aside for a moment. In another mixing bowl, beat the egg whites just until light peaks form. Fold the whites into the batter. Pour the batter into 2 nonstick or greased miniloaf tins. Bake for 30 to 40 minutes or until the bread turns a golden brown. Cool on wire racks.

Prepare the apple-corn relish. Mix all of the relish ingredients in a bowl, adjusting seasonings and adding a little water if a thinner consistency is desired. Set the relish aside.

Prepare the duck. Season with the salt, pepper, and sugar and place skin-side down in a heated sauté pan, cooking over medium-low heat just a few minutes until most of the fat is rendered. (Do not sauté the duck on the other side as you do not want to cook the breasts, just render the fat.)

Place the breasts in a 2-inch-deep skillet and cover with maple syrup. Allow to marinate for at least 4 hours in the refrigerator. Smoke over hickory chips for 20 minutes or until tender, or cook over a barbecue grill. (The duck is at its optimum flavor when cooked medium rare.) Cool the duck in the refrigerator and thinly slice on the bias when ready to serve.

Slice the Sally Lunn bread, toast lightly, and place a piece on each individual serving plate with a few slices of the duck and some apple-corn relish.

Yield: 4 to 6 servings

*CLIFTON COUNTRY INN*

*Bedtime Stories* (continued)

• Even in warm weather, be sure to have at least a lightweight blanket tucked into the bed along with the sheets.

Be sure to dust underneath the guest bed. An otherwise clean room with dust balls under the bed is unpleasant.

• If your guest is a child, place some stuffed animals or just a teddy bear on the bed. It makes the youngster feel right at home.

Cook over an open fire

# Wild-Mushroom Napoleon

*Each Napoleon is composed of two layers of breadcrumb-coated phyllo dough that sandwiches a variety of sautéed mushrooms flavored in a vegetable broth.*

VEGETABLE STOCK
1 carrot, cut into large pieces
1 medium onion, cut into large dice
2 ribs celery, cut into large dice
2 bay leaves
1 sprig fresh thyme
6 black peppercorns

FILLING
¼ cup plus 2 tablespoons olive oil
1 tablespoon chopped garlic
1 pound each: shiitake, crimini, portobello, and oyster mushrooms, sliced
1 teaspoon each: chopped fresh thyme, sage, rosemary, and marjoram
Salt and pepper
1 tablespoon butter
½ cup diced red bell pepper
12 sheets phyllo dough
Olive oil
¼ cup plain breadcrumbs
30 sugar snap peas, blanched

Make a vegetable stock. Place the carrot, onion, celery, bay leaves, sprig of thyme, and peppercorns in a small stockpot with 2 quarts of water. Bring the vegetables to a boil. Simmer for 20 minutes and then strain, saving the vegetable stock and discarding the vegetables.

Heat the olive oil in a saucepan and sauté the garlic until lightly browned. Add all of the mushrooms along with the thyme, sage, rosemary, and marjoram, and sauté until the mushrooms soften. Add enough of the vegetable stock to cover the mushrooms. Season all with salt and pepper and simmer for at least 20 minutes, adding more stock as necessary. While the mushrooms simmer, heat the butter in a small skillet and sauté the red pepper just until tender (not browned). Set aside, keeping warm.

Preheat the oven to 400°. Brush a sheet of phyllo dough with olive oil. Dust with the breadcrumbs and fold the dough into a rectangle 2 x 3 inches. (Note: Fold each sheet of phyllo dough in half and in half again and in half again to get a 2- x 3-inch piece. There will be 2 sheets of phyllo per Napoleon.) Repeat the oil and breadcrumb steps for each of the remaining 11 sheets of phyllo.

Place the Napoleons on a cookie sheet and bake 8 to 10 minutes or until golden brown.

To serve, place a rectangle of phyllo on each individual serving plate. Drain the mushrooms and divide them equally overtop each phyllo. Add a second phyllo rectangle. Place 5 of the sugar snap peas around each plate, sprinkling the red bell pepper overall.

Yield: 6 servings

*BEE & THISTLE INN*

## Onion Tart

*Easy to prepare, this makes a tasty side dish or appetizer, or it can be served with a salad for a lunch.*

10 tablespoons unsalted butter
 4 large Spanish or Vidalia onions, peeled and thinly sliced
   Salt and freshly ground pepper
 1 sheet puff pastry, thawed

1 tablespoon country-style (grainy) mustard
3 egg yolks
¼ cup heavy cream
   Chives for garnish

Melt the butter in a large nonstick skillet over low heat. Add the onions and stir well to coat. Cover the skillet and cook the onions over low heat for 10 minutes. Remove the cover, raise the heat to medium-high, and sauté the onions, stirring occasionally, until they are tender and just beginning to turn golden brown (approximately 25 minutes). Season with salt and pepper.

While the onions are cooking, preheat the oven to 375°. Roll out the puff pastry to an ⅛-inch thickness. Place it in an 11-inch tart pan and crimp the edges. Trim excess as you crimp the edges. Line the pastry with aluminum foil, and fill it with dried beans or pie weights so that the pastry won't puff up when baking. Bake the tart shell for 25 minutes. Remove the weights and foil.

Spread the mustard over the bottom of the baked shell. Stir together the egg yolks and cream until smooth (about 30 seconds) and add to the onions. Pour the mixture into the prepared pastry shell. Bake the tart for another 30 minutes or until golden brown.

Remove the tart from the oven. Slice it into 8 pieces and garnish each piece with chives (preferably with blossoms). Serve immediately.

Yield: 8 servings

*NEWCASTLE INN*

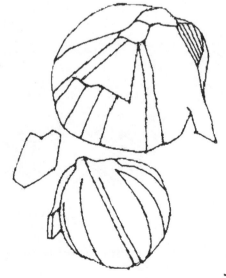

Vermont~Cherry
Amaretto
Glaze

Pheasant with
Wild Rice
Stuffing

# ENTRÉES

## Penne with Chicken, Sausage, and Hot Peppers in a Dijon Mustard Cream Sauce

2½ cups penne pasta
1 teaspoon olive oil
1½ cups chicken stock or broth
1 tablespoon butter, softened
1 tablespoon all-purpose flour
2 teaspoons Dijon-style mustard
1 cup half-and-half
  Salt and pepper
¼ pound Italian sausage, cut into bite-size pieces
¼ pound boneless chicken, cut into bite-size pieces
2 jalapeño peppers, seeded and finely chopped
⅓ cup white wine
1 bunch scallions, chopped
1 tomato, diced
  Chopped Italian parsley for garnish

In a large pot of boiling salted water, cook the pasta. Drain and rinse with cold water; toss with the olive oil and set aside.

In a small saucepan, bring the chicken stock to a gentle boil. Combine the butter and flour, and stir into the boiling stock, whisking until smooth. Simmer for 3 to 4 minutes. Add the mustard and the half-and-half. Season with salt and pepper. Bring to a rolling boil and simmer for 5 minutes more, whisking constantly. Set aside.

In a large nonstick skillet, sauté the sausage and chicken for 5 to 7 minutes. Add the jalapeños and the wine. Add the sauce, pasta, and scallions, and simmer for 3 minutes to blend flavors and to heat the pasta. Place on individual serving plates; top each portion with 1 tablespoon of chopped tomato and a sprinkling of parsley.

Yield: 4 servings

*WHITE OAK INN*

## Homemade Gnocchi Parmesan with Fresh Sage

*The easiest way to make this dish is to employ a potato ricer, which crushes the food to vaguely resemble rice.*

1 pound potatoes (about 2 medium, white Russets)
Salt
1 egg yolk
½ cup all-purpose flour, plus more for kneading
2 teaspoons kosher salt
½ teaspoon freshly ground pepper

2 tablespoons sweet butter
24 leaves fresh sage, whole or chiffonade
Grated Parmigiano-Reggiano or other quality Parmesan cheese

Place the potatoes in a large saucepan of cold water. Season the water with ½ teaspoon or so of salt. Heat to boiling over high heat. Reduce the heat to medium. Cover the pan and boil until the potatoes are very tender, about 45 minutes. Drain the potatoes; return them to the empty pan off the heat and keep them tightly covered.

When the potatoes cool down enough to handle, after about 30 minutes, peel them and pass them into a large bowl through a potato ricer, a food mill, or a large, fine-mesh sieve such as a china cap. Set aside.

In a small bowl, beat the egg yolk with a few drops of water. Pour over the potatoes. Sprinkle the flour and coarse salt and ground pepper over the potatoes. Mix with a fork until the mixture forms a dough. Turn the dough out onto a generously floured surface. Knead with the heels of your hands, adding flour as necessary to prevent sticking. Knead just until the dough is evenly blended and only slightly sticky. Do not over-knead. Allow the dough to rest in a bowl, covered with a tea towel, for about 10 to 15 minutes.

Heat a large pot of generously salted water to boiling. Divide the gnocchi dough into eight pieces. Roll each section with the palms of your hands on a floured surface to form a cylinder shape, about ½ inch in diameter. Cut into ¾-inch lengths. Hold the tines of a fork diagonally to each mini-cylinder and press to flatten into a rectangle, forming a diagonal-ridged pattern. Transfer the gnocchi to a tray lined with a lightly floured kitchen towel. Repeat with the remaining dough.

Carefully slip half the gnocchi into the boiling water. In about 1 minute, the gnocchi will bob to the surface. Continue to cook for 30 seconds. Meanwhile, heat the butter in a medium sauté pan until hot. Add the sage leaves and gnocchi to the pan. Season with more salt and pepper. Toss with freshly grated Parmesan cheese and serve.

Yield: 8 servings

*CHECKERBERRY INN*

## Fettucine Florentine in a Spicy Tomato and Cheddar Sauce

*The Settlers Inn gets its Cheddar from an Amish cheese maker who still uses wooden rakes and an old-fashioned method in preparing the cheese.*

1 teaspoon olive oil
1 leek, cut into thin strips
2 cloves garlic, minced
3 tomatoes, peeled and chopped
2 tablespoons minced chives
1 tablespoon ketchup
1 tablespoon Dijon-style mustard
1 tablespoon Worcestershire sauce
Salt and pepper
2½ cups heavy cream
¾ pound extra sharp Cheddar cheese, grated; plus more for garnishing
1 pound fettucine
10 ounces fresh spinach, cut into strips

Heat the olive oil in a large nonstick sauté pan. Add the leeks and the garlic and cook until they are limp but not brown (about 7 minutes). Add the tomatoes, chives, ketchup, mustard, Worcestershire sauce, salt, and pepper, and cook for 5 minutes. Add the heavy cream and heat the mixture to a boil. Remove the pan from the heat, mix in the cheese, and keep warm.

Cook and drain the fettuccine. Add the cooked pasta and spinach strips to the sauce. Toss until the pasta and spinach are well-coated. Garnish with freshly grated Cheddar.

Yield: 6 servings

*SETTLERS INN*

## Roasted Vegetable Lasagne with Cheese and Pesto Filling

*A vegetarian's delight for a main course, this is a delicious pasta entrée that incorporates the full-bodied flavor of roasted vegetables. If you want to save time, skip the first step for making your own tomato sauce and buy a fresh sauce from a gourmet market. You will need at least two cups of sauce. This recipe makes three cups, so you can add more, or reserve for another dish. The recipe also calls for a pesto sauce for the filling; buy pre-made pesto or see recipe on page 220. Chef Patrick Runkel makes this dish at the inn with fresh lasagne, but feel free to use dried.*

### SAUCE
- 3 tablespoons olive oil
- 1 cup finely chopped onions
- 1 tablespoon finely chopped garlic
- 4 cups Italian plum tomatoes (fresh or canned), coarsely chopped and liquid reserved after chopping
- 1 6-ounce can tomato paste
- 1 tablespoon dried oregano
- 1 tablespoon dried basil
- 1 bay leaf
- 2 teaspoons sugar
- 1½ teaspoons salt
- Freshly ground black pepper

### FILLING
- 1 medium red onion, diced
- 2½ cups Ricotta cheese
- 4 ounces Mozzarella cheese, grated
- 6 ounces Parmesan cheese, grated, plus more for serving
- 1 tablespoon pesto sauce
- 1 clove garlic, chopped
- Olive oil for coating
- Black pepper

### ROASTED VEGETABLES
- 1 small eggplant, unpeeled
- Olive oil
- 2 red bell peppers
- ¾ pound fresh spinach

### ASSEMBLY
- 1 pound fresh lasagne sheets

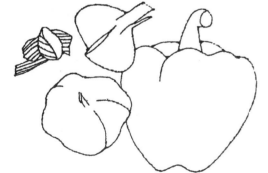

In a large saucepan, heat the olive oil and cook the onions over medium heat, stirring frequently for 7 or 8 minutes, or until the onions are transparent. Add the chopped garlic and cook for another 1 to 2 minutes, stirring. Add the tomatoes and their liquid, the tomato paste, herbs, bay leaf, sugar, salt, and a few grinds of black pepper. Bring the sauce to a boil, turn heat to low, and simmer uncovered, stirring occasionally, for about 1 hour or until the sauce is thickened. Remove and discard the bay leaf.

In a large bowl, combine the filling ingredients (except the extra Parmesan for serving) until well incorporated. Set aside and prepare the vegetables.

Slice the eggplant into thin rounds (about ¼ inch or so, not too thin). Lightly brush one side of the eggplant with olive oil. Broil, oiled-side up, until browned. Turn the eggplant, brush the other side, and broil until browned.

To roast the red peppers, place under the broiler and turn at intervals until the skin is blackened on all sides. Place in a plastic bag to steam for about 15 minutes. Remove from the bag and peel away the skin and seeds. Slice into thin strips.

Place the spinach in a large colander. Pour boiling water over the spinach to wilt slightly.

Preheat the oven to 375°. Bring a large pot of water to a boil. Add the fresh pasta to the water and cook slightly. (If using dried lasagne, cook to *al dente*, or about 10 minutes.) Drain and toss lightly with olive oil. Cut the lasagne sheets to fit a 9x13-inch pan.

Layer a thin coating of the tomato sauce over the bottom of the pan. Next, arrange a layer of pasta and spoon half of the filling in an even layer overtop. Add half of each of the vegetables. Follow with another layer of pasta, more sauce, and repeat with the remainder of the filling and then vegetables. Place a final layer of pasta on top, add more sauce, and sprinkle with additional Parmesan cheese. Bake 45 to 50 minutes or until heated through and just slightly bubbly.

Yield: 6 to 8 servings

*OCTOBER COUNTRY INN*

# Lasagne of Roasted-Red-Pepper Pasta with Gorgonzola and Pesto

## Pasta Advice

Cook pasta in a lot of water and you won't need to add oil. The water dilutes the starch that causes the stickiness, because the starch dissolves during cooking.

*This is a white herbed cream-style lasagne with several interesting components, from the flat pasta sheets made with roasted bell peppers to the unusual filling of Gorgonzola, all baked piping hot and served in a pool of red pepper purée. In this recipe, Chef Francis Brooke-Smith offers a step-saver by not having you boil the pasta first.*

RED PEPPER PASTA
- 1 24-ounce can roasted red peppers, wiped dry with a towel
- 4 cups all-purpose flour
- 1 cup semolina flour
- 1 teaspoon salt
- 4 eggs, slightly beaten
- 1 tablespoon olive oil

RED PEPPER PURÉE
- 4 large red bell peppers
  Salt and pepper
- 1 tablespoon olive oil

FILLING
- 3 pounds Ricotta cheese
- 1½ pounds Gorgonzola cheese, crumbled
- 2 cups heavy cream
- 4 eggs, slightly beaten
  Salt and pepper
  Butter for greasing

ASSEMBLY
- 1 cup or more pesto sauce, premade or see recipe page 220
  Freshly grated Parmesan cheese
  Deep-fried basil leaves (basil cooked until crisp in olive oil), optional

Begin by making the pasta. Purée the peppers in a blender until very fine. In a bowl of an electric mixer, add the flours, salt, and the puréed peppers, and mix until well blended. Add the eggs a little at a time. Add the olive oil. The mixture should be fairly dry (not sticky); so add more or less flour to reach this consistency. Form the dough into a ball and place it in a bowl. Cover with plastic wrap and allow to sit for at least 20 minutes. Then cut ¼ of the dough and roll it out to ¼-inch thick. Continue rolling until the dough is ⅛-inch thick. Repeat with each remaining quarter of the dough. All finished sheets should be about 9x13 inches. Set the pasta sheets aside, covered to keep moist.

Prepare the red pepper purée. Blacken the skin of the red peppers on a gas flame or grill. Place the peppers in a paper bag until cool. Remove all of the skin and seeds. In a blender, purée the red peppers with salt and pepper and the olive oil until smooth. Set aside and preheat the oven to 350°.

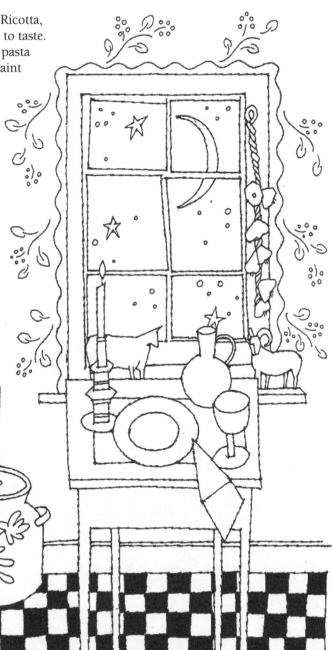

Prepare the filling. In a large bowl, combine the Ricotta, Gorgonzola, heavy cream, eggs, and salt and pepper to taste. Butter a 9x13-inch pan. Layer 1 sheet of red pepper pasta (uncooked) to cover the entire bottom of the pan. Paint the pasta with pesto sauce, using a wide pastry brush. Follow with ⅓ of the cheese filling. Repeat with layers of pasta, pesto, and cheese mixture. Finish with a fourth and final layer of pasta. Sprinkle with Parmesan cheese.

Bake for 45 minutes or until the center is firm. Cut into individual servings and serve on a pool of red pepper purée. Garnish the plate with fried basil leaves.

Yield: 8 servings

*BEE & THISTLE INN*

## Yukon Gold Potato-and-Truffle Ravioli with Butternut Squash Sauce

*Chef Gerard Thompson's ravioli is easy to make with won-ton wrappers. If winter truffles are not available, add a little truffle flavoring to the mix or omit.*

RAVIOLI
- 3 Yukon Gold potatoes, peeled
- 2 tablespoons extra virgin olive oil
- 1 shallot, finely diced
- 1 winter truffle, chopped
- 2 tablespoons sherry
  Kosher salt
  Freshly ground pepper
- 4 ounces goat cheese
- 1 tablespoon chopped fresh thyme
- 40 won-ton wrappers
- 2 eggs, mixed with a teaspoon of water

SAUCE
- 1 ounce extra virgin olive oil
- 2 cups medium-diced butternut squash
- 1 onion, chopped and caramelized
  Salt and pepper
- 4 cups vegetable broth
- 1 teaspoon fresh thyme
- ½ cup chopped chives

Begin by making the ravioli filling. Quarter the potatoes and place them in 2 quarts of cold, salted water. Bring the potatoes to a boil and lightly simmer until soft. Meanwhile, heat the olive oil in a small skillet over medium-high heat and sauté the shallots and truffles. Cook for 3 to 5 minutes. Add the sherry and cook for an additional 2 minutes. Season with salt and pepper. Remove from the heat and set aside.

Drain the potatoes and, while still hot, add the truffles, goat cheese, and thyme, and whip with electric mixer and paddle attachment until potatoes are lumpy.

Place each won-ton wrapper on a flat work surface. Brush each wrapper with the egg wash. Place about 1 scant tablespoonful of the potato mixture onto each wrapper. Fold in half on the diagonal and seal with water. Repeat until all of the wrappers are filled.

Prepare the sauce. Heat the olive oil in a medium skillet and add the squash. Cook for 1 to 2 minutes or just until translucent. Add the onion and season with salt and pepper. Cook until the squash is soft, about 15 to 20 minutes. Remove from the heat and add the broth and thyme. Pour the squash into a blender and purée until smooth. Adjust seasonings to taste.

To assemble, cook the ravioli in boiling salted water for 3 to 5 minutes or until *al dente*. Remove the pasta from the water with a slotted spoon and drain on paper towels. Arrange 5 ravioli on each of 8 individual serving plates. Ladle the sauce over the pasta and sprinkle with chopped chives.

Yield: 8 servings

*SAN YSIDRO RANCH*

## Classic Spaetzle

*This dish is one of the supreme contributions of German cuisine to world cooking. If you don't have a spaetzle maker, you can make a homemade version: Clean and wash a medium-sized tin can. Punch holes in the bottom of the can about the size of a pencil. Put the mix in the can and push it through the holes with a ladle. Spaetzle will keep for about four days in the refrigerator.*

4 eggs
¼ cup cold water
¼ teaspoon salt
¼ teaspoon grated nutmeg
1¾ cups all-purpose flour
Butter for sautéing

In a medium-size bowl, combine the eggs, water, salt, and nutmeg. Beat with a wire whisk until frothy. Add the flour slowly until the mixture is stiff and gathers around the whisk. Remove any mixture from the whisk and continue stirring with a spoon until it pulls away from the sides of the bowl.

Bring salted water to a boil. Put the mix into a spaetzle maker, dropping the spaetzle directly into the water. Bring the water back to a boil and simmer for 2 minutes. After cooking, remove the spaetzle from the boiling water, strain, and rinse under cold water. Drain well. Line a pan with a dry, cotton dish towel. Place the spaetzle on the towel and cover to store until ready to use.

To serve, heat some butter and sauté the spaetzle, being careful not to brown. Spaetzle can also be served with pan gravy.

Yield: 4 to 6 servings

*SCHUMACHER'S NEW PRAGUE HOTEL*

*Note:*

While sautéing, you can make a number of variations on this famous dish by adding chopped parsley, bacon bits, salt, and nutmeg; or sautéing minced onions or shallots; adding Parmesan cheese; or combining all of the above.

## Pasta Pomodoro with Blackened Chicken, Prosciutto, and Peas in Parmesan Herb Sauce

*Chef Sharon Ashburn's pasta entrée was inspired by The Polo Restaurant in Baltimore, Maryland, where she worked before joining Antrim 1844 as executive chef. The blackened chicken with the pasta is a signature dish of Polo's that Sharon has adapted for Antrim 1844.*

BLACKENING SPICE
- 4 tablespoons paprika
- 2½ teaspoons salt
- 1 teaspoon onion powder
- 1 teaspoon garlic powder
- 1 teaspoon cayenne pepper
- ¾ teaspoon each of white and black pepper
- ½ teaspoon oregano
- ½ teaspoon thyme
- 1 tablespoon chili powder

CHICKEN
- 3 pounds skinned, boneless chicken breasts

PARMESAN HERB SAUCE
- 1 cup butter, room temperature
- ¾ cup heavy or light cream, at room temperature
- 2 tablespoons chopped fresh herbs of choice
- ½ cup grated Parmesan cheese
  Salt and pepper

ASSEMBLY
- 2 large ripe tomatoes, peeled, seeded, and chopped
- ¼ cup diced prosciutto
- 1 cup frozen peas, thawed
- 1 pound cooked penne pasta

Combine all of the blackening spice ingredients and set aside. Place a heavy-bottomed skillet (preferably a cast-iron skillet) over high heat. Meanwhile, coat the chicken breast on each side with the spice mixture. Add some butter to the skillet and sauté each breast on both sides. Keep the chicken on warm and prepare the sauce.

Whip the butter in a mixer on medium speed until fluffy. Gradually add the cream, beating until smooth. Reduce the speed of the mixer and add the fresh herbs and cheese. Season with salt and pepper to taste.

To assemble the dish, slice the chicken in half lengthwise. In a large skillet, gently heat the tomatoes, prosciutto, and peas. Add the pasta and chicken and remove from the heat. Stir in the Parmesan herb sauce and serve.

Yield: 8 servings

*ANTRIM 1844*

## Cod Filets with Spinach and Dal

*In India, dal means any variety of dried pulses, including peas, mung beans, and lentils. When I was deciding what recipes from October Country Inn to show on camera, it was hard to choose. The inn is known for serving a variety of complete ethnic meals. This main course from Chef Patrick Runkel's Indian menu is both healthy and delicious.*

1 cup red lentils, washed and drained
3 cups water
1 ½-inch piece ginger, peeled and grated
½ teaspoon ground turmeric
2 pounds fresh spinach
3 tablespoons clarified butter, or oil
¾ cup chopped onion
3 cloves garlic, chopped
1 teaspoon cumin seeds
1 teaspoon black mustard seeds
1 teaspoon ground coriander
¼ teaspoon cayenne pepper
2 tablespoons chopped cilantro
Juice of 2 lemons
½ teaspoon salt
3 pounds large cod fillets
White wine
Lemon wedges for garnish

Prepare the dal first. In a medium-size nonstick saucepan, combine the lentils with the water. Add the ginger and turmeric, and bring to a boil. Skim the foam, turn the heat to low, and simmer, partially covered, for 45 to 60 minutes until the lentils are tender. Stir frequently to prevent sticking, especially when nearing the end of the cooking time. While the dal is cooking, clean and cook the spinach until wilted. Squeeze dry.

In a large skillet, heat the clarified butter or oil. Sauté the onions and garlic until they are translucent. Add the cumin and the mustard seeds and cook 30 seconds more, stirring constantly. Add the ground coriander and the cayenne and stir for a few seconds more. Add the cooked lentils and stir well to combine. Add the cilantro, lemon juice, and salt. Taste for seasonings. Remove from heat and set aside.

Preheat the oven to 400°. Place the fish in a single layer in a 9x13-inch baking dish. Place the spinach on top of the fish. Top with the dal. Sprinkle with the white wine. Cover the dish with foil and bake for 20 to 30 minutes until the fish is cooked through. Serve with lemon wedges.

Yield: 6 to 8 servings

*OCTOBER COUNTRY INN*

# Cod Cakes

*Cod was served at the first Thanksgiving feast in America, and it's still served at this inn today as a bow to Randall's past when it was a tavern or ordinary. On camera during the filming of* Country Inn Cooking, *historian-chef Cindy Clark, showed us how to use a hanging griddle as she cooked the cod over the open hearth. Here is a recipe for doing it over your stovetop.*

| | |
|---|---|
| 2½ pounds fresh codfish | 1½ tablespoons dried tarragon |
| 1½ pounds peeled white potatoes | 3 tablespoons chopped parsley |
| 1 medium onion, chopped | 1 egg |
| 2 tablespoons butter | 1 cup breadcrumbs |
| 1½ teaspoons salt | 3 tablespoons oil |
| ½ teaspoon white pepper | |

Place the codfish and potatoes in a large saucepan and add water to cover. Simmer about 20 minutes or until tender. Drain the fish and potatoes and set aside.

In a small nonstick skillet, sauté the onion in the butter and add the salt, pepper, tarragon, and parsley. Combine the onion mixture in a large bowl with the fish and potatoes. Add the egg and breadcrumbs and mix well with your hands. Shape the mixture into equally portioned patties. In a large nonstick skillet, heat the oil. Fry the patties in the oil for 3 to 4 minutes on each side. Pat any excess oil with paper towels. Serve immediately.

Yield: 4 to 6 servings

*RANDALL'S ORDINARY*

## Halibut in Barbecue Sauce
## with Watermelon Salsa

*Finally, a great way to literally spice up a watermelon! The salsa may be used on any barbecued seafood.*

SALSA
- ¼ watermelon (rind discarded), seeded and cut into 1-inch chunks
- 1 red onion, sliced
- ½ bunch Italian parsley leaves, chopped
- 1 bunch cilantro, chopped
- ¼ cup champagne vinegar
- ¼ cup extra virgin pure olive oil
- 6 green chilies, seeded and sliced julienne style
- 4 small plum tomatoes, cut into quarters

SAUCE
- 1 tablespoon olive oil
- 1 yellow onion, sliced
- 4 cloves garlic
- 4 chipotle chilies, seeded
- 2 cascabel chilies, seeded
- 6 ancho chilies, seeded
- ¼ cup molasses
- 2 tablespoons honey
- 3 cups water
- 1 bunch cilantro, chopped
  Juice and zest of 2 oranges
  Juice and zest of 2 limes

FISH
- 4 to 6 7-ounce halibut steaks or filets

Combine all of the salsa ingredients in a bowl. Season to taste, and chill extremely well.

Heat the olive oil in a saucepan. Sauté the onions and garlic until tender. Add the chilies and continue to sauté for 2 minutes. Add the molasses, honey, and water, and simmer for 10 minutes. Purée until the mixture is smooth, then cool. Fold in the cilantro and the zest and juices of the oranges and limes. Dip the halibut in this sauce and grill on a stovetop grill or over wood coals or chips (about 1 to 2 minutes on each side). Season with salt while cooking. Serve with watermelon salsa.

Yield: 4 to 6 servings

*INN OF THE ANASAZI*

# Salmon-and-Cheese-Filled Roulade with Dijon Sauce

*You will be making a savory, cakelike outer shell and a delicious seafood-mixture filling, topped with a satisfying sauce.*

SHELL
- 7 eggs, separated
- ¼ cup dried dill
- ¼ cup all-purpose flour
- 2 tablespoons sour cream
- 1 egg white
- ¼ teaspoon cream of tartar
- 3 tablespoons vegetable oil

FILLING
- 1 pound fresh or canned salmon, chopped
- ½ cup sour cream
- ½ teaspoon seasoned salt
- 1 cup smoked Cheddar cheese
- ⅓ cup mayonnaise

DIJON SAUCE
- ¼ cup butter
- ¼ cup all-purpose flour
- ½ cup dry white wine
- 1 cup chicken stock
- 1 tablespoon Dijon-style mustard
- 1 teaspoon brown mustard
- 2 tablespoons fresh chives
- ½ cup heavy cream
  Fresh dill and lemon for garnish

Preheat the oven to 375°. Prepare the shell. Mix the egg yolks with the dill, flour, and sour cream. Set aside.

Beat the 8 egg whites just until fluffy. Add the cream of tartar and beat until stiff. Fold in the egg-yolk mixture. Pour the vegetable oil into a nonstick 9x13-inch jellyroll pan. Heat the pan in the oven for 5 minutes. Remove the pan from the oven and spread the egg mixture evenly in the pan. Return it to the oven and bake 10 minutes or until the cake is golden brown and the sides begin to pull away from the pan. Remove the pan from the oven and cover with a clean towel. Put an inverted pan of the same size on top of the towel, then flip the pan so that the cake comes out on the towel.

Prepare the filling. Combine the salmon, sour cream, salt, cheese, and mayonnaise, and mix well. Spread the filling evenly on the cake. Then roll up the cake in jellyroll fashion. Wrap it tightly in plastic wrap and refrigerate for several hours.

To bake, preheat the oven to 325°. Unwrap the roulade and place it on a nonstick cookie sheet. Bake for 25 minutes.

Meanwhile, prepare the Dijon sauce. Melt the butter in a nonstick skillet. Whisk in the flour and stir over medium heat until the flour is golden brown. Slowly add the wine, chicken stock, mustards, and chives, stirring constantly. Continue cooking over medium heat for about 15 minutes. Reduce the heat; add the cream and cook until slightly thickened. Season to taste. Place 1 slice of the salmon roulade on a serving plate. Top with about 2 tablespoons of the cream sauce. Garnish with fresh dill and a slice of lemon.

Yield: 8 servings

*ROWELL'S INN*

Salmon & Cheese-filled Roulade

Dijon Sauce

fresh dill & a slice of lemon

## Smoked Salmon Tartare with Creamed-Dill Rösti Potatoes and a Bouquet of Young Field Lettuce

### Guest Towels

• If you have a dedicated guest or spare room in the house, mount a permanent towel bar across the back of the room's door. Keep guest towels hanging here if you have guests quite frequently. This saves you a step when preparing for their visit. The towels are always there.

• If you don't want to use the towel bar method, keep the towels in a basket.

• Towels should be extra large—a bath sheet for each guest, a small towel and one washcloth for each night of their stay. (Keep the extra washcloths in a small basket in the room.)

• If you have more than one guest, provide each with a different colored set of towels so they can keep track of their own.

• Be sure there is a peg rail or some sort of a rack for them to dry their towels for the next day, either in the bedroom or bathroom. (Continued on next page)

*Rösti potatoes are of Swiss origin and popular today as a way of serving food with a base, as they are cooked up like a galette or potato pancake. In this case, they form a casing for stuffing.*

**RÖSTI**
1 pound white potatoes, washed and peeled
¾ cup vegetable oil
Salt and pepper

**TARTARE**
½ pound fresh salmon filet, bones and skin removed
2 shallots, finely chopped
½ tablespoon ground coriander
1 tablespoon finely chopped fresh dill
¼ cup virgin olive oil
Salt and freshly ground pepper
Juice of ½ lemon
8 slices smoked salmon

**DILL CREAM**
3 tablespoons crème fraîche
Juice of ½ lemon
1 tablespoon freshly chopped dill, reserve some sprigs for garnish
Salt and freshly ground pepper
1 teaspoon caviar

**SALAD**
¼ pound assorted young lettuces (such as arugula and radicchio), washed
¼ cup walnut oil
3 tablespoons balsamic vinegar
Sugar, salt, and freshly ground pepper

Cut the potatoes into very thin, julienne-style strips. Pour and heat equal parts of the vegetable oil into 4 small nonstick skillets, and cover the bottom of each with about ¼-inch layer of potato sticks. Brown to a golden color on each side. Season with the salt and pepper. Remove the potato pancakes to drain on a paper towels, but keep them warm.

Meanwhile, prepare the tartare. Chop the fresh salmon into very fine cubes, and place into a glass bowl. Add the remaining tartare ingredients, except the smoked salmon. Combine well, and adjust seasoning to taste.

Place 2 slices of the smoked salmon on each rösti, and top with the tartare mixture. Once soft enough, roll each pancake gently over like a book, delicately pressing together the open end. With a small, sharp kitchen knife, carefully cut a round opening in the center of each of the rösti.

In a small bowl, mix all of the dill cream ingredients, except the caviar, until smooth. Put 1 teaspoon of the cream into the opening of each rösti. Top with the caviar and a sprig of fresh dill.

Make the lettuce marinade by combining the walnut oil and vinegar, and the sugar, salt, and pepper to taste. Toss over the lettuce. Serve with the rösti.

Yield: 4 servings

*CHÂTEAU DU SUREAU*

## Steamed Filet of Fresh Salmon on Creamed Scallions

*The scallion is one of the oldest and perhaps finest members of the onion family. Because of its subtleness, the scallion is perfect when overpowering flavors cannot be tolerated, as in delicate fish dishes such as this.*

| | |
|---|---|
| 1½ pounds scallions, white and green parts | 2 bay leaves |
| 2 tablespoons butter | 2 cloves garlic |
| Salt | 2 tablespoons fresh tarragon |
| ½ cup crème fraîche | 4 salmon filets (8 ounces each) |
| Water or fish stock | Salt and white pepper |
| | Lemon juice |

Slice the white part of the scallions julienne-style and set aside. Chop the green parts of the scallions and sauté them in butter just until translucent; season with salt, and combine them with the crème fraîche to make a sauce. Set aside, but don't allow to cool.

Into a steamer, place the water or fish stock, the bay leaves, garlic, and tarragon. Cover with the screen insert and place the fish filets on top. Cover and steam for about 5 minutes. Uncover the steamer. Remove the fish, and discard the stock, bay leaves, garlic, and tarragon. Season the fish with the salt, pepper, and fresh lemon juice. Warm the sauce for serving.

To serve, make a bed of the uncooked white strips of scallions on a plate, place the fish on top and coat lightly with the sauce. Serve immediately.

Yield: 4 servings

*CHÂTEAU DU SUREAU*

• Even though inns change your linens every day, change your guests' towels after the second day of use. Sheets, by the way, need only be changed once a week. Always change them between guests, however.

• Even though you may have a rug outside of the bathtub/shower area, always include a clean terry bath mat.

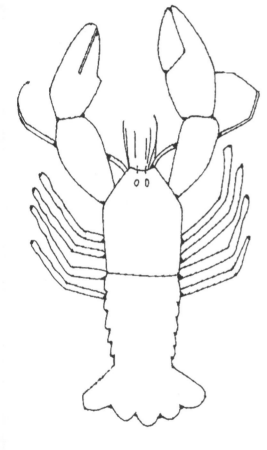

## Salmon and Lobster en Croûte with a Sweet-Pea Sauce

### STUFFING

- 2 tablespoons butter
- 1 tablespoon chopped shallots
- 1 tablespoon chopped mixed herbs (parsley and dill)
- 1½ tablespoons brandy
  Salt and pepper
- ¼ teaspoon Old Bay seasoning
- 3 tablespoons lobster broth (substitute with white wine or fish broth)
- ¾ pound lobster meat
- ¼ cup plain breadcrumbs or as needed

### SAUCE

- 6 tablespoons butter
- 2 small shallots, minced
- ⅓ cup white wine
- 1½ cups fish broth
- 1½ cups fresh, shelled sweet peas
- 1 teaspoon fresh lemon juice

### SALMON

- 1 4½-ounce filet
- 3 to 4 sheets puff pastry
- 2 eggs lightly beaten (for egg wash)

Begin the recipe by preparing the stuffing. In a small skillet, melt the butter over medium heat, and sauté the shallots until translucent. Add the herbs and flame with the brandy. Season with salt and pepper. Add the Old Bay and then the lobster broth. Bring the mixture to a boil. Stir in the lobster meat and breadcrumbs and adjust the seasoning if necessary.

Prepare the sauce. In a small saucepan, heat the butter. Add the shallots and sauté until translucent. Add the white wine and reduce by ¾. Add the fish stock and peas. Bring the mixture to a boil and cook until the peas are tender, about 5 minutes. Transfer the mixture to a food processor and pulse until a smooth purée forms. Pass through a chinois or fine mesh sieve to extract the pea skins. Season with salt and pepper. Stir in the lemon juice. (Note: If the sauce is too thick, add additional fish broth.)

Preheat the oven to 400°. Roll the pastry out to ¼-inch thickness. Cut out 6 8-inch disks. Onto each disk, evenly divide the stuffing. Place 1 salmon filet onto the stuffing. Gather the pastry to the center and cover the salmon with the dough, overlapping slightly so that it is completely encased. (Note: Trim any excess dough or it will not cook through.) Seal the dough with water. Flip the bundle over and brush with egg wash. Place on a nonstick baking sheet or cover a baking sheet with parchment. Place in the oven and bake for 30 minutes.

Remove from the oven and let rest for 10 minutes. Pool some sauce in the center of the serving plate and add a pastry bundle to the dish.

Yield: 6 servings

*STONEHEDGE INN*

## Chardonnay Oak-Barrel-Planked Salmon

*You must make a trip to your local winery or lumber store to make this recipe work exactly as Chef Gerard Thompson does it at the ranch. The flavor imparted by the oak is worth the trip, and think of what your guests will say. This is a real conversation recipe. If you cannot find oak planks from a winery, oak or cedar planks from a lumber yard will do.*

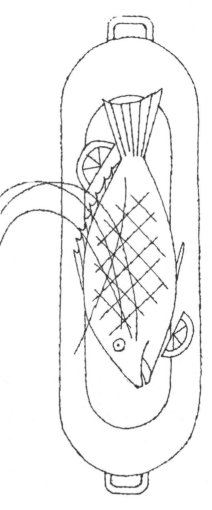

SALMON
8 Chardonnay oak barrel planks
½ cup vegetable oil
8 salmon fillets (6–7 ounces)
¼ cup unsalted butter, softened
   Salt and white pepper

SAUCE
2 cups dry white wine
1 bay leaf
2 shallots, sliced
6 white peppercorns
1 sprig fresh thyme
1 cup heavy cream
1 pound unsalted butter, cut
   into 10 pieces
   Salt
   Juice of ½ lemon
¼ cup chopped fresh chives

Rub the oak planks with the vegetable oil and place them onto a cookie sheet in a 400° oven. Let the planks roast for 20 minutes. Season both sides of the salmon with salt and pepper. Rub the top of the fish with the butter and place on the preheated (smoking) boards. Roast in the same oven for 12 to 15 minutes.

Prepare the sauce. Place the white wine, bay leaf, shallots, peppercorns, and thyme into a small saucepan. Cook, reducing the liquid until 1 tablespoon remains. Add the cream and bring to a boil. Turn the heat to low and slowly add the butter, 1 piece at a time, until all of it is incorporated. Strain and season with salt and lemon juice. Add the chives just before serving.

Yield: 8 servings

*SAN YSIDRO RANCH*

## Knot of Salmon with Green-Onion Sauce and Olive Tapenade

*Tying strips of salmon into a knot makes the presentation on the plate elegant and simple with the knot sitting primped up in the center of the plate. The knot of salmon is a trademark dish of the Bee & Thistle Inn.*

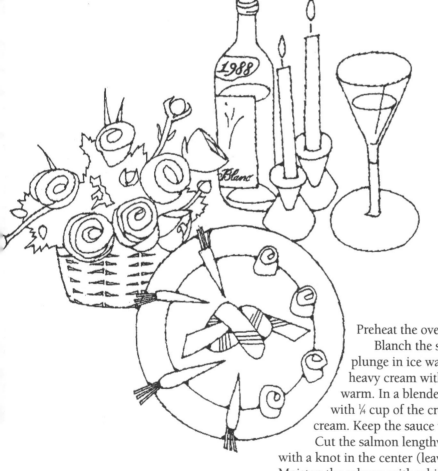

**GREEN ONION SAUCE**
3 bunches scallions
2 ounces fresh spinach leaves
1⅜ cups heavy cream
2 tablespoons dry sherry
¼ teaspoon minced garlic

**SALMON**
7 to 8 pounds fresh salmon, boned and skinned
1 cup white wine
½ cup olive oil

**TAPENADE**
1 cup kalamata olives, pitted
¼ ounce fresh basil
¼ ounce fresh oregano
6 cloves garlic, roasted
¼ cup olive oil (preferably the oil used to roast the garlic)

Preheat the oven to 400°. Prepare the green onion sauce. Blanch the scallions and spinach until tender and plunge in ice water. In a nonstick saucepan, scald the heavy cream with the sherry and garlic. Cool until just warm. In a blender, combine the scallions and spinach with ¼ cup of the cream mixture. Slowly add the rest of the cream. Keep the sauce warm.

Cut the salmon lengthwise into 8 7-ounce strips. Tie each strip with a knot in the center (leaving 1 free end on each side of the knot). Moisten the salmon with white wine and drizzle with olive oil. Roast in a baking pan for about 7 minutes or until medium rare.

Prepare the tapenade. Purée all of the tapenade ingredients in a food processor with half of the oil, adding the rest if necessary, until it reaches a creamy consistency for piping through a pastry bag. Set aside.

To assemble the dish, place the tapenade in a pastry bag fitted with a star tip. Pipe 4 rosettes in a semicircle on half of the plate. Place about ¼ cup of the warm green onion sauce onto the plate. Place the knot of salmon in the center.

Yield: 8 servings

*BEE & THISTLE INN*

## Baked Bundles of Sole, Mushrooms, and Tomatoes

*This is one of the Newcastle Inn's most popular fish entrées, and it's wonderful to make ahead for a dinner party. You will need kitchen parchment paper, which is available in kitchen specialty shops and some supermarkets. Steaming in parchment enhances flavor and helps food retain its nutrients during cooking.*

½ pound fresh shiitake mushrooms, sliced ½-inch thick
¼ cup olive oil
1 pound tomatoes, peeled, seeded, and chopped
¾ cup crème fraîche
1 tablespoon country-style mustard
Salt and finely ground pepper
1½ pounds gray sole filets

*Note:*

A substitute for real crème fraîche is to mix together 1 cup of heavy cream with 2 tablespoons of buttermilk in a glass container. Cover and let stand at room temperature until it thickens (8 to 24 hours).

Sauté the mushrooms in the oil until just tender. Add the tomatoes, and cook until the mixture is nearly dry. Let it cool.

In a small bowl, stir together the crème fraîche, mustard, salt, and pepper, and then stir this mixture into the mushroom-and-tomato mixture.

Preheat the oven to 500°. Fold six 11x15-inch sheets of parchment in half. Divide the filets evenly among the sheets of parchment, placing the filets inside against the fold. Divide the sauce among the fish packages, spreading it over the filets. Seal the filets in the parchment by rolling the cut edges toward the fish. Place the bundles on a cookie sheet and bake them 10 minutes or until they puff.

Serve the bundles unopened so your guests can fully enjoy the fragrance that will rise as they cut through the parchment.

Yield: 6 servings

*NEWCASTLE INN*

## Shiitake-Coated Red Snapper with Tomato Purée and Grilled Zucchini

*A dusting of finely ground shiitake mushrooms with the world-class taste of red snapper sums up this easy-to-prepare yet elegant dish. Chef Jim Overbaugh's recipe is an example of how simple ingredients, used inventively, make for creative and inspiring dishes. This one is a cinch with memorable results. Be sure to use a very sharp blade in order to coarsely grind the mushrooms.*

1½ cups dried shiitake mushrooms
    (substitute with other dried
    wild mushrooms)
⅓ cup all-purpose flour

### TOMATO PURÉE
¼ cup olive oil
1 tablespoon chopped shallots
¼ teaspoon finely chopped garlic
¼ cup white wine
1 pound ripe yellow tomatoes
    (substitute with red)
    Salt and pepper

### ZUCCHINI
2 medium-to-large zucchini
    Salt and pepper to taste
¼ cup olive oil

### FISH
6 6-ounce pieces red snapper
    filets, boned and skinned
    Salt and pepper
½ cup olive oil
¾ cup white wine

Pulverize the mushrooms into a flourlike consistency in a blender with sharp blades. Transfer to a bowl and mix the ground mushrooms with the flour. Set aside.

Make the yellow tomato purée. In a medium-sized saucepan, heat the ¼ cup of olive oil and sweat the shallots and garlic over medium heat just until they turn translucent. Add the white wine and then the tomatoes. Simmer the vegetables until the tomatoes have cooked tender. Transfer the contents of the saucepan to a food processor and whirl until puréed. Season with salt and pepper and set aside.

Cut the zucchini lengthwise into 12 thin slices or sheets. Season with salt and pepper and brush with the olive oil.

Grill the zucchini on a charcoal cooker or sauté in a frying pan. Once the vegetable is lightly browned, set aside and keep warm.

Preheat the oven to 375°. Season the red snapper filets with salt and pepper and dredge them in the shiitake mushroom flour. Heat a straight-sided skillet with the ½ cup of olive oil until the slightest haze of smoke is visible. Sauté the snapper on both sides until golden brown. Add the white wine and place the pan in the oven for 10 min-

utes or just until the fish is opaque when you separate it slightly at the thickest part. To serve, arrange the zucchini on a plate with the tomato purée and a snapper filet in the center.

Yield: 6 servings

*STONEHEDGE INN*

## Mediterranean Red Snapper

¼ cup fresh lemon juice
2 tablespoons olive oil
1½ teaspoons chopped garlic
1 teaspoon dried oregano, divided
2 pounds (6) red snapper filets

1 teaspoon salt
Freshly ground black pepper
2 medium, firm, ripe tomatoes, sliced
Chopped fresh parsley

Preheat the oven to 400°. Combine the lemon juice, olive oil, garlic, and ½ teaspoon of the oregano in a shallow glass baking dish, just large enough to hold the filets in 1 layer (at least a 9x13-inch dish). Stir until the ingredients are well blended.

Pat the snapper dry with paper towels and season both sides with salt and a few grinds of black pepper. Add the fish to the lemon mixture and turn to moisten each piece. Place the tomato slices over the snapper and sprinkle the remaining oregano overtop.

Bake in the oven for 15 to 20 minutes or until the filets flake easily with a fork. Sprinkle with parsley and serve.

Yield: 6 servings

*OCTOBER COUNTRY INN*

# Swordfish Risotto

*Arborio is a short-grain rice whose plump size holds a large amount of starch, which is released by cooking the grains slowly, resulting in a creamy texture. Making risotto is a bit of a slow but worthwhile process. Usually, risotto needs to be prepared just before serving time. That means standing over the stove for thirty minutes, stirring constantly while your guests or family members arrive. To expedite, cook the rice up until five minutes before it is ready. Spread the cooked rice over a baking sheet. Cover and refrigerate. Then, five minutes before serving time, place it back in a saucepan and add one more ladleful or so of chicken stock. The rice will be the same as if it were just cooked.*

*Chef David Blessing's recipe includes traditional risotto with tomatoes and swordfish and a garnish of Parmesan wafers.*

### ROASTED GARLIC
1 bulb garlic
1 tablespoon olive oil

### TOMATOES
6 medium, ripe-red plum
  tomatoes
1 tablespoon olive oil

### PARMESAN CRISPS
1 cup shredded Parmesan
  cheese
  Nonstick vegetable spray

### RISOTTO
⅓ cup olive oil
2 cups chopped onion
2 bay leaves
1 pound Arborio rice
1½ quarts fish broth (substitute
  with chicken broth)
  Salt and pepper

### FISH
6 swordfish steaks (6–8 ounces
  each)
2 tablespoons olive oil

### ASSEMBLY
½ cup olive oil
¾ cup diced tomatoes
2 cups fish stock (substitute
  with chicken broth)
½ cup grated Parmesan cheese
1 tablespoon chopped flat-leaf
  parsley
6 small bouquets of watercress

Preheat the oven to 450°. Begin the recipe by roasting the garlic. Oil the garlic bulb and place it in a glass or ceramic ovenproof shallow dish. Bake in the oven until soft and browned on the outside (about 20 to 30 minutes). Be sure not to overcook the garlic. The meat inside the bulb needs to be soft to get that sweet garlic flavor. Remove from

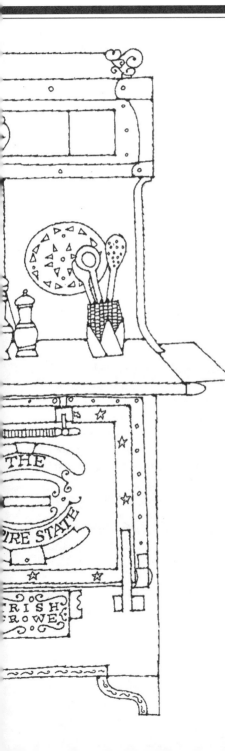

the heat and let cool. Slice off the bottom of the bulb and squeeze out the meat, discarding the outer skin. Set aside.

In the same oven, roast the tomatoes. Brush the tomatoes with oil and place them in a shallow baking pan. Bake for 15 minutes, or until the peels are loose and the tomatoes are soft. Remove the tomatoes from the heat and let them cool enough to handle. Remove and discard the peels. Set aside.

Prepare the Parmesan crisps. Spray vegetable coating onto a nonstick baking sheet. Spread the Parmesan cheese in 6 small piles on the baking sheet. Place under a broiler for a few minutes (watch constantly) until melted and just turning light brown.

Remove from the boiler. Slice each Parmesan crisp off the baking sheet with a spatula, turning it out onto a plate. Set aside. Meanwhile, prepare the risotto.

In a medium skillet with high sides (nonstick preferred), heat the olive oil and sweat the onions. When the onions have become translucent, stir in the Arborio rice. Add the bay leaves. Add the fish broth a ladleful at a time, adding each ladle only at intervals. Slowly add more liquid as it is absorbed by the rice. Add up to 1½ quarts. Stop adding liquid when the rice is *al dente*. Season the risotto to taste. Cool the risotto by spreading it out onto a sheet pan and setting it aside. Remove and discard the bay leaves. (To prepare this earlier in the day, see the recipe introduction above.)

To assemble the dish, in a large skillet, sauté the roasted garlic very lightly along with the mushrooms. Add the risotto and the diced tomatoes. Coat with the oil. Add the fish stock and bring to a simmer. Fold in the Parmesan, parsley, and season with salt and pepper. Keep warm.

Brush the swordfish with olive oil. Place on a grill, cooking the fish for about 8 to 10 minutes or until the fish turns opaque.

Plate the dish by first putting the risotto onto the individual serving dishes and leaning the swordfish against it. Place a bunch of watercress at the top of the plate, topped by a roasted tomato. Position a Parmesan crisp between them. Repeat for each serving.

Yield: 6 servings

# Brook Trout Mousse in Crêpes of Fresh Flowers

*In this unique recipe, you are incorporating edible flowers into the batter to form the crêpes.*

### CRÊPES
1 cup all-purpose flour
⅔ cup milk
⅔ cup cold water
3 large eggs
¼ teaspoon salt
3 tablespoons butter, melted, plus more if needed

### EDIBLE FLOWERS
A few handfuls of a large assortment of nasturtiums, pansies, violas, and scarlet bees (avoid dark-colored flowers and buds, as the colors bleed).

### TROUT MOUSSE
2 8- to 10-ounce smoked trout, cleaned
2 8- to 10-ounce fresh trout, cleaned
⅛ teaspoon salt
⅛ teaspoon pepper
2 egg whites
1 cup heavy cream

Prepare the crêpes. In a food processor, blend all of the ingredients except the melted butter. Let the batter stand for an hour before cooking. (The batter can also be made ahead and refrigerated for 1 day.)

Heat an 8-inch nonstick skillet until hot. Drizzle in the melted butter. Add some of the flowers (face down and pressed flat with a spatula). After a moment, add some of the crêpe batter to the middle of the pan. With a spatula, gently swirl to disperse the batter and just coat the pan. Cook the batter until it first bubbles and the batter becomes firm. Turn the crêpe out onto wax paper. Repeat this process with the remaining flowers and batter.

Prepare the trout. Peel the skin from the trout. In a food processor, add the trout and the salt and pepper. Mix until blended, then add the egg whites, and gradually add the cream until the mousse is well blended. Chill until ready to use.

Assemble the crêpe. Place each crêpe flower-side down. Spread a thick layer (¼ to ⅜ inch) of the trout mousse on half of each crêpe. Fold the other half over to create semi-circles. Cut each semi-circle in half, then pinch the edges together, sealing in the mousse. Lightly oil a baking sheet and place the crêpes on the sheet. Bake for 10 to 12 minutes until the mousse inside is firm and cooked and the crêpe becomes firm.

Yield: 8 servings

*SETTLERS INN*

# Peanut Trout with Curried Mango Butter

*CURRIED MANGO BUTTER*
 2  cups unsalted butter, softened
1½ tablespoons curry powder
¼  cup mango chutney
½  tablespoon fresh cilantro,
    chopped
    Salt and pepper

*TROUT*
 6  fresh boneless trout
 2  cups buttermilk
 2  cups dry-roasted peanuts
 1  cup all-purpose flour
    Salt and pepper
 2  cups unsalted butter, clarified

Make the mango butter. Combine all of the ingredients in a blender and mix until combined. Roll the mixture into a ball, wrap in a piece of parchment paper or plastic wrap, and refrigerate.

Prepare the trout. Preheat the oven to 350°. Place the trout in the buttermilk and set aside while preparing the peanut coating. Grind the peanuts in a food processor until fine. Add the flour and the seasonings, and grind a bit more.

Dredge each trout in the peanut mixture and then sauté in a hot skillet with the clarified butter until golden brown. Flip carefully and finish in the oven for 5 minutes or until cooked through.

Slice the mango butter into 6 disks. Place a disk on top of each trout. Flash under the broiler just until the butter begins to melt. Serve immediately.

Yield: 6 servings

*BEE & THISTLE INN*

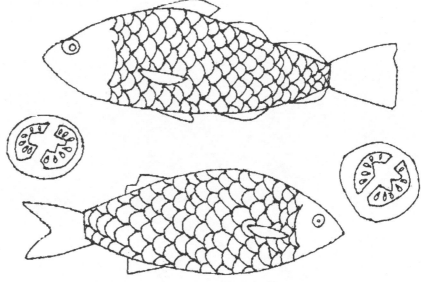

## Grilled Tuna with Tomatoes and Arugula Over Straw Potatoes and a White Herbal Sauce

### VEGETABLES
3 tablespoons balsamic vinegar
½ cup olive oil
½ cup diced onions
½ cup assorted fresh herbs
  Salt, pepper, and sugar
8 thick slices of ripe red tomatoes
2½ cups arugula, minced

### STRAW POTATOES
2 medium, white potatoes, julienned
  Oil for frying

### TUNA
4 5-ounce tuna steaks (yellowfin preferred)
  Salt and pepper
  Olive oil

### SAUCE
½ cup white wine vinegar
½ cup dried onion flakes
1 cup assorted, freshly chopped herbs
½ pound butter

In a small mixing bowl, combine the balsamic vinegar, olive oil, onions, herbs, salt, pepper, and sugar. Using an electric mixer, blend the ingredients until incorporated. Place the tomatoes in a bowl and pour most of the balsamic marinade over them. Add the remaining marinade to the arugula in a separate small bowl. Allow to marinate for at least 15 minutes. Then roast the tomatoes on a grill or under the broiler, just to flash heat them and soften slightly. Remove the tomatoes and set aside.

Prepare the potatoes. In a large frying pan, heat the oil and fry the potatoes until crisp tender. Drain and set aside.

Prepare the tuna. Cut each tuna steak on the thick and narrow so that you have 8 steaks. Season with salt and pepper. Brush with olive oil. Roast on a grill or in a skillet for about 3 minutes per side (more if you prefer). Keep warm.

Prepare the white herbal sauce. In a small saucepan, add the white vinegar, the onion flakes, and the cup of herbs, and reduce over medium-high heat until almost dry. Whisk in the butter a little at a time. (Make sure to keep the sauce warm and be ready to serve immediately.)

To assemble the dish, place a little of the sauce in the center of each individual serving plate. Place 2 slices of the tomato (shingled) on top of the sauce. Place a handful of arugula on top of the tomatoes, followed by the tuna. Drizzle the sauce around the outside of the tuna. Arrange some straw potatoes on the outside.

Yield: 8 servings

*CLIFTON COUNTRY INN*

## Fresh Crab Roulade with Red Pepper Cream Sauce

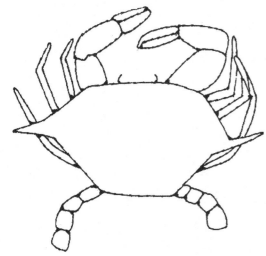

### FILLING

8 ounces cream cheese
1 tablespoon sour cream
1 teaspoon freshly chopped chives
1 teaspoon freshly chopped thyme
1 teaspoon freshly chopped dill
1 cup fresh crabmeat
  Salt and white pepper

### ROULADE

4 eggs, separated
⅓ cup sugar
¼ teaspoon cream of tartar
⅔ cup cake flour, sifted

### SAUCE

2 red bell peppers
½ cup white wine
4 scallions, finely chopped
2 cloves garlic, minced
2 cups heavy cream
  Salt
¼ teaspoon white pepper

Prepare the filling. In a small bowl, whip the cream cheese with the sour cream, chives, thyme, and dill. Fold in the crabmeat and then add the salt and pepper. Set aside in a cool place.

Prepare the roulade. Preheat the oven to 350°. Lightly grease and flour an 11x15-inch jellyroll pan. Line the bottom with parchment paper.

In a large bowl, beat the egg yolks to break them up. Add the sugar and continue to beat until the mixture falls from the beater in a ribbon. In a separate, large copper or stainless steel bowl, beat the egg whites until just foamy. Add the cream of tartar. Continue beating until stiff, glossy peaks form. Fold the flour into the yolk mixture in three stages. Then fold in ⅓ of the whites to lighten. Very gently fold in the remaining whites. Fill the prepared pan with the batter and bake until the top springs back when gently pressed with a finger (about 15 minutes). Cool in the pan for 5 minutes.

Turn the cake out onto a kitchen towel covered with a sheet of parchment paper. Remove the paper from the cake bottom and discard. Trim the crusts all around. Carefully roll up the cake in the parchment, wrap with a kitchen towel to secure, and cool completely on a wire rack. After cooling, gently unroll, then spread the crab filling to within 1 inch of the edges of the cake. Gently roll again, then refrigerate the roulade for 2 hours. Remove from the refrigerator and bring to room temperature.

Prepare the sauce. Roast the red peppers under the broiler or over a gas flame until the skins blacken. Remove the skins. Purée the peppers in a food processor. Leave them in the processor.

In a medium saucepan, sauté the wine, scallions, and garlic and reduce over medium heat until about 2 tablespoons of the wine remain. Add the cream and reduce until the mixture thickens. Add the salt and white pepper. Add the cream mixture to the red pepper purée already in the food processor. Purée completely, then strain through a fine mesh.

To serve, cut the roulade into 1-inch-thick slices, spoon the sauce overtop, and garnish as desired.

Yield: 6 to 8 servings

*CARTER HOUSE*

## Gingered Scallops with Capers and Bell Peppers

3 tablespoons extra virgin olive oil
1 tablespoon finely diced shallots
2 cups julienned green, red, and yellow bell peppers
1½ pounds sea scallops
1 teaspoon freshly grated ginger
1 tablespoon crushed garlic
2 tablespoons capers
½ teaspoon finely chopped saffron (or turmeric)
1 teaspoon Pernod liqueur
Salt and white pepper
Coarsely cut Italian parsley for garnish

In a heavy saucepan, heat 2 tablespoons of the olive oil. Sauté the shallots and peppers until the shallots are transparent. Remove from the saucepan and strain through a fine-mesh sieve, saving the juice and olive oil. Set aside the strained shallots and peppers. Pour the juice back into the saucepan. Add the remaining tablespoon of olive oil and heat.

Quickly sauté the scallops. (Do not overcook scallops, as they become tough and lose their natural juice.) Add the ginger, garlic, capers, and saffron; mix. Splash with the Pernod and add the sautéed shallots and peppers. Season to taste with salt and white pepper. Serve in scallop shells or on a decorative plate, and garnish with the parsley.

Yield: 4 to 6 servings

*HERITAGE PARK B&B INN*

## Potato-Crusted Shrimp with Black Bean Sauce and Chayote Squash Relish

*SAUCE*
⅛ cup vegetable oil
1 yellow onion, diced
1 chipotle chili (canned)
10 cups dry black beans, soaked
   overnight
6 cups shrimp or chicken stock
   Kosher salt
1 head garlic, roasted

*RELISH*
1 chayote squash
1 roasted ear of corn, kernels
   removed and cob discarded
1 cup cooked black beans,
   reserved from the sauce

1 red bell pepper, diced
1 clove garlic, chopped
½ jalapeño pepper, very finely
   chopped
2 tablespoons corn oil
1 tablespoon lime juice
   Kosher salt

*SHRIMP*
4 eggs
¼ cup water
1 cup cornstarch
8 Idaho potatoes, peeled and
   soaking in water
32 prawns, peeled
   Peanut oil for deep frying

Heat the vegetable oil and sauté the onion for 3 minutes. Add the chili, beans, and stock, and cook on low heat until the beans are soft (about an hour). Remove 1 cup of the beans and put aside for the relish; allow the beans to cool. Season with salt. Remove from the heat. Add the bean mixture and the roasted garlic and purée until smooth.

Prepare the relish. Peel and core the chayote squash, then dice it into 1-inch pieces and place in a medium bowl. Add the remaining ingredients and season with the salt. Set aside.

Prepare the shrimp. Mix the eggs with the water. Place the cornstarch in a shallow dish. Shred 1 potato on a mandoline or the heavy side of a cheese grater. Working quickly, dip 4 shrimp at a time, first in the cornstarch (brushing off any excess), then into the egg, and then into the shredded potato. Wrap the potato around the shrimp very carefully, making sure to cover the entire shrimp. Set aside after dusting with a little more cornstarch. Continue until all of the shrimp are coated. Cover and refrigerate.

Preheat the oven to 250°. Heat the oil in a large skillet with high sides. Be sure the oil is very hot and at least 3 inches deep in the pan. Using a mesh basket or strainer, place 4 shrimp at a time in the hot oil, lowering them gently. Cook for 3 to 5 minutes or until just golden brown. Drain on a paper towel and place in the oven to keep warm. Repeat with the remaining shrimp.

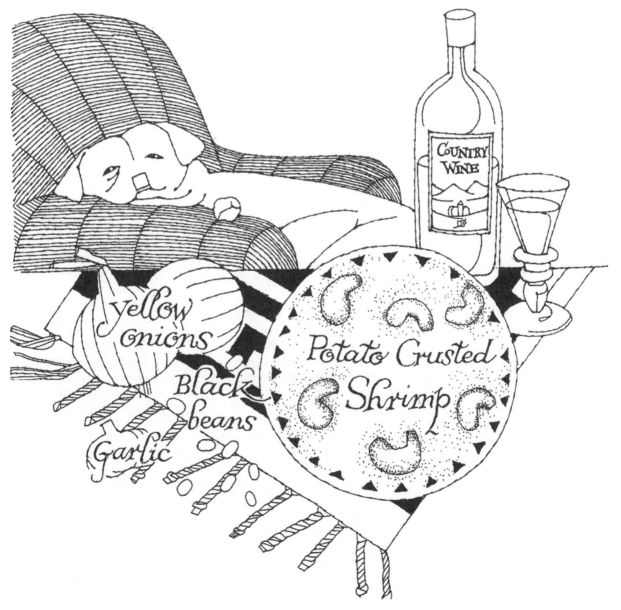

When all of the shrimp have cooked, divide the black bean sauce among 8 individual serving plates and top each with 4 of the shrimp. Top each of the shrimp with the chayote squash relish.

Yield: 8 servings

*SAN YSIDRO RANCH*

## Pecan-Crusted Catfish, Shrimp, and Crayfish with Zippy Francisco Sauce

*The sauce was created by Chef Larc Lindsey in honor of another cook at the inn whose middle name was Frances. Frances had a lot to do with inspiring this unusual, tasty sauce.*

### SAUCE
1 cup white wine
1 cup red wine
4 cups water or substitute 1 quart very concentrated homemade fish stock
2 tablespoons fish bouillon or fish stock
2 tablespoons shrimp bouillon or stock
4 cups clam juice
⅔ cup tomato paste
2 scallions, coarsely chopped
2 ribs celery, coarsely chopped
2 cloves garlic, coarsely chopped
1 large sprig parsley
½ teaspoon oregano
1 small carrot, coarsely chopped
½ teaspoon thyme
1 small onion, coarsely chopped
⅛ teaspoon cayenne pepper
¼ teaspoon white pepper
¼ teaspoon black pepper
3 bay leaves
8 whole black peppercorns
2 teaspoons salt
1 tablespoon cornstarch

### CRUST
1 cup toasted pecans or pecan pieces
½ cup seafood breading mix or all-purpose flour
1 teaspoon dried basil
1 teaspoon dried oregano
2 tablespoons chopped fresh parsley
½ teaspoon Hungarian paprika
1 teaspoon salt
½ teaspoon white pepper
½ teaspoon black pepper
⅛ teaspoon cayenne pepper

### SEAFOOD
6 5-ounce fresh catfish filets
1 pound peeled and deveined large shrimp, with tail on
1 pound crayfish tail meat
¼ cup clarified butter

Prepare the sauce. In a large stockpot, combine and boil all the sauce ingredients, except the cornstarch, until reduced by ½. Strain the remaining liquid. Return to a low boil and thicken by combining the cornstarch with some water and adding to the pot. Set aside.

Prepare the crust by combining all of the crust ingredients in a food processor and blending until the flour and nuts are thoroughly incorporated and finely chopped. Transfer the mixture to a large mixing bowl.

Prepare the fish. Moisten the catfish, shrimp, and crayfish with water, then toss each one into the pecan-crust mixture, coating all sides well. Heat a large skillet with about half of the clarified butter. Sauté the catfish 3 or 4 minutes or until done. Remove and keep warm. Repeat this process with the shrimp and the crayfish. (Sauté time for the shrimp should be 2 to 3 minutes and the crayfish just less than 2 minutes. Each should be moist inside and slightly crunchy on the outside.)

To serve, arrange several pieces of shrimp and crayfish over each catfish, and ladle 4 to 6 tablespoons of the sauce overtop. Serve immediately.

Yield: 6 servings

*HIGHLAND LAKE INN*

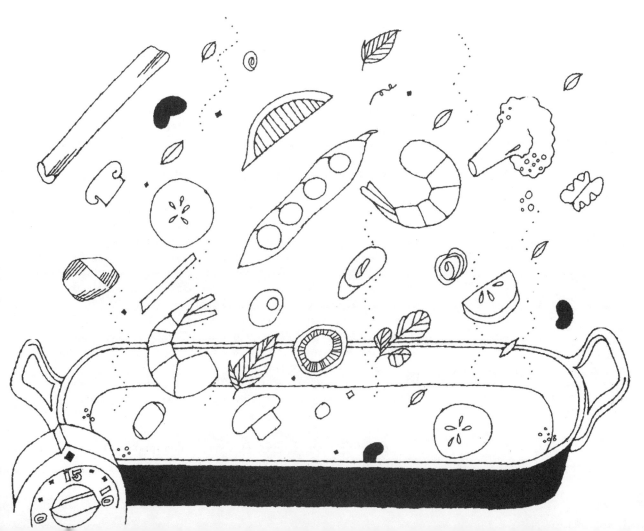

113

## Black Tiger Shrimp with Tomato Compote and Wilted Spinach

*SAUCE*
1 small onion, chopped
1 tablespoon chopped basil
2 ounces domestic mushrooms, chopped
½ cup fish stock (substitute with white wine)
2 tablespoons white wine
1 cup heavy cream
1 bunch fresh basil
1 tablespoon unsalted butter, softened
1 teaspoon white wine vinegar

*COMPOTE*
1 tablespoon olive oil
3 shallots, finely chopped
4 cloves garlic, mashed

2 medium vine-ripened tomatoes, blanched, peeled, seeded and diced
1 tablespoon chopped thyme
1 tablespoon chopped chives
Salt and pepper

*SHRIMP*
20 black tiger shrimp, peeled and deveined
½ pound goat cheese

*SPINACH*
1 tablespoon unsalted butter
12 ounces fresh spinach, washed and trimmed
2 tablespoons white wine

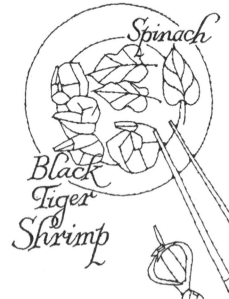

Prepare the sauce. In a small saucepan, combine the onion, half of the basil, the chopped mushrooms, fish stock, and the white wine and reduce by half. Add the heavy cream and reduce until the mixture is thick enough that it coats the back of a spoon. Purée the mixture in a blender with the remaining basil. Whisk in the butter and vinegar.

Make the compote. Heat the oil in a small saucepan and saute the shallots and garlic. When the shallots turn translucent, add the chopped tomatoes. Cook until the liquid evaporates. Add the thyme and chives and season with salt and pepper.

Preheat the oven to 475°. Butterfly the shrimp and fill the crevices with the goat cheese. Place on an oiled baking pan. Season with salt and pepper. Roast in the oven for about 7 minutes, or until done. Keep the shrimp warm.

In a small saucepan, heat the butter and cook the spinach a few minutes, just until it wilts. Add a splash of white wine.

To serve, place the spinach in the center of an individual serving plate. Place a spoonful of the tomato compote on top of the spinach. Spoon the sauce all around and top with the shrimp, divided evenly among the plates.

Yield: 4 servings

114

## Flambé of Lobster Ragout

2 whole lobsters (1½ pounds each)
½ cup plus 3 tablespoons unsalted butter
3 leeks, white part only, chopped finely
1 garlic clove, minced
10 ounces peeled plum tomatoes, drained and coarsely chopped
¾ cup dry white wine

2 tablespoons tomato paste
1 small onion, minced
2 tablespoons white wine vinegar
¼ cup heavy cream
Salt and freshly ground pepper
⅓ cup cognac
Boiled rice, made from 1 cup dry rice

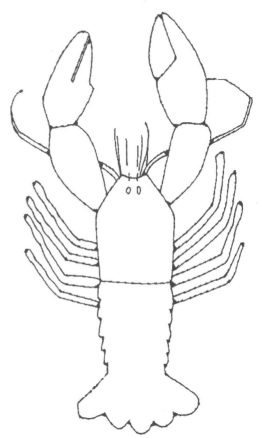

In a large kettle, bring 2 inches of salted water to a boil. Plunge the lobsters into the kettle; cover the kettle, and steam the lobsters for 13 to 15 minutes, until they have turned red. Transfer the lobsters to a bowl, reserving the cooking liquid. Let the lobsters cool slightly, then snap off the claws and remove their meat, keeping the meat whole. Split the underside of the tail shells lengthwise, and remove the tail meat. Cut each tail into 2 pieces.

Prepare the tomato mixture. In a nonstick skillet, melt 2 tablespoons of the butter. Add the leeks and garlic, and sauté until they are soft, about 5 minutes. Add the tomatoes, ½ cup of the white wine, and 2 tablespoons of the reserved cooking liquid. Bring the mixture to a boil, reduce the heat, and cook for 15 minutes, or until the mixture is thick. Add the tomato paste and stir well. Keep the tomato mixture warm.

Prepare the sauce. In a small saucepan, combine the onion, the remaining white wine, white wine vinegar, and ¼ cup of the reserved lobster liquid. Bring the mixture to a boil, and boil until it is reduced to ¼ cup. Whisk in the heavy cream, and boil until the mixture is again reduced to ¼ cup.

Cut the ½ cup of butter into small pieces. Whisk the butter into the mixture, 1 piece at a time. Set the sauce aside.

In a nonstick skillet, melt the remaining 1 tablespoon of butter. Add the lobster meat. Season with salt and pepper and heat gently for 2 to 3 minutes. Add the cognac, and ignite it by touching a lit match to the edge of the skillet. Remove the skillet from the heat.

Divide the boiled rice among 4 plates. Spoon the tomato mixture over the rice. Spoon the lobster over the tomato mixture, and top with the sauce.

Yield: 4 servings

*NEWCASTLE INN*

## Pistachio-Stuffed Amish Chicken Breasts with Cider Cream Sauce

*The Checkerberry Inn sits woven into a patchwork quilt of Amish farm-land. The inn buys its poultry and other farm-raised products from the area's Amish. The chicken is stuffed with a filling of ground thigh meat, cream, and pistachios. Note: You may skip the deboning and chicken preparation steps by having your butcher prepare the poultry according to the recipe.*

2 large whole chickens (3½ to 4
    pounds each)
⅓ cup heavy cream
¼ cup shelled pistachio nuts
1 teaspoon salt
½ teaspoon pepper

*SAUCE*
¼ cup dry vermouth
½ cup apple cider
3 cups chicken broth
½ cup light cream
    Salt and pepper

Remove the excess fat and skin from the breast area. Debone the breasts, leaving the tenderloins intact. Refrigerate the chicken.

Begin to make the filling. Disjoint the rear quarters and remove the skin and excess fat. Separate the legs from the thighs. Remove the thigh meat from the bone. Repeat this process with the remaining chicken parts. Place only the meat in the freezer to chill. When the thigh meat is almost frozen, place the meat in a food processor. Add salt and pepper and whirl until the mixture comes together like ground chicken.

While processing the meat, add the heavy cream slowly, using a spatula to make sure that it is well combined. Add the pistachios and pulse a few times. Remove the filling and refrigerate.

Preheat the oven to 400°. Make 4 6-inch squares of heavy-duty aluminum foil. Coat 1 side of the foil with a nonstick spray. Place the chicken tenderloins onto the squares, spooning the filling under the tenderloins, between the breast and tenderloins. Season with salt and

pepper. Carefully roll the chicken into a cylinder, twisting each end of the foil to seal. Roast in a shallow pan or on a rack in the oven 12 to 18 minutes or until firm.

While the chicken bakes, prepare the cider cream sauce. In a medium saucepan, boil the vermouth until almost dry. Add the apple cider. Boil the cider and reduce the mixture to about 3 tablespoons. Add the broth and reduce again until ½ cup remains. Finally, add the light cream and reduce the mixture until a sauce consistency is obtained, another few minutes. Season with salt and pepper.

To assemble the dish, remove the foil from the chicken. Place the chicken on individual serving plates and pour the sauce overtop.

Yield: 4 servings

*CHECKERBERRY INN*

## Texas Fried Chicken

*This is a classic recipe that cannot be beat.*

2 fryer chickens (about 2½ pounds each), cut into serving pieces (reserve back and necks for making stock)
Salt and pepper

7 eggs
¼ cup evaporated milk
3 cups all-purpose flour
Shortening for deep frying (about 2 pounds)

Season the chicken pieces with salt and pepper and place them in a colander over a large bowl.

Break the eggs into a mixing bowl and whisk in the evaporated milk. Place the flour in another mixing bowl. Melt the shortening in a deep heavy skillet or Dutch oven to a depth of not more than halfway up the sides of the pan. Heat the shortening to a temperature of about 350°.

Dredge the chicken pieces heavily with flour, then dip in the egg batter, then once again in the flour. Place a few pieces at a time in the hot shortening, but do not crowd. Cook until golden brown, about 15 minutes, turning with tongs. The chicken is ready when it floats.

Remove the chicken from the pan and keep it warm in a 150° oven until ready to serve.

Yield: 8 servings

*Y. O. RANCH*

## Apricot Pecan Chicken Breasts

*Chef Yvonne Martin serves this dish often at White Oak Inn. It is low in fat and calories as well as fast and simple to prepare. Garnished with apricot and pecan halves, it allows for very pretty plate presentation. Although the sauce is sweet, the small amount used for each serving keeps the calorie count down on this dish.*

2 pounds canned apricot halves, juice reserved
1 cup apricot preserves
2 teaspoons Dijon-style mustard
¼ cup dry sherry, white wine, or apple juice
2 teaspoons freshly chopped rosemary (or 1 teaspoon dried)
¾ teaspoon freshly ground pepper
¼ cup pecan halves (save 8 for garnish, chop the rest)
8 boneless, skinless chicken breasts (6 to 8 ounces each), fat trimmed
1 tablespoon olive oil
Paprika

Drain the apricots, saving about half of the juice. Reserve 8 of the apricot halves for garnish. Put the remainder in a blender or food processor and add the reserved juice, the preserves, mustard, and sherry; then purée. Mix in the rosemary and pepper. Pour the mixture into a saucepan, and simmer gently for about 30 minutes, stirring occasionally. (If the sauce becomes too thick, dilute it with more sherry or apple juice.) Add the chopped pecans just before serving. Meanwhile, prepare the chicken. Preheat the oven to 350°.

Place the chicken breasts in a greased baking pan. Brush them with the olive oil and then sprinkle lightly with the paprika. Bake for about 20 minutes and then pour about 1 tablespoon of the sauce over each breast. Return the chicken to the oven and bake for another 10 minutes.

To serve, make a pool of sauce on the plate. Place the chicken in the center. Garnish with apricot and pecan halves and serve with extra sauce on the side.

Yield: 8 servings

*WHITE OAK INN*

118

# Chicken Marsala with Morel Mushrooms and Angel Hair Pasta

*Although this recipe requires a full bottle of wine, don't worry; it will be reduced by half.*

| | |
|---|---|
| 1 bottle (750 ml) Marsala cooking wine | 6 jumbo, dried morel mushrooms |
| 1 beef bouillon cube | 6 8-ounce chicken breasts, bones removed, skin on |
| ½ teaspoon fresh garlic juice | 1½ pounds fresh angel hair pasta |
| 1 pint heavy cream | |

In a heavy saucepan, reduce the Marsala by half. Add the bouillon, garlic juice, and cream, and whisk until completely blended. Add the dried mushrooms and simmer at a low boil until the sauce is thick enough to coat the back of a spoon without dripping.

Grill the chicken breasts until the skin is golden brown and the meat has turned white. Move to a warm oven to hold the temperature.

In a large saucepan, boil salted water. Then add the pasta and cook *al dente*.

To serve, place individual portions of pasta on each plate, add ¼ to ½ cup of the Marsala sauce, and top with a morel mushroom. Place a chicken breast next to the pasta, and serve.

Yield: 6 servings

*VICTORIAN VILLA*

119

## Garlic-Crusted Chicken

2 cups seasoned breadcrumbs
½ cup grated Parmesan cheese
¼ cup chopped parsley
  Salt and pepper

2 cloves garlic, minced
1 cup butter, melted
8 boned, skinless chicken
  breasts

Preheat the oven to 375°. In a medium bowl, combine the bread-crumbs, Parmesan cheese, parsley, and salt and pepper to taste. Add the garlic to the melted butter. Dip the chicken in the butter and then in the crumbs. Place in a 9x13-inch or larger glass baking dish. Bake for 45 to 50 minutes or until golden brown.

  Yield: 8 servings

*OCTOBER COUNTRY INN*

## Fruit and Sage-Stuffed Boneless Breast of Turkey

*Most turkey breasts are sold with the bone in. Ask the butcher to remove the bone but keep the skin intact. You will need a twelve-inch piece of cheesecloth and toothpicks to hold the stuffing in while the turkey bakes. Only about half of the stuffing will bake inside the breast; the other may be placed in a casserole dish and baked one hour along with the turkey.*

STUFFING
1 cup golden raisins or ¾ cup
  raisins and ¼ cup dried cherries
½ cup white wine
2 cups day-old unseasoned
  breadcrumbs
2 cups crumbled cornbread
1 tart apple, peeled and diced
⅓ cup finely chopped parsley
1 clove garlic, finely chopped

½ teaspoon chiffonade of fresh
  sage
2 tablespoons melted butter
1 cup or less chicken broth
  Salt and pepper

TURKEY
½ cup butter, melted
1 6-pound turkey breast,
  deboned
  Salt and pepper

Soak the raisins in the white wine until soft, about 30 minutes, or heat for about 1 minute in the microwave. In a large bowl, combine the plain and cornbread crumbs with the raisins, apple, parsley, garlic, and sage. Add the butter and enough chicken broth to make a moist stuffing that will hold together. Season with salt and pepper to taste. Set the stuffing aside and prepare the turkey.

120

Preheat the oven to 325°. Dip the cheesecloth in the melted butter and spread the cheesecloth out onto a baking pan. Brush the skin of the turkey with the remaining butter. Sprinkle generously with salt and pepper. Place the turkey skin-side down in the center of the cheesecloth. Spread at least half of the stuffing out evenly over the meat. Press the 2 halves of the breast together; then bring the cheesecloth up over the turkey to enclose it completely.

Fasten the edges of the cheesecloth together with strong toothpicks, tucking the ends of the cloth in securely and cutting off any excess cloth.

Bake the turkey in the lower (not the lowest) level for 2 hours (20 minutes to the pound) or until the internal temperature reaches 170°. Baste occasionally with melted butter and juices from the pan.

When the turkey is cooked, remove it from the oven and allow to sit for 20 minutes. Carefully remove the cheesecloth, trying not to tear the skin. Slice carefully, keeping the stuffing inside.

Yield: 8 to 10 servings

*GLEN-ELLA SPRINGS INN*

Pecking turkey toy

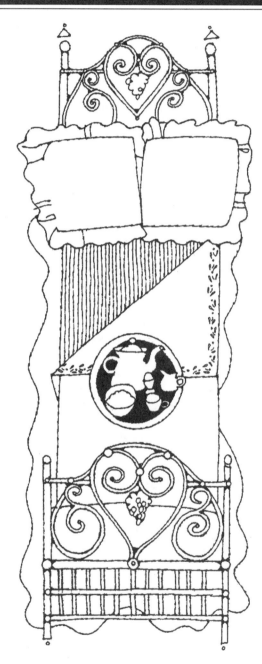

## Seasoned Pheasant Cacciatore in Burgundy Wine

*This easy but elegant main course would also go well with the inn's potato gratin recipe on page 165.*

| | |
|---|---|
| 1 2½- to 3-pound pheasant | Pepper |
| 1 onion, coarsely chopped | 2 tablespoons clarified butter or |
| 1 carrot, coarsely chopped | olive oil |
| ⅛ teaspoon thyme | ¼ cup all-purpose flour |
| 1 bay leaf | 2 tablespoons tomato paste |
| Salt | 2 cups Burgundy wine |
| ½ teaspoon ground rosemary | 2 ounces wild mushrooms, |
| ¼ teaspoon curry powder | chopped (optional) |
| ¼ teaspoon ground juniper | ¼ cup heavy cream (optional) |

Joint the pheasant. First remove the legs, then cut away the 2 breast sections down along the backbone. Cut the 2 leg sections in half at the joint and cut each breast in half. Trim off the wing section. Place all the boned sections in a large stockpot with the onion and the carrot; add the thyme and bay leaf, and salt to taste. Add water to cover. Cook for about 1 hour at a slow simmer. Strain and reserve the stock.

Mix the rosemary, curry powder, and juniper together; add salt and pepper to taste. Sprinkle the seasonings over the pheasant pieces. In a large sauté pan, heat the clarified butter and quickly sauté the pheasant pieces until they are brown on all sides. Add the flour, browning slightly. While stirring, add the tomato paste, wine, and some of the reserved stock to just cover the pheasant. Cook uncovered at a slow simmer for 45 minutes to 1 hour or until tender and cooked through. (Add a little more stock if necessary.)

If desired, add the wild mushrooms and the heavy cream about 10 minutes before the dish is done.

Yield: 4 servings

*SIGN OF THE SORREL HORSE*

# Pheasant with Wild Rice Stuffing and Vermont Cherry Amaretto Glaze

PHEASANTS
- 2 pheasants (3½ pounds each)
- 2 teaspoons unsalted butter (to be added to pheasant preparation later)
- 1 cup no-salt chicken stock (to be added to pheasant preparation later)

STUFFING
- 2 cups cooked wild rice
  Meat from 4 slightly smoked pheasant thighs (smoked is optional), chopped
- 2 tablespoons chopped garlic
- 2 tablespoons chopped shallots
- 1 tablespoon freshly chopped rosemary
- 2 eggs
- 1 cup toasted seasoned bread-crumbs

GLAZE
- 2 tablespoons chopped shallots
- ¼ cup amaretto liqueur
- 1½ cups cherry amaretto preserves or other cherry preserves
- ½ cup no-salt chicken stock
- 2 teaspoons unsalted butter

### Stuffing No-No

The cavities of wild birds contain bacteria. It is better to cook stuffings separately than inside the fowl.

*SCHUMACHER'S NEW PRAGUE HOTEL*

Preheat the oven to 400°. Bone the pheasants, leaving the skin and the tenderloin up to the first knuckle of the wings. Set aside.

Make the stuffing. In a large bowl, mix together the stuffing ingredients. Season to taste with salt and pepper. Set stuffing aside and prepare the glaze.

In a medium, nonstick skillet, add the shallots and amaretto. Cook over medium-high heat, reducing by half. Add the cherry preserves and the chicken stock. Whisk in the butter. Bring down to a simmer, then just keep warm.

Turn the pheasant meat skin-side down, flipping the tenderloin to the outside (leave intact). With a boning knife, butterfly the opposite side of the breast to make a pocket.

Stuff the pheasants, using ½ cup of the stuffing per bird. Fold the butterflied pheasant over the stuffing. Place on a baking sheet, skin-side up. Baste with the 1 cup of chicken stock and place 1 teaspoon of the butter on each pheasant. Bake for 20 to 25 minutes, basting frequently, until the breasts are firm and golden brown. Remove from the oven and let rest. Slice and serve with the sauce.

Yield: 6 servings

*KEDRON VALLEY INN*

*Man with Grapes*

## Mango-and-Macadamia-Stuffed Pheasants in a Honey-Tarragon Sauce

*STUFFING*
2 cups bread cubes (about ⅛-inch thick)
¼ cup mango purée
¼ cup diced mango
¼ cup macadamia nuts, chopped
3½ ounces finely chopped prosciutto
2 egg whites

*PHEASANTS*
6 pheasant breasts, washed and patted dry

*GLAZE*
½ cup honey
2 sprigs fresh tarragon
¼ cup water

Preheat the oven to 375°. Prepare the stuffing. In a medium bowl, mix all of the stuffing ingredients together and set aside.

Prepare the pheasant breasts. Cut a deep pocket lengthwise along the thick side of each of the breasts. Place some stuffing inside each breast pocket. Place the breasts in a nonstick or greased roasting pan and set aside.

Prepare the glaze. In a small saucepan, mix the glaze ingredients and cook to reduce by about half. Pour ½ of the glaze over the stuffed breasts and bake for 10 minutes. Pour the remaining glaze over the breasts and bake for an additional 15 minutes or until browned.

Yield: 6 servings

*SIGN OF THE SORREL HORSE*

### Bubble Up

To keep the effervescence in an opened bottle of champagne until the next day, place the straight end of a metal spoon in the neck and store the bottle in the refrigerator. Wine connoisseurs don't know why this is so. Do you?

## Crispy Roasted Hen Rolls with Sage-and-Pancetta Stuffing

*Free-range hens should be available from your butcher or gourmet market. If you prefer, have the butcher bone the hen, and if so, skip the first part of the recipe method and just go on to preparing the stuffing. You will need four pieces of kitchen string, each one foot long.*

2 3-pound free-range hens
¼ cup pancetta, chopped medium fine (tasso or prosciutto hams may be substituted)
¼ cup chopped scallions
3 tablespoons clarified butter
1 tablespoon chopped fresh sage
1 tablespoon finely chopped fresh parsley

4 cups toasted coarse cubed
bread (any leftover bread will
do, but white French loaves
are best)

½ cup chicken broth, concentrated preferred
Salt and white pepper

Begin by removing the bones from each of the hens. Starting at the
breastbone, split the hen through the flesh only. Cut the breast meat
and wing away from the central carcass and cut the thighbone free.
Try to keep the flesh and skin intact as much as possible. Remove the
breast meat, wing, and thigh/leg away from the central carcass along
with the skin, then remove the wing entirely. Remove the leg and
thighbones by making 1 long slit in the skin and carefully cutting the
bones out with a minimum of damage to the flesh and skin; remove
the tendons from the lower leg. You now have 2 pieces of meat; the
breast and the thigh/leg attached to a large piece of skin. Arrange the
half-hen, skin-side down, with the dark and white meats lying side by
side looking up. Pound the breast slightly to even the thickness.
Sprinkle the meat with salt and white pepper. Repeat the process for
the remaining 1½ hens.

Prepare the stuffing. In a nonstick skillet, sauté the pancetta and
green onion in the butter for 1 to 2 minutes. Add the sage and parsley.
Sauté until the pancetta and onions are translucent. (The pancetta
should not be crispy.)

In a large mixing bowl, combine the bread cubes with the sautéed
mixture, mixing thoroughly. Sprinkle chicken broth in to moisten the
stuffing. Season with salt and white pepper to taste. Preheat the oven
to 375°.

Place 1 cup of the stuffing between each of the dark and white
meat halves, encircling the stuffing with the meat. (The skin holds
everything in place as you tie the hens.) Using 1 piece of butcher's
twine, tie the packet near the end so as to close. Tie a second string
approximately 1½ inches from the first knot, using the loose ends to
tie the first and second knots together. This secures the first string in
place. Repeat the procedure at the other end of the packet.

Roast the stuffed hen rolls for 20 to 22 minutes or until the hens are
very crispy on the outside and juicy on the inside. Serve immediately.

Yield: 4 servings

*HIGHLAND LAKE INN*

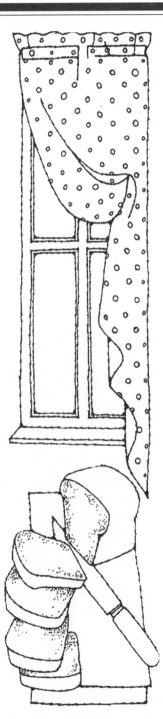

Three Birds
Baked
in a
Pie

# Three Birds Baked in a Pie

*Chef Larc Lindsay's wonderful recipe calls for three different poultry types. But you may make this pie with any one or two or whatever poultry you desire to use.*

FILLING
5 ounces lean bacon, diced
1½ cups coarsely sliced shiitake
  or portobello mushrooms
  Olive oil
2 cups diced onions
1 tablespoon minced garlic
½ teaspoon freshly chopped
  thyme
½ cup freshly chopped parsley
½ teaspoon freshly chopped tarragon
½ cup all-purpose flour
½ cup quality brandy
½ cup beef broth
½ cup concentrated poultry
  stock
1 cup Burgundy wine

1 cup veal demi-glace, or make
  1 cup from Knorr's demi-glace
  sauce mix
  Salt and white pepper
2 pounds cooked duck meat,
  cut into ½-inch cubes
1 pound cooked chicken, cut
  into ½-inch cubes
1 pound cooked turkey, cut into
  ½-inch cubes
1 8-ounce can pearl onions in
  water

CRUST
1 17¼-ounce package frozen
  puff pastry
1 egg, beaten
1 tablespoon water

In a 4-quart, heavy-bottomed saucepan, sauté the bacon until cooked, but not crisp. Remove the bacon with a slotted spoon and set aside. Drain most of the fat from the pan, reserving it for later. Using the same pan, sauté the mushrooms. Remove the mushrooms when just cooked, and set aside. Combine the reserved bacon fat with enough olive oil to make 1 cup total. Place the oil mixture back in the pan and cook the diced onions until caramelized; add the garlic and the fresh herbs. Cook for about 1 minute more. Add the flour, continuing to stir for 2 or 3 minutes to make a roux. Add the brandy, broth, stock, wine, and demi-glace, stirring until the sauce thickens. Taste the sauce and add salt and white pepper to taste. Thicken the sauce by either adding a roux (1 tablespoon butter and 1 tablespoon flour cooked together into a paste) or simply reduce the sauce until it thickens naturally. Add the cooked poultry, bacon, mushrooms, and pearl onions; mix and pour into a large iron skillet or a 4-quart casserole.

Preheat the oven to 350°. Prepare the pie shell. Roll 1 piece of thawed puff pastry about ⅛-inch thick to fit the skillet or casserole.

Cut to the correct shape, place overtop of the filling, and crimp the edges to seal. Cut 3 vents in the crust. In a small bowl, beat the egg with the water. Brush the crust with the egg mixture. Bake for 25 minutes or until the pastry is golden brown and the filling is bubbly hot.

Yield: 6 to 8 servings

*HIGHLAND LAKE INN*

# Foie Gras with Field-Ripened Pineapples in a Ginger Sauce

*SAUCE*
¼ cup soy sauce
¼ cup sweet rice wine
  or dry sherry
¼ cup plus 1 tablespoon water,
  divided
2 tablespoons sugar
1 tablespoon rice wine vinegar
  or sherry vinegar
3 slices ginger root
1 clove garlic, mashed
1 tablespoon cornstarch

*ASSEMBLY*
¾ pound foie gras, cut into
  4 even pieces
  Olive oil for sautéing
4 ½-inch slices ripe pineapple
¼ cup demi-glace (available in
  gourmet stores or see recipe
  for Quick Brown Sauce, page
  222)
12 ounces fresh spinach, trimmed

In a small saucepan, combine the soy sauce, rice wine, ¼ cup of the water, sugar, vinegar, ginger, and the garlic. Heat to a slow simmer. Mix the cornstarch with the 1 tablespoon of water, and slowly whisk the mixture into the simmering sauce. Continue whisking the sauce for a few minutes, strain and set aside.

Brown both sides of the foie gras in a very hot sauté pan with a little olive oil. Remove the foie gras from the pan, and keep warm. Caramelize the pineapple slices in the remaining fat. Place each pineapple slice on a warm plate. Deglaze the sauté pan with the ginger sauce and demi-glace. Add the spinach and cook until just wilted.

To assemble the dish, arrange the spinach in the center of the pineapple. Add the foie gras on top of the spinach. Pour the ginger sauce overall and serve.

Yield: 4 servings

*OLD DROVERS INN*

127

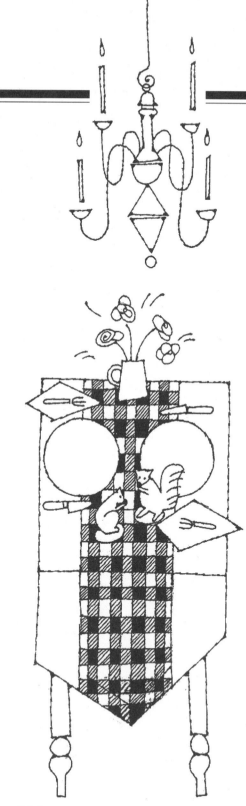

## Medallions of Pork with Cider Cream and Glazed Apples

*Simple to make, this dish makes a gourmet impression.*

1 pound pork tenderloin, trimmed and cut into 1-inch thick slices
5 tablespoons butter
4 medium baking apples (such as Granny Smith), peeled, cored, and sliced ½-inch thick
1 teaspoon sugar
Salt and pepper
2 large shallots, chopped
1 tablespoon chopped fresh thyme
½ cup apple cider, divided
1 cup heavy cream

Place pork slices between 2 sheets of plastic wrap, and, using a mallet, pound the pork into ¼-inch-thick medallions.

Melt 2 tablespoons of the butter in a large, nonstick skillet over medium-high heat. Add the apples and sugar to the skillet and sauté until the apples turn a golden brown. Set aside.

Melt 2 tablespoons of the butter in another large, nonstick skillet over high heat. Season the pork with salt and pepper. Add the meat to the skillet and sauté until just cooked through (about 2 minutes per side). Transfer to a serving plate and keep warm.

Melt the remaining tablespoon of the butter in the same skillet over medium heat. Add the shallots and the thyme and sauté 2 minutes. Deglaze the pan by adding ¼ cup of cider, and boil until reduced to a glaze. Stir in the cream and remaining cider and boil until the mixture thickens to a sauce consistency. Season with salt and pepper. Arrange a few pork slices on each plate and add the sauce. Top generously with the sautéed apple (reheated if necessary).

Yield: 4 servings

*ROWELL'S INN*

# Pork Chops with Cider-and-Crabapple Sauce

*When cider is left to ferment, it develops an alcohol content and is called
"hard" cider. Crabapples come to the inn from a nearby orchard. Call your
local orchard or gourmet shop for the apples, or you may substitute with
very tart apples.*

2 tablespoons olive oil
8 pork chops, 1½-inches thick
    Salt and pepper
1 cup hard cider
2 cups sweet cider
1 cup strong chicken stock
2 tablespoons cornstarch

1 sprig fresh Italian parsley,
    chopped
24 very small crabapples, left
    whole, but cores and stems
    removed (or substitute 2 tart
    red apples, cored and diced
    with skins on)

Preheat the oven to 350°. Heat the oil in a large skillet. Sprinkle the
pork chops with salt and pepper. Sear both sides of the chops in the
hot oil. Place them in a baking pan and bake 30 to 40 minutes or until
they are done but juices still run a little bit.

In a medium saucepan, combine the ciders and chicken stock and
bring to a rolling boil. Dissolve the cornstarch in ¼ cup cool water.
Slowly stir enough of the cornstarch mixture into the boiling sauce
until the sauce is slightly thickened. Add the chopped parsley and the
apples. Cook until the apples are slightly soft (about 5 minutes). Place
the pork chops on a serving plate and spoon the sauce over them
(apples and all).

Yield: 8 servings

*SETTLERS INN*

## Casserole of Curried Butternut Squash with Apples and Italian Sausage

2 medium butternut squash, peeled, seeded, and cut into ¾-inch cubes
¼ cup clarified butter
½ pound Italian sausage, crumbled
2 medium yellow onions, cubed
2 red cooking apples, cut into medium cubes, seeded but not peeled
½ cup finely diced celery
½ cup finely diced green bell pepper

1 teaspoon curry
⅓ teaspoon Caribbean Jerk seasoning (available at supermarkets)
½ teaspoon ground rosemary
¼ teaspoon celery salt
⅓ teaspoon salt, preferably sea salt
¼ teaspoon ground basil
¼ teaspoon white pepper
¼ cup grated Parmesan cheese

In a medium saucepan, steam the squash until just done but not mushy. Set aside.

Preheat oven to 350°. In a large sauté pan or cast-iron skillet, sauté the squash in the clarified butter with the sausage, onions, apples, celery, and green pepper. Add all the seasonings, mixing occasionally until the sausage is cooked and the onions are lightly browned. (Do not overcook or overstir.) Taste for additional salt and pepper. Place the entire mixture into a large iron skillet or 9x13-inch baking dish and sprinkle with Parmesan cheese. Bake for 5 to 10 minutes just to heat thoroughly and semimelt the cheese. Serve immediately.

Yield: 8 servings

*HIGHLAND LAKE INN*

## Veal Chop and Mushroom Bake with Glazed Bananas

¾ cup butter, divided
2 medium onions, thinly sliced
2 cups sliced fresh mushrooms
Celery salt
½ cup dry vermouth
Salt and pepper

4 veal chops (6–8 ounces each)
All-purpose flour for dusting
2 cups chicken broth
1 cup sour cream
2 bananas
Brown sugar to taste

Preheat the oven to 300°. Melt 2 to 3 tablespoons of the butter in a skillet and sauté the onions until tender. Remove and set aside in a bowl. Add 3 or so more tablespoons of the butter to the skillet and sauté the mushrooms until barely tender. Sprinkle the mushrooms with some celery salt to taste and pour the mushrooms into the bowl with the onions. Deglaze the skillet with a little of the vermouth; then pour the remaining wine over the onion and mushrooms.

Salt and pepper the veal chops and dust each with flour on both sides. Place the veal into a Dutch oven and add the chicken broth. Bake for 40 minutes or until the veal is tender. Add the mushrooms, onions, and sour cream and bake until heated through, about 10 minutes.

Meanwhile, slice the bananas. In a clean skillet, melt 2 or more tablespoons of the butter and quickly sauté the fruit slices, sprinkling them with brown sugar. In a few minutes, the bananas should be browned and ready. Arrange the bananas on individual serving plates and add the veal chops with mushrooms and onions.

Yield: 4 servings

*CHALET SUZANNE*

## Skewered Veal with Fresh Sage

1 pound veal cutlets, cut into very thin pieces
Salt and pepper
2 tablespoons freshly squeezed lemon juice
¼ pound prosciutto, thinly sliced
½ pound sliced bacon
¼ medium loaf French bread, sliced in ½-inch slices
4 leaves fresh sage
2 teaspoons butter, melted

Preheat the oven to 350°. Cut the veal into pieces about 6 inches square. Sprinkle the salt, the pepper, and a few drops of the lemon juice on each piece. Place 1 slice of the prosciutto on each piece of veal and roll up. Wrap each roll with the bacon strips. On metal or wooden skewers, place a slice of bread, a leaf of sage, and a veal roll; then sage, bread, and veal until the skewers are full. Brush with the melted butter and place in the oven for approximately 30 minutes, turning once.

Yield: 4 servings

*HERITAGE PARK B&B INN*

# Cameos of Veal with Pink Peppercorn Sauce

*Pink peppercorns have a delightful tangy taste that wakes up the palate gently. I've included John Schumacher's recipe for brown sauce here, or see my recipe for a quick brown sauce on page 222.*

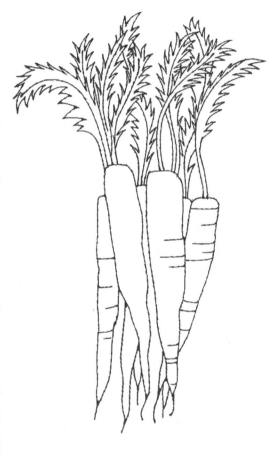

### BROWN SAUCE
- 6 tablespoons butter
- 1 cup diced onions
- ½ cup diced celery
- ½ cup diced carrots
- ½ scant cup all-purpose flour
- 6 cups double-strength beef stock (reduce 12 cups of stock to the 6 cups double strength by rapidly boiling in a large saucepan)
- ¼ cup tomato purée
- 1 bay leaf
- 1 teaspoon salt
- ¼ teaspoon black pepper

### VEAL
- 2 pounds veal loin, sliced into 24 pieces and pounded with a mallet to ⅛-inch thickness
- 2 cups all-purpose flour seasoned with 2 teaspoons salt and ½ teaspoon black pepper
- ½ cup clarified butter (see page 220)
- ⅔ cup minced shallots
- 2 tablespoons fresh lemon juice
- 3 cups brown sauce
- 2 cups dry white wine
- 4 teaspoons pink peppercorns
- 1 teaspoon salt
- ½ teaspoon black pepper
- 4 teaspoons freshly chopped parsley

In a heavy saucepan, heat the butter to a fast bubble and sauté the onions, celery, and carrots until the onions are translucent. Add the flour and cook 2 minutes on low heat, stirring often with a wooden spoon. In another saucepan, heat the beef stock and then add to the sautéed vegetables. Add the tomato purée, bay leaf, salt, and pepper. Cook for 30 minutes. Pour the brown sauce through a fine strainer. Set aside and prepare the veal.

Dredge the veal in the seasoned flour. In a large sauté pan, heat the clarified butter to a fast bubble. Add the veal slices and shallots, and sauté for 1 minute. Turn the veal slices over and sauté for 30 seconds, taking care not to brown the shallots. Add the lemon juice, brown sauce, wine, peppercorns, salt, and pepper. Reduce the heat and simmer on low for 15 minutes, gently stirring occasionally to keep from sticking. Add the parsley. Adjust the sauce consistency with white wine if necessary. Bring to a boil and serve.

Yield: 6 to 8 servings

*SCHUMACHER'S NEW PRAGUE HOTEL*

# Grilled Lamb Chops with Beet-and-Eggplant Bulghur-Wheat Pilaf

*Unlike the more common cracked wheat, bulghur wheat has a tender, chewy texture and makes an excellent pilaf. Just the pilaf portion of this recipe is delicious alone, served cold with lemon juice or vinaigrette in the summer.*

PILAF
¾ cup olive oil
2 cloves crushed garlic
1 small onion, minced
1 medium fresh beet, trimmed, peeled, and finely diced
2 medium eggplants, 1 of them peeled and diced and 1 with peel, diced
1½ cups bulghur wheat
2- 3 cups chicken broth

¼ teaspoon ground cardamom
½ tablespoon coriander
Salt and pepper
2 tablespoons fresh lemon juice
Quality extra virgin olive oil

LAMB
1 tablespoon fresh rosemary, chopped
1 tablespoon olive oil
12 lamb chops

In a large skillet, heat the olive oil and sweat the garlic and onions. Add the beets and all of the eggplant. Sauté the vegetables over low heat until the beets are completely cooked and the eggplant is tender. Add the bulghur wheat, making sure to coat with any residual oil. Add half the chicken stock. Simmer and stir until the stock is absorbed. Continue adding stock slowly, stirring until the wheat is cooked (soft and tender). Season with cardamom, coriander, and salt and pepper. Add the lemon juice. Set aside. (When ready to serve, sprinkle the wheat with a drizzle of olive oil.)

Mix the rosemary and the oil together in a small bowl. Season the lamb chops with salt and pepper. Brush them with the seasoned oil. Grill the chops on a charcoal grill until desired doneness.

To assemble the dish, place the chops over a bed of the pilaf and serve. (Remember to sprinkle the pilaf with a little olive oil.)

Yield: 6 servings

*STONEHEDGE INN*

## Lamb-and-Tomato Country Inn Stew

*This is a nice, old-fashioned dish with a kick from the horseradish and a full body from the red wine. Serve with crusty bread and brown wild rice.*

6 slices bacon
All-purpose flour
Salt and pepper
4 lamb shanks (about 12 ounces each)
1 28-ounce can tomatoes, chopped and with juice
1 cup chopped celery
½ cup chopped Italian parsley
2 medium onions, finely chopped
1 clove garlic, finely chopped
1 teaspoon Worcestershire sauce
1 tablespoon freshly grated horseradish
1 cup dry red wine
½ pound fresh, small-button mushrooms, stems and heads separated

In a Dutch oven, sauté the bacon until crisp. Remove and dice the bacon into bits, leaving the renderings in the pot.

Season the flour generously with the salt and pepper. Coat the lamb shanks with the flour and brown them in the bacon fat, turning on all sides until nicely browned. Add the tomatoes and juice, bacon bits, celery, parsley, onions, garlic, Worcestershire sauce, horseradish, and wine. Cover the mixture and let it simmer for 2 hours. After simmering, add the mushrooms and cook for at least another 30 minutes.

Check to see if the liquid has thickened to desired stage. If not, make a flour paste (2 tablespoons flour and a little water mixed) and thicken the gravy.

Yield: 4 to 6 servings

*CHALET SUZANNE*

## Roasted Leg of Lamb with Dijon and Rosemary Marinade

1 8-ounce jar quality Dijon-style mustard
¼ cup rosemary-infused olive oil
4 cloves garlic, finely minced
¼ teaspoon salt
¼ teaspoon pepper
1 tablespoon soy sauce
1 leg of lamb (6–8 pounds), boned, rolled, and tied

Whisk together the mustard, olive oil, fresh garlic, salt, pepper, and soy sauce. Set aside. Preheat the oven to 425°. Place the leg of lamb in an open roasting pan. Pour half of the mustard mixture over the rolled leg of lamb and brush on evenly with a pastry brush. Bake for 1 hour.

Remove the lamb from the oven and reduce the temperature to 375°. Pour the remaining mustard mixture over the browned meat, cover with foil, and return to the oven for 1½ hours, or until the meat reaches a temperature of 175°. Serve immediately.

Yield: 6 to 8 servings

*VICTORIAN VILLA*

## Tajine of Lamb and Green Beans

*A tajine is a deep-glazed, earthenware dish with a conical lid. It is used for preparing and serving a variety of recipes that are cooked slowly and result in a ragout, such as October Country Inn's lamb stew. Serve this dish over a bed of Moroccan pasta or couscous, a semolina-based starch discovered by the French in Algeria during Charles X's conquest. Couscous is the national dish of Algeria, Morocco, and Tunisia.*

| | |
|---|---|
| 6 tablespoons olive oil | 2 cinnamon sticks |
| 4 pounds lamb stew meat, cubed | ¾ cup freshly chopped parsley |
|    Salt and freshly ground pepper | 8 tomatoes, peeled and chopped |
| 4 onions, chopped | 6 tablespoons tomato paste |
| 2 cloves garlic, chopped | 1½ cups water |
| 2 teaspoons cumin | 2 pounds green beans, sliced |
| 1 teaspoon each: ginger, |    lengthwise |
|    turmeric, thyme | 2 tablespoons toasted sesame |
| 2 bay leaves |    seeds |
| ⅛ teaspoon cayenne pepper | |

In a large casserole dish heat the oil and brown the meat (in batches, if necessary). Remove the lamb from oil and season it with salt and pepper. Set it aside.

In the same casserole sauté the onions and garlic until lightly browned. Add the spices, parsley, tomatoes, tomato paste, and water, and blend well. Add the reserved lamb. Cover the casserole and simmer for 1½ to 2 hours or until the meat is tender. Stir occasionally. In a saucepan, blanch the green beans in boiling salted water until nearly tender. Preheat the oven to 400°. Add the beans to the casserole. Cover and bake the tajine for 15 minutes or until the beans are tender. Remove the tajine from the oven. Remove the bay leaves and cinnamon sticks. Sprinkle with sesame seeds.

Yield: 8 servings

*OCTOBER COUNTRY INN*

## French-Canadian Tourtière Meat Pie

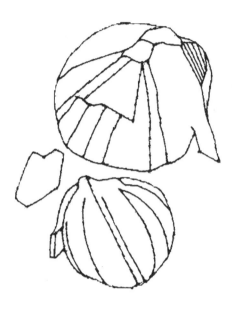

*Excellent with chutney or plum sauce, this recipe can be served warm or cold. If desired, make small, individual-serving pies. Tourtière originally referred to a round mold of variable diameter, slightly wider at the top, with high fluted sides. It was used for cooking tourtes or tarts and pies.*

| | |
|---|---|
| 1 pound ground pork | ¼ teaspoon each: pepper, thyme, |
| ½ pound ground beef | ground nutmeg, ground |
| 1 medium onion, chopped | cloves, and ground cinnamon |
| 2 small white potatoes, peeled | 1 small bay leaf |
| and finely chopped | 1½ cups water |
| 1 teaspoon salt | Pastry for 2-crust (9- or 10- |
| | inch) pie (see page 221) |

In a heavy saucepan, lightly brown the pork and the beef, stirring to break the meat up into small pieces. Drain off the fat. Add the onion, and sauté lightly. Add the potatoes, salt, spices, bay leaf, and water, and simmer for 30 minutes. Add more water, if necessary. Remove the pan from the heat and discard the bay leaf. With a fork, mash the potatoes into the meat mixture; cool the mixture to lukewarm.

Preheat the oven to 400°. Line a 9- or 10-inch pie plate with the pastry. Fill it with the meat and potato filling. Dampen the edge of the bottom crust and cover with the top crust. Crimp the edges to seal, and cut air-vent slits in the top. Bake for about 30 minutes or until the pastry is golden brown.

Yield: 6 to 8 servings

*WHITE OAK INN*

## Beer-and-Onion-Marinated Beef Fajitas

| | |
|---|---|
| 1 large onion | 12 to 14 flour tortillas or more |
| 5 pounds fajita meat (tender | Pico de gallo sauce |
| beef strips) | Guacamole |
| Fajita seasoning | Lettuce |
| 3 12-ounce cans of beer | Tomatoes |

Mince the onion and set aside. Sprinkle the meat with the fajita seasoning. In a large bowl, marinate the beef with the onion and the beer for at least 1 hour. The longer the meat marinates, the more intense the flavor.

Cook the beef over a mesquite grill until medium rare. Remove the meat from the grill and cut into bite-size pieces. Serve with warmed tortillas, pico de gallo sauce, guacamole, lettuce, and tomatoes.

Yield: 8 servings

*Y. O. RANCH*

## Grilled Drovers Steak with Sweet Potato Hay in Bourbon Sauce

*SAUCE*
1 shallot, finely chopped
1 teaspoon butter
¼ cup Jack Daniels or other quality bourbon
1 cup demi-glace (see recipe for Quick Brown Sauce, page 222)
¼ cup crème fraîche (or see recipe, page 220)
1 clove garlic, mashed
1 teaspoon chopped fresh thyme
1 teaspoon chopped fresh rosemary
Sea salt and pepper

*POTATOES*
2 sweet potatoes
Oil for frying

*STEAK*
4 Black Angus tenderloin steaks (12 ounces each)

In a medium skillet, sauté the shallot in the butter. Deglaze the pan with the bourbon and the demi-glace. Cook over medium-high heat, reducing the mixture to 1 cup. Whisk in the crème fraîche. Add the garlic and herbs. Add salt and pepper to taste.

Using a mandoline or a very sharp knife, cut the potatoes into shoestring-thin slices. Deep fry in enough oil to cover the potatoes. Drain well and season with salt and pepper. Set aside, keeping warm.

Grill the steaks to desired doneness. Place each steak in the center of a warm individual serving plate. Pour some of the sauce to cover the steak. Add a mound of the sweet potato hay on top of the steak.

Yield: 4 servings

*OLD DROVERS INN*

## Fried Beef Steak with Cream Gravy

*Serve this with mashed potatoes and a basket of hot biscuits, and you will have a traditional Texas treat. Usually, this recipe is called Chicken-Fried Steak with Cream Gravy because it employs the same batter cooks use for chicken. I decided to avoid the confusion for those of us who do not live in Texas.*

6 portions cube steak, tender-
   ized round steak, or any other
   tender beef (7 ounces each)
   Salt and pepper
5 eggs
1 12-ounce can evaporated
   milk, divided

2 to 3 cups shortening or
   vegetable oil
3 tablespoons all-purpose flour,
   plus more for dredging
2 cups water

Season the steaks with salt and pepper. Set aside.

In a medium bowl, beat the eggs and ½ cup of the evaporated milk. Heat the shortening in a heavy, deep-sided skillet to about 350°.

Dredge the steaks with flour and dip them in the batter, then in the flour again, lightly shaking off the excess flour. When the oil is hot, add the steaks a few at a time. Be careful not to add too many at a time or they will lower the temperature of the oil. Fry for 4 minutes on 1 side, or until golden brown, then turn with tongs and fry on the other side. Drain on a paper towel and set aside, keeping warm until ready to serve.

To make the gravy, discard all but ¼ cup of the shortening from the skillet and turn the heat to low. Add 3 tablespoons of flour and cook over low heat, stirring constantly, for 3 minutes; be careful not to burn the flour. Add the remaining evaporated milk, whisking until smooth and scraping the pan to release any small bits clinging to the bottom. (A nonstick pan is a good choice for this recipe.) Begin adding the water gradually, stirring constantly, until the gravy is smooth and of desired thickness. Add salt and pepper to taste and pour the gravy into a bowl to serve with the steaks.

Yield: 6 servings

*Y. O. RANCH*

# Roasted Stuffed Filet Mignon with Red-Onion Marmalade and Mustard Vinaigrette

*MARMALADE*
- 6 large red onions, peeled and thinly sliced
- 2 tablespoons olive oil
- 6 tablespoons sugar

*VINAIGRETTE*
- ¼ cup whole-grain mustard
- ¾ cup olive oil
- 1 tablespoon sherry vinegar
- 1 cup Madeira wine
  Salt and pepper

*STUFFING*
- 1 small onion, diced
- 1½ teaspoons chopped garlic
- 2 teaspoons chopped fresh sage
- 2 tablespoons olive oil
- 1 pound prosciutto, very finely diced
- 4 egg whites

*BEEF*
- 6 beef filets (7 ounces each)

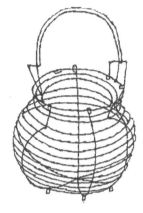

In a medium skillet, over moderate heat, slowly sauté the onions in the olive oil and sugar. When lightly browned, remove from the heat and set aside.

Prepare the vinaigrette. Whisk together all of the vinaigrette ingredients in a small mixing bowl and set aside.

Preheat the oven to 450°. Make the stuffing. Sauté the onion, garlic, and sage in 1 tablespoon of the olive oil. Mix with the prosciutto. Add the egg whites and place all into a food processor, pulsing until the mixture forms a smooth paste. Make a ½-inch-round incision in the center of each filet, pivoting the knife to enlarge the cavity without penetrating the outer walls of the filet. Place the stuffing paste into a pastry bag. Fill the cavity and surrounding area with the stuffing. Use your fingers to pack it in firmly.

Sear and brown each filet in the remaining olive oil. Finish in the oven for about 7 minutes or until medium rare.

To serve, cover a plate with a thin layer of the mustard vinaigrette. Place the stuffed meat in the center of the plate. Evenly position the onion marmalade next to the meat.

Yield: 6 servings

*BEE & THISTLE INN*

# Cabbage-and-Beef Roulades with Tomato Chutney

*Savoy cabbage offers several advantages: it is easier to digest than other types from the same vegetable family; it is wonderful for steaming, roasting, and frying; and it combines well with fish, game, red meats, and all fowl. These rolled-up bundles of ground beef in a wrap of cabbage are easy to make.*

## CABBAGE
1 Savoy cabbage head (select dark green and medium size)

## FILLING
1 cup milk
½ loaf dried French bread, crust removed and bread cubed
3 tablespoons vegetable oil
2 cloves garlic, crushed
1 large onion, peeled and thinly sliced
½ cup parsley, stems removed and leaves coarsely chopped
1 pound quality lean ground beef
¼ cup pine nuts
2 eggs, slightly beaten
Marjoram

## CHUTNEY
5 tablespoons olive oil
2 medium onions, diced
5 ripe large tomatoes, seeded, peeled, blanched, and cut into cubes
1 clove garlic, crushed
2 sprigs fresh thyme
2 ripe pears, cored, peeled, and cut into small cubes
1 14½-ounce can peeled tomatoes, drained and cut into cubes
2 tablespoons apple cider vinegar
1 tablespoon dark molasses
Salt and pepper
1 tablespoon diced fresh basil

Remove the cabbage leaves, wash well, and blanch in salted water. Drain and refresh in ice water.

In a small saucepan, heat the milk and drop the bread cubes in to soak. In a nonstick skillet, heat the vegetable oil. Add the garlic and the onion, and sauté until golden; add the parsley. Remove from the burner and let cool. In a separate bowl, mix together the beef, soaked bread, and onion mixture. (Discard any milk not absorbed.)

In a hot skillet, quickly toss the pine nuts to brown lightly; fold into the meat mixture followed by the eggs and marjoram; mix well.

Preheat the oven to 300°. Remove the cabbage leaves from the ice water and dry with paper towels. Select the 10 best large leaves; remove the center veins if too tough. Spread the leaves out in a row and equally divide the meat onto them. Fold the leaves like a package; tie with kitchen string. In a nonstick skillet, heat the olive oil and brown the cabbage roulades, turning them often and cooking slowly to a golden color. Then bake the roulades for 10 minutes or until they are heated through. Meanwhile, prepare the chutney.

Sauté the onions, fresh tomato cubes, garlic, and thyme in the same skillet as the roulades. Add the pears and the canned tomatoes. Add the vinegar and molasses and allow to simmer lightly. Season with salt and pepper and add the diced basil.

Remove the roulades from the oven and discard the kitchen string. Spoon the chutney onto a platter, top with the roulades, and serve.

Yield: 5 servings

*CHÂTEAU DU SUREAU*

Cabbage

Tomato Chutney

Beef Roulades

## Mushroom-Crusted Beef with a Shiitake Ragout

BEEF
- 1 beef tenderloin (3½ pounds)
  Salt, pepper, and sugar
- 1 tablespoon olive oil
- ½ cup Dijon-style mustard
- 2 cups assorted dried mushrooms, finely crumbled
  Herbes de Provence
- 1 tablespoon cornstarch

RAGOUT
- ½ cup diced shallots
- 2 tablespoons olive oil
- 6 tablespoons mixture of diced red, yellow, and green bell peppers
- 2 cups fresh shiitake mushrooms, quartered
- 1 tablespoon freshly ground pepper
- 1 tablespoon sugar
- 1 cup dry red wine
- 1 tablespoon balsamic vinegar
- 2 cups demi-glace (or see recipe for Quick Brown Sauce, page 222)
- 1 tablespoon chopped fresh parsley

Preheat the oven to 400°. Season the beef with salt, pepper, and sugar. Sear the loin in a pan in the 1 tablespoon or so of olive oil until dark brown on all sides. Spread the outside of the meat with the mustard. In a food processor, make crumbs out of the dried mushrooms, season with salt and pepper, sugar, and *herbes de Provence*. Add the cornstarch. Place the crumbs on a sheet pan and roll the mustard-coated beef around the pan, coating the meat evenly with the crumbs. Bake for 30 minutes or until the internal temperature reaches 130°. Remove from the oven.

Meanwhile, prepare the ragout. In a medium skillet, sauté the shallots in the olive oil for a few seconds. Add the bell peppers and sauté for about 1 minute more. Add the mushrooms, pepper, and sugar, and sauté for another minute. Add the wine and the vinegar, and reduce until almost dry. Add the demi-glace and reduce to slightly thick. Add the fresh parsley and keep warm. Slice the beef and add to a serving platter with the ragout.

Yield: 8 to 10 servings

*CLIFTON COUNTRY INN*

## Stuffed Beef Roulade with a Red-Wine Sauce

8  3x6-inch steaks from top
    round or sirloin, each ½-inch
    thick
8  slices bacon

*FILLING*
½  pound ground pork
½  pound ground beef
½  pound ground veal
1  teaspoon salt
¼  teaspoon marjoram
½  teaspoon black pepper
1  teaspoon Dijon-style mustard
½  cup seasoned breadcrumbs
1  egg

*SAUCE*
2  cups beef stock
½  cup red wine
2  tablespoons ketchup
2  tablespoons
    Worcestershire sauce
2  teaspoons cornstarch
1  tablespoon water

*GARNISH*
8  tablespoons sour cream
    Chopped Italian parsley

Pound the steaks to ¼-inch thickness. Combine the filling ingredients.
Divide the filling into 8 equal portions, placing 1 portion on each
steak. Roll the steaks up around the meat mixture. Wrap a slice of
bacon around each roll, and tie with kitchen twine. Sear the roulades
in a nonstick skillet over high heat, turning to cook on each side.
Remove to a shallow casserole dish. Pour off the bacon fat.

Preheat the oven to 350°. Prepare the sauce. Pour the beef stock,
wine, ketchup, and Worcestershire into a skillet. In a bowl, mix the
cornstarch and water together, then whisk the mixture into the broth.
Bring to a boil and simmer for 2 to 3 minutes. Pour the sauce over the
roulades. Cover and bake 1½ hours, turning the rolls every 20 minutes.

To serve, remove the twine. Spoon 1 tablespoon of sour cream
overtop each roulade and garnish with the parsley.

Yield: 8 servings

*WHITE OAK INN*

## Wyoming Buffalo in an Orange-Curry Ragout

2¼ pounds buffalo stew meat,
    cubed
    Salt and pepper
2 teaspoons curry powder
    Olive oil, as needed
1 Spanish onion, diced

1 cup orange juice
4 cups brown stock
    Zest of 1 orange
1 pound canned whole tomatoes,
    juice drained
1 pound mushrooms

Season the meat with salt, pepper, and one teaspoon of the curry powder. In a Dutch oven, add enough oil to cover the bottom of the pot, and heat until the oil just begins to smoke. Add the meat and sear on all sides, repeating the process until all the meat is seared. Remove the meat and set aside.

In the same pan, sauté the onion just until it is translucent. Deglaze the pan with the orange juice and the brown stock.

Add the zest, the remaining curry powder, the tomatoes, and the meat, and bring to a simmer. Continue to simmer, stirring occasionally, for 1½ hours or until the meat is fork tender. Add the mushrooms 15 minutes before the meat is done. Serve immediately.

Yield: 6 servings

*SIGN OF THE SORREL HORSE*

## Venison in Red Currant Sauce

*This delicious and rich way to prepare venison also works well with flattened boneless chicken breasts, veal or pork tenderloins, or any other wild game loin.*

1 pound venison loin or round
1 cup all-purpose flour, sea-
    soned with salt and pepper
¼ cup clarified butter
½ cup shallots, diced ¼ inch

⅓ cup red currant jam or jelly
½ cup cream sherry
2 cups brown sauce
4 fresh apricots, cut in half

Remove the fat and silver skin from the venison. Slice into 12 slices, ½-inch thick. Flatten each slice with a mallet. Dredge the slices in the flour. In a heavy sauté pan, heat the butter to a fast bubble. Add the shallots and the venison. Sauté until the venison slices are brown. Turn and sauté for 30 seconds, being careful not to brown the shallots.

Add the currant jelly, the sherry, and the brown sauce. Simmer 20 minutes on low heat, stirring gently occasionally to prevent sticking.

To serve, place 3 slices of the venison on a hot serving plate, and top with the sauce. Garnish each plate with 2 apricot halves filled with the currant jelly.

Yield: 4 servings

*SCHUMACHER'S NEW PRAGUE HOTEL*

## Colorado Elk Loin in Lingonberry and Cassis Sauce

2 pounds each of elk and veal bones
2 pounds of elk (or venison) loin
1 pint veal stock
2 carrots, halved
2 onions, halved
2 celery stalks, halved

1 bouquet garni: 3 sprigs thyme, 2 bay leaves, 1 celery heart, and 1 casing from a leek
1 cup Cassis liqueur
¼ pound lingonberries, or substitute with dried cranberries
Salt and pepper
Olive oil as needed

Preheat the oven to 425°. Place the bones in a roasting pan and roast them until a deep caramelized color, turning them periodically. Remove from the oven.

Place the bones into a stockpot with 3 quarts of water. Bring to a slow simmer and continue cooking for 4 hours. When cooked, add the carrots, onions, celery, and bouquet garni. Cook for 30 minutes. Strain the mixture through a chinois or fine-mesh sieve. Return the liquid to a saucepan, add the Cassis and the veal stock and reduce to about 1 pint. Add the lingonberries and simmer for 2 minutes or until the sauce coats the back of a spoon.

Preheat the oven to 350°. Season the elk with salt and pepper. Coat an ovenproof pan with olive oil. Place the pan over high heat and when the oil just begins to smoke, add the elk loin and sear until browned. Place the pan in the oven and finish cooking the elk for about 25 to 30 minutes or until tender and cooked to desired doneness. Slice into portions and serve with the sauce.

Yield: 6 servings

*SIGN OF THE SORREL HORSE*

# SIDE DISHES

## Black Bean Terrine with Pesto-Pumpkin Vinaigrette

*Chef Peter Zimmer is known for coming up with incredible concoctions, and they all work. Who would think of a dish such as this one?*

**VINAIGRETTE**
- 1 bunch Italian parsley
- 4 cloves garlic
  Juice of 1 lemon
- 1 cup pumpkin seeds, toasted
- 2 cups olive oil
  Salt, pepper, cayenne pepper

**TERRINE**
- 1 tablespoon olive oil
- 1 red onion
- 1 celery stalk, sliced
- 2 jalapeño peppers, diced
- 2 carrots, peeled and diced
- 8 cups black beans, soaked in water overnight then drained
- 4 quarts vegetable stock
- 2 bunches cilantro, chopped
- 1 tablespoon cumin
- 1 tablespoon coriander
- 4 eggs, slightly beaten
- 2 cups heavy cream or milk
  Salt, pepper, cayenne pepper

Prepare the vinaigrette. Place all of the ingredients except the olive oil into a blender. With the blender on, add the oil; emulsify. Season to taste. Set aside.

Preheat the oven to 350°. Prepare the terrine. In a stockpot, sauté the olive oil, onion, celery, jalapeños, and carrots for 3 to 5 minutes. Add the beans and the vegetable stock, and cook until the beans are tender, about 30 minutes. Add the cilantro, cumin, and coriander. Reserve 2 cups of the bean mix. Purée the remaining mixture in a food processor until smooth. Fold in the eggs, cream, and the reserved bean mixture. Season to taste. Place the mixture in a buttered terrine mold and bake in a water bath for 25 to 30 minutes. Remove from oven and cool. Chill to set. Slice and serve with pesto-pumpkin-seed vinaigrette.

Yield: 8 to 10 servings

*INN OF THE ANASAZI*

# Y. O. Ranch Beans

*People on the Texas prairie thrive on this recipe served as a side dish to chicken, beef, or game meats. You will need to prepare this three hours ahead of serving time.*

2 cups dried pinto beans
4 slices bacon

Salt and pepper

Place the beans in a colander and wash them under cold running water for about 2 minutes, picking over them to discard any stones or broken, discolored, or shriveled beans.

Place the beans in a large pot and fill with hot water to 4 inches above the beans. Add the bacon and bring the water to a boil. Turn down the heat, cover, and simmer for 3 to 3½ hours. Remove the lid during the last hour of cooking. Add more water if necessary, 1 cup at a time. Check seasonings and serve when the beans are tender.

Yield: 8 to 10 servings

*Y. O. RANCH*

## Easy Veggie Cleaning

The best way is to fill your sink or a large bowl with cold water and add a generous amount of salt. Put vegetables in water and swish and clean. Rinse and drain.

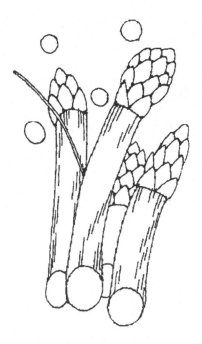

# Cold Purée of Fresh Fennel and Broccoli

1 head fresh broccoli (florets only)
1 head fresh fennel
¼ cup heavy cream
1 medium onion, chopped

Clarified butter
3 tablespoons chopped assorted fresh herbs, your choice
Salt and pepper

Parboil the broccoli for about 3 minutes. Slice the fennel, julienne style, and parboil for about 5 minutes or until tender. While both the broccoli and the fennel are still warm, purée them together in a food processor with the heavy cream.

In a medium saucepan, sauté the onion in the butter over high heat until the onion is golden brown, almost caramelized. Add the onion to the broccoli-fennel mixture and purée again until all of the ingredients are well mixed. Mix the fresh herbs together, add to the purée, and toss well. Season to taste with the salt and pepper. Chill to set before serving.

Yield: 8 to 10 servings

*CARTER HOUSE*

## Steamed Brussels Sprouts with Fresh Parmesan and Toasted Almonds

*It's been said, "In England, everyone eats sprouts, but alas, not everyone knows how to cook them." Rest assured, the Victorian Villa knows how to cook the garden favorite—this wholesome vegetable dish proves the point!*

3 pints fresh Brussels sprouts
   (or two 16-ounce packages
   frozen Brussels sprouts)
⅓ cup coarsely shredded
   Parmesan cheese

¼ cup toasted, slivered almonds
Butter
Salt and pepper

Trim the stems from the Brussels sprouts, and remove and discard any wilted leaves. Rinse the sprouts under cool, running water; then cut any large sprouts in half lengthwise.

Place the sprouts in a steamer basket, and place the basket over, but not touching, boiling water. Reduce the heat, cover, and steam for 15 to 20 minutes or until just tender.

Put the sprouts in a serving bowl. Sprinkle the cheese and toasted almonds overtop, dot with butter, and season to taste with the salt and pepper.

Yield: 8 servings

*VICTORIAN VILLA*

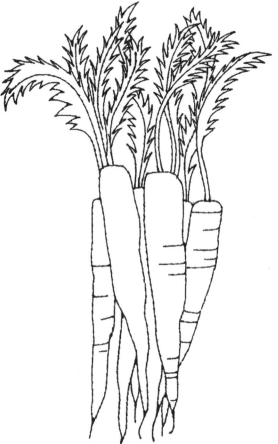

## Creamed Minted Carrots

1½ cups water
1½ pounds carrots, peeled and
  quartered
1½ tablespoons butter
½ teaspoon salt
1 cup heavy cream
2 tablespoons butter, softened

2 tablespoons sugar
Pepper
2 tablespoons freshly chopped
  peppermint or spearmint
  leaves (or 2 teaspoons dried
  chopped mint)

Place the water, carrots, butter, and salt in a medium saucepan. Bring to a boil and cover. When the carrots are nearly done (cooked just tender), most of the water should have evaporated. If not, drain the carrots. Warm the cream and then add it to the almost-dry carrots. Simmer a few minutes until the carrots are tender. Add the softened butter, sugar, pepper, and mint. Stir well until the butter is incorporated. Serve immediately.

Yield: 8 servings

*RANDALL'S ORDINARY*

## Corn and Clam Hash

*Chef Gerard Thompson likes to cook this dish in two separate pans so that he can get the mixture crisp (without risking letting the ingredients sweat) and to keep them from burning.*

64 littleneck clams, soaked and
  scrubbed clean
4 cups white wine
1 tablespoon chopped garlic
¼ cup corn oil
1 sweet potato, peeled and diced
4 new potatoes (with peel),
  oven roasted, cut into eighths

4 strips apple-smoked bacon,
  cooked and chopped
½ red bell pepper, diced
  Kernels from 1 ear fresh corn
1 bunch scallions, chopped

Place the clams, wine, and garlic in a large pot and cover with a lid, steaming until the clams open. Remove the clams from the heat and allow them to cool. Remove the clams from the shells and set aside.

Use 2 14- or 16-inch nonstick sauté pans and place half of the corn oil into each. Turn the heat up to high. When the oil is hot, add half of the sweet potato to each pan. Brown for about 3 to 5 minutes. Lower the heat and add the new potatoes, half to each pan, and cook 3 minutes. Divide the clams between each pan as well as the bacon. Cook 3 to 5 minutes, stirring occasionally. Divide the red pepper, corn, and scallions to each pan and raise the heat to high. Continue cooking 3 to 5 minutes longer until the mixture is crisp.

Yield: 8 servings

Note: To oven-roast potatoes, rub the skins with olive oil, salt, and pepper, and bake in a 350° oven until fork tender.

*SAN YSIDRO RANCH*

## Cornbread and Cheddar Pudding

Vegetable shortening
1 cup yellow cornmeal
½ teaspoon baking soda
¾ teaspoon salt
1 cup buttermilk
2 eggs, beaten
½ cup butter, melted
1 medium onion, finely chopped

3½ cups yellow cream-style corn
1 cup grated sharp Cheddar cheese
2 tablespoons canned chopped mild green chilies or to taste
1 jalapeño pepper, chopped

Preheat the oven to 350°. Brush a 9-inch square or round baking pan heavily with vegetable shortening. Place the dish in the oven until piping hot (about 6 minutes).

Meanwhile, in a large mixing bowl, combine the cornmeal, baking soda, salt, buttermilk, eggs, butter, and onion. Beat quickly and thoroughly. Fold in the corn. Pour half of the batter into the hot pan. Sprinkle the cheese overtop and add the chilies and jalapeño. Top with the remaining batter and bake 50 minutes to 1 hour or until golden and slightly browned on the edges.

Yield: 6 to 8 servings

*OCTOBER COUNTRY INN*

## Braised Dill-Cucumber Vegetable Dish

*The English cucumber usually comes well wrapped in clear plastic and has a lighter texture than its less expensive (regular) cucumber counterpart. This dish is an easy, refreshing one that can be served almost all year.*

1 medium English cucumber, unpeeled
1 small onion, finely diced
2 tablespoons olive oil
1 medium carrot, peeled and shredded

2 tablespoons finely chopped fresh dill
½ teaspoon sugar
Salt

Cut the cucumber in half lengthwise and then slice each half into ¼-inch slices. In a medium sauté pan, sauté the onions in the olive oil until the onions are translucent. Add the cucumber slices and shredded carrots, and mix. Cover the pan and let the vegetables braise for approximately 3 to 5 minutes, or until *al dente* (chewy and crunchy). Stir in the dill and sugar, and season to taste with the salt.

    Yield: 4 to 6 servings

    *HERITAGE PARK B&B INN*

## Chèvre and Roasted-Garlic Soufflés with Tomato-Basil Sauce

*ROASTED GARLIC*
4 whole heads fresh garlic, peeled (about 4 ounces)
1 cup dry white wine
2 tablespoons extra virgin olive oil

*GOAT CHEESE SOUFFLÉS*
3 tablespoons butter
3 tablespoons all-purpose flour
1¼ cups milk
12 ounces goat cheese or chèvre, crumbled
5 large eggs, separated

*SAUCE*
2 tablespoons extra virgin olive oil
1 clove garlic, minced
1 28-ounce can Italian tomatoes, crushed
¼ teaspoon salt, optional
½ teaspoon freshly ground black pepper
2 tablespoons fresh basil, shredded (or 1 tablespoon dried basil)
½ cup grated Parmesan or Romano cheese

Preheat the oven to 350°. Prepare the roasted garlic. In a small oven-proof dish, place the garlic cloves, the wine, and the olive oil. Roast until the garlic is soft and most of the liquid has evaporated (about 20 minutes). Remove from the oven but keep the oven at 350°. Cool and mash the garlic to a purée.

In a nonstick sauté pan, melt the butter and whisk in the flour. Add the roasted garlic purée and cook slowly for 2 minutes, stirring constantly. Whisk in the milk and bring to a boil, cooking until thickened. Remove from the heat and whisk in the goat cheese. Cool slightly and whisk in the egg yolks.

In a bowl, beat the egg whites until stiff but not dry, then fold them into the cheese-garlic sauce. Butter jumbo muffin tins or 6-ounce custard cups, and fill with the soufflé mixture. Bake for 20 to 30 minutes until browned on top and cooked all the way through (when knife inserted in center comes out clean). Cool slightly and remove carefully from the tins, turning out upside down onto a greased baking sheet while still warm. (These may be prepared ahead and refrigerated.)

Prepare the tomato-basil sauce. In a small saucepan, heat the oil, add the garlic, and cook, stirring until golden brown. Add the tomatoes, salt and pepper, and dried basil, if using. Cook at a slow simmer for about 20 minutes until slightly thickened. Add the fresh basil just before serving.

To serve, sprinkle the soufflés with the grated cheese and reheat in the same oven for about 10 minutes or until warmed through. Pool a small amount of the warm tomato sauce in the center of a plate and top with the soufflé. Garnish with fresh basil.

Yield: 10 to 12 servings

*GLEN-ELLA SPRINGS INN*

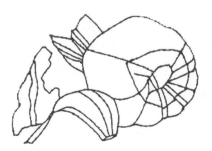

# Rosettes of Roasted Garlic and Pumpkin

*Swirled mixtures of pumpkin and potato make an easy, impressive dish.*

1 head garlic
3 cups cubed fresh pumpkin,
   cut into 1-inch cubes, or any
   squash, if fresh pumpkin is
   not available
2 tablespoons olive oil
5 large russet potatoes

6 tablespoons butter
½ cup sour cream
   Salt and white pepper
¼ cup instant potato flakes or
   cooked potatoes
1 tablespoon honey, if needed

Preheat the oven to 350°. Place the entire head of garlic and the pumpkin pieces in a 9x13-inch baking dish with about ⅛ inch of water and the oil in the bottom. Cover the dish with foil and roast for 1 hour or until the pumpkin is tender.

While the pumpkin and garlic are roasting, peel, cut, and boil the potatoes until tender. Whip the potatoes with the butter and the sour cream and season to taste with salt and white pepper. (Be sure to whip the mashed potatoes until they are free of lumps, but be careful not to overwhip.)

When the pumpkin is tender, squeeze the roasted garlic head so as to release the soft garlic from the husk. Place the pumpkin and all of the garlic into a food processor and purée, adding the potato flakes. Also, add a little or all of the honey if you find that the pumpkin is lacking flavor or sweetness. Season the mixture with the salt and white pepper to taste.

At serving time, heat the mashed potato and the pumpkin mixture separately. (A microwave works great.) The two mixtures should be of a similar consistency when heated. Load some of the hot mashed potatoes and the hot pumpkin into a pastry bag fitted with a star tip. Do this by placing the bag on its side and filling 1 side with the potatoes and the other side with the pumpkin mixture. (The ratio of mashed potato to pumpkin should be about 4 or 5 to 1.) When the mixture is piped out, it will make a lovely rosette with an orange and white swirl.

Yield: 6 to 8 servings

*HIGHLAND LAKE INN*

# Fried Green Tomatoes with Roasted Pepper Purée

*Chef Barrie Aycock cooks many dishes that are low in fat, but I persuaded her to do a demonstration on this most southern of dishes. Leave it to Barrie to add her gourmet touch with the red pepper sauce. You can make the sauce a day ahead of time.*

ROASTED PEPPER PURÉE
- 2 red bell peppers, seeded and cut into quarters
- 1 teaspoon hot sauce (such as Tabasco) or more if desired
- 2 to 4 tablespoons heavy cream
  Salt

TOMATOES
- 3 medium green tomatoes
- 2 cups all-purpose flour, seasoned with salt and pepper
  Vegetable oil for frying
  Crumbled goat cheese or Feta cheese to garnish, optional

Make the purée. Place the peppers skin-side up on a baking sheet and broil until the skins are blackened all over. (Or place skin-side down on a char-grill and do the same.) Then put the peppers in a plastic or paper bag and close the top. Let stand for about 10 minutes. Peel skins off with a sharp knife. Place the peppers in the bowl of a food processor and purée, adding the hot sauce and heavy cream until smooth and seasoned to taste. (Refrigerate if not using right away. Return to room temperature before serving.)

Wash the tomatoes and cut into ¼-inch slices (should have at least 12 slices). Dredge the slices in the flour. In a deep fryer, heat the oil. Fry the tomatoes, a few slices at a time, until brown and crisp on both sides. Place on a paper-towel-lined baking sheet in a warm oven while frying the rest.

To serve, arrange the tomatoes on a platter, drizzle the purée over-top, and sprinkle with crumbled cheese. Serve immediately.

Yield: 6 servings

Note: This inn has made up its own breading mix of 1 cup packaged, seasoned croutons with 1 cup Bisquick, ground into fine crumbs in a food processor. For the 2 cups of seasoned flour, you may substitute the Glen-Ella mix.

*GLEN-ELLA SPRINGS INN*

# Wood-Grilled Mushrooms with Vegetable Pestos and Potato Tumbleweeds

*Be creative and use the pestos for a variety of food such as pastas or other vegetables. I love Chef Peter Zimmer's idea of eating tumbleweeds! Prepare the recipe by making the sauces first. Cook fresh beets and purée for the beet pesto. Delicious. Use a juicer for the carrot pesto or buy juices at a gourmet shop.*

### BEET PESTO
1 cup chopped and roasted hazelnuts
2 tablespoons freshly chopped fresh mint leaves
1 cup beet juice
1 red onion, grilled and finely diced
½ cup olive oil

### CARROT PESTO
1 cup chopped roasted peanuts
1 tablespoon fresh chopped oregano
1 cup carrot juice
½ cup olive oil
2 dry chipotle chilies, seeded, and finely chopped
Juice of 2 limes

### CILANTRO PESTO
2 small bunches of cilantro, finely chopped
Juice of 2 limes
½ cup chopped roasted pumpkin seeds
½ cup chopped roasted pine nuts
½ cup grated Parmesan cheese
1 cup olive oil

### POTATO TUMBLEWEEDS
1 tablespoon sugar
1 tablespoon cracked coriander seeds
1 tablespoon cinnamon
¼ teaspoon salt
¼ teaspoon cayenne pepper
1 Idaho potato, julienned
1 sweet potato, julienned
2 cups canola oil

### MARINADE
½ bunch Italian parsley, chopped
4 cloves garlic, minced
Juice and zest of 1 lime
2 chipotle chilies, chopped and seeded
3 tablespoons olive oil
3 pounds bolete mushrooms (portobellos or shiitake)

Prepare each pesto one at a time in the same manner. Combine all ingredients in a blender. Season to taste with salt and freshly cracked white pepper. Set aside.

Prepare the tumbleweeds. Combine the sugar, coriander, cinnamon, salt, and pepper, and set aside. In a medium-size, nonstick saucepan, fry the potatoes in the oil until they are golden and crispy. Strain the potatoes and dust them with the dry spice mix. Set aside.

Prepare the mushrooms. Combine all the marinade ingredients except the mushrooms. Set the marinade aside. Remove the stems of the mushrooms and slice them lengthwise to ½-inch thickness. Toss the mushroom heads and the stems in the marinade and let stand 4 to 6 hours at room temperature or overnight in the refrigerator. Grill over wood or briquettes for 2 to 3 minutes on each side while seasoning with salt and pepper. Arrange the mushrooms in the center of a plate. Use a spoon to splash the 3 color vegetable pestos on and around the mushrooms. Garnish with the potato tumbleweeds.

Yield: 4 to 6 servings

*INN OF THE ANASAZI*

## Baked Vegetables au Gratin

2 cups chopped onions
2 tablespoons chopped garlic
½ cup quality extra virgin olive oil
6 fresh plum tomatoes, cored and sliced
4 medium zucchini, sliced diagonally (¼-inch thick)

4 medium, yellow squash, sliced diagonally (¼-inch thick)
2 medium eggplants, sliced diagonally (¼-inch thick)
2 tablespoons fresh thyme
Freshly ground black pepper
1 cup grated Parmesan cheese

Preheat the oven to 350°. Sauté the onions and garlic in ¼ cup of the olive oil until translucent. Transfer the onions to an 8x11-inch glass baking dish and spread to cover the bottom of the dish. Spread a layer of tomatoes in the dish, then a layer of zucchini, a layer of yellow squash, and a layer of eggplant. Repeat this process until the vegetables are all tightly packed into the dish. Sprinkle with the thyme, pepper, and Parmesan, and drizzle with the remaining olive oil.

Bake for 20 to 25 minutes or until the vegetables are soft and the cheese is light brown. Let rest 5 minutes. Slice lengthwise and serve, making sure to scoop up the garlic on the bottom of the dish.

Yield: 6 servings

*KEDRON VALLEY INN*

# Chilled, Spiced Marinated Vegetables

*The chef and owner of Rowell's Inn, Beth Davis, makes her own version of seasoned salt. I don't dare ask for her secret recipe because she packages and sells her salt. Substitute with commercial seasoned salt, or I'm sure Beth would be happy to send you hers.*

¼ cup white wine vinegar
6 tablespoons vegetable oil
2 cups water
1 clove garlic, peeled
1 shallot, peeled
2 sprigs Italian parsley
1 bay leaf
6 peppercorns
1 teaspoon Rowell's Inn
   seasoned salt
½ teaspoon tarragon
½ teaspoon thyme
¼ teaspoon marjoram

2 carrots
½ head cauliflower
1 green bell pepper
1 zucchini (green squash)
1 yellow squash
1 purple onion
½ pound fresh mushrooms
1 cup chopped celery
   Tomato and parsley for
   garnish
   Bibb lettuce leaves for
   assembly

Combine the vinegar, oil, and water in a nonstick saucepan. Make a bouquet garni by tying the garlic, shallot, parsley, bay leaf, and peppercorns in a small cheesecloth bag. Place it in the saucepan along with the seasoned salt and the remaining herbs.

Cut the carrots into ½-inch chunks. Separate the cauliflower into small florets and cut the green pepper into 1½-inch pieces. Slice the zucchini and yellow squash into 1-inch slices. Slice the onion and mushrooms into thin slices.

Bring the marinade to a boil. Drop the carrots into the boiling liquid and cook, covered, for 6 minutes. Add the cauliflower and cook 2 to 3 minutes more. Add the zucchini and yellow squash and continue to cook until all the vegetables are just barely tender, about 3 minutes.

With a slotted spoon, remove the cooked vegetables to a shallow glass dish. Add the green pepper, celery, onion, and mushrooms to the marinade and continue boiling until the mixture is reduced by about half. Remove the bouquet garni and pour the liquid over the vegetables. Let the food cool to room temperature. Cover and allow to chill and marinate for 4 hours or overnight. Garnish with tomato wedges and parsley. Serve on Bibb lettuce.

Yield: 4 to 6 servings

*ROWELL'S INN*

## Indian Spiced Vegetable Casserole in Phyllo with Yogurt Sauce

**VEGETABLES**
2½ pounds red potatoes, peeled and diced
1 tablespoon olive oil
1 cup shredded carrots
1 cup finely chopped onions
2 teaspoons minced fresh ginger
1 cup peas, fresh or frozen (thawed)
2 tablespoons chopped fresh cilantro
2 tablespoons freshly squeezed lemon juice
3 to 4 teaspoons curry powder
½ teaspoon cumin
¾ teaspoon salt
¼ teaspoon pepper
⅛ teaspoon cayenne pepper

**PHYLLO**
7 sheets phyllo dough
Melted butter

**SAUCE**
2 cups plain yogurt
2 cloves garlic, finely chopped
½ cup cilantro, chopped

Boil the potatoes until just tender (don't overcook). Drain and set aside. Preheat the oven to 400°.

In a large nonstick skillet, heat the olive oil. Sauté the carrots, onions, and ginger until tender. Add the remaining vegetable ingredients and cook together for 3 to 5 minutes. Add the potatoes.

Transfer the vegetables to a 9x13-inch baking pan, and cover with 7 sheets of phyllo dough, 1 at a time, brushing each layer with the melted butter. Bake for 20 to 30 minutes or until golden.

Prepare the sauce by combining all of the ingredients and mixing well. Serve the sauce on the side.

Yield: 8 to 10 servings

*OCTOBER COUNTRY INN*

### Easy Butter Roses

Just shave cold butter, forming decreasing circles. Dip butter into paprika on the edges for color.

## Sicilian Braised Vegetables with Pine Nuts and a Sweet Vinaigrette

1 medium eggplant (about 1½ pounds), unpeeled and cut into ¾-inch cubes
Coarse salt
⅓ cup olive oil, or more if necessary
2 large red onions, peeled and thinly sliced
2 large cloves garlic, minced
1 red bell pepper, cored, seeded, and cut into ¾-inch cubes
1 yellow bell pepper, cored, seeded, and cubed
Salt and freshly ground black pepper

3 small zucchini, trimmed and cut into ¾-inch cubes
2 large red, ripe tomatoes, peeled, seeded, and diced
3 tablespoons balsamic vinegar
1½ tablespoons sugar
½ cup golden raisins, plumped in hot water and drained
2 to 3 tablespoons pine nuts, toasted
2 tablespoons finely minced Italian parsley

Place the eggplant in a bowl of ice water with 1 tablespoon of the coarse salt. Set aside for 30 minutes.

Meanwhile, in a large, cast-iron skillet, heat 3 tablespoons of the olive oil over high heat. Sauté the onions and garlic for 2 to 3 minutes. Reduce the heat and simmer, partially covered, for 25 to 30 minutes, stirring often until vegetables turn very soft.

Drain the eggplant; dry thoroughly and set aside.

Add the red and yellow peppers to the onion mixture and continue simmering until the peppers are tender. Transfer the mixture to a bowl.

Add 3 tablespoons of the olive oil to a skillet and, when hot, sauté the eggplant over medium heat until nicely browned. Add more oil if necessary. Season with salt and pepper. Transfer to a bowl with the onion mixture.

Add 2 tablespoons more of the oil to the skillet and, when hot, sauté the zucchini for 3 to 5 minutes or until browned. Season with salt and pepper.

Return all of the vegetables to the skillet. Add the tomatoes and simmer for another 5 minutes.

In a bowl, blend the vinegar and sugar thoroughly. Add the vinaigrette to the vegetable mixture with the plumped raisins and cook for

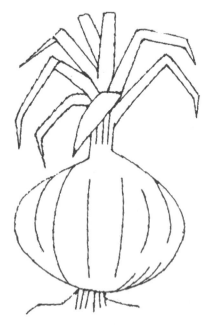

5 minutes more. Fold in the pine nuts and parsley. Remove the vegetable mixture from the heat and cool. Serve at room temperature.

Yield: 8 to 10 servings

*OCTOBER COUNTRY INN*

*Potatoes*
*Milk*
*Garlic*
*Parmesan & Swiss Cheeses*
*Nutmeg*

## Baked Scalloped Potatoes Layered with Swiss Cheese and Mustard

3 large russet potatoes, peeled and sliced into ¼-inch-thick slices
Salt and pepper
Yellow mustard
¼ pound Swiss cheese, thinly sliced

3 medium onions, thinly sliced
¼ cup freshly cooked bacon, diced into bits
½ cup dry vermouth
¼ cup seasoned breadcrumbs
Parmesan cheese
¼ cup butter

Preheat to 350°. In a buttered 8x8-inch glass baking dish, place a layer of potatoes on the bottom of the dish in shingled fashion. Season with salt and pepper. Spread a thin layer of mustard over the potatoes and follow with a layer of Swiss cheese and then onions. Add another layer of potatoes, cheese, and more mustard and onions. Sprinkle with some bacon and repeat the layers until the dish is full.

Pour the vermouth overall. Spread the breadcrumbs on top and sprinkle with Parmesan cheese. Dot with butter. Cover the dish with foil and bake 20 minutes. Remove the foil and bake another 10 minutes or until the top browns. Serve hot.

Yield: 6 servings

*CHALET SUZANNE*

Since this is a book that may inspire you to travel as well as cook, I have included some tips for taking to the road. You may want to make a copy of this list for friends traveling to your house.

• Keep gloves in the trunk for pumping gas or changing a flat tire.

• Pack the family up the day before to relieve tension on traveling day.

• Pack toiletries in a separate bag for easy accessibility at any time during your travel.

• If you find yourself daydreaming when on a long drive, bring along an alarm clock and set it to go off at intervals to remind you to stay alert.

• Wrapping garments in layers of tissue paper really does keep your clothes from getting crushed.

• Drench house plants in water and then wrap them in clear plastic for a greenhouse effect. This way you lessen the chance of their drying out. There are also gels on the market that release moisture into house plants slowly. Check with your local nursery.

(Continued on next page)

## Twice-Baked Maple Yams

*When selecting yams or sweet potatoes, choose those with smooth, unblemished skins.*

6 medium yams or sweet potatoes
3 tablespoons butter, plus more
  for greasing
¼ cup pure maple syrup
1 teaspoon salt
1 tablespoon sherry
  Fresh parsley, chopped, for
  garnish

Preheat the oven to 400°. Scrub the potatoes well. Prick the skins with a fork and lightly grease with butter. Bake 45 to 60 minutes or until tender.

Cut the tops off the potatoes and scoop out the pulp, leaving the shells intact. In a mixer bowl, combine the pulp with the 3 table-spoons of butter, maple syrup, salt, and sherry, and whip until well combined and fluffy. Spoon the mixture back into the potato shells. Return the potatoes to the oven for 10 to 15 minutes or until heated through. Garnish with chopped fresh parsley.

Yield: 6 servings

*ROWELL'S INN*

## Potato, Leek, and Cheese Casserole

4 large russet potatoes
3 eggs
1 cup milk
½ cup half-and-half
¼ teaspoon nutmeg
1 cup shredded Swiss cheese or
  any similar hard cheese
2 teaspoons salt
1 teaspoon pepper
1 teaspoon butter
½ cup thinly sliced leeks, white
  part only
¼ cup Parmesan cheese plus
  more for garnishing

Peel and slice the potatoes thinly (about ¼-inch thick). Immediately after slicing, submerge the potatoes in water. Beat the eggs with the milk and the half-and-half. Add the nutmeg and stir in the Swiss cheese. Season with 1 teaspoon of the salt and all of the pepper.

Coat a 6x12-inch glass baking dish with a nonstick spray. Preheat the oven to 325°.

In a nonstick skillet, heat the butter and sauté the leeks until soft, about 3 to 5 minutes. Set them aside. Drain the potatoes and discard the water. Place the potatoes in the baking dish. Add the leeks. Add the remaining salt and cover the potatoes and leeks with the egg-and-cheese mixture. Flatten the potatoes with your hand to submerge into the mixture. Top with Parmesan cheese and bake for 25 to 35 minutes or until browned on top. Cool for a few minutes before serving. Cut into squares and serve.

Yield: 6 to 8 servings

*CHECKERBERRY INN*

## Roasted Garlic Mashed Potatoes in a Savory Phyllo Shell

| | |
|---|---|
| 5 white potatoes, peeled and chopped | 1 medium head garlic |
| 4 12x16-inch phyllo pastry leaves | 1 cup butter |
| 1 cup olive oil (not all will be used) | 1½ cups heavy cream |

Preheat the oven to 400°. Boil the potatoes until soft; strain. While the potatoes are boiling, arrange the phyllo pastry 1 sheet at a time. Brush each sheet entirely with a thin layer of olive oil. Place the next sheet directly overtop the brushed sheet. Repeat the process until all 4 sheets are coated with the oil. Cut the sheets in 6 equal pieces; then stagger each brushed stack in a muffin tin, skipping a muffin section in-between each. Bake for about 10 minutes or until golden brown. Remove from the oven and let rest.

Meanwhile, cut the head of garlic in half and roast in 2 tablespoons of the olive oil in a pie tin until soft. Over medium heat, melt the butter with the cream in a medium saucepan. After the garlic has cooled, squeeze out the cloves and discard the skin; purée the cloves.

In the bowl of an electric mixer, beat the puréed garlic, potatoes, and the cream-and-butter mixture on slow speed for 1 minute. Raise the speed until desired consistency is achieved. Season with salt and pepper for taste. Remove the phyllo shells from the muffin tin and fill with the garlic mashed potatoes.

Yield: 6 servings

*KEDRON VALLEY INN*

### On the Road (continued)

• Always have on hand an entire set of United States road maps. Not only are they handy for traveling and for putting on the dashboard to keep out the sun, but they are a veritable encyclopedia for looking up a number of geographic matters. We keep our set in a map holder my father created for us.

• Before you swim in a chlorinated pool, apply a little baby oil to your hair to prevents the chemical from seeping into your hair. Shampoo after swimming.

• To keep baggage to a minimum, try to stick to one color scheme, which will help cut down on accessories.

• Don't tangle with tailgaters. Move over as soon as it is safe and let them pass you.

• If you have been away from your house for a week or longer, hydrogen gas can accumulate in the water heater. Turn on all hot water faucets for about two minutes to release any buildup. I also let the cold water run for a while, as some water sits in the pipes while you're away.

## Potato Dumplings

5 medium to large potatoes, peeled, boiled, mashed, and cooled
4 cups bread flour or all-purpose flour
1 tablespoon farina
1 teaspoon salt
1 egg, beaten
¼ cup butter, melted

In a large bowl, mix all of the ingredients (except the butter) by hand. Let dough stand for 5 minutes. Shape into 4-inch-long (3-ounce) cylinder dumplings.

In a large saucepan, bring salted water to a boil. Add the dumplings, and stir them gently to keep them from hugging the bottom of the pan. Bring to a boil, cooking 15 minutes more or until the dumplings are fluffy and white when slicing one through the middle. Remove the dumplings from the water carefully with a slotted spoon. Make a slit in the center of each and brush with melted butter.

Yield: 10 dumplings

*SCHUMACHER'S NEW PRAGUE HOTEL*

## Potato-and-Cheese Casserole

1 cup heavy cream
1 cup milk
2 tablespoons salt
1 teaspoon freshly ground pepper
1 teaspoon freshly ground nutmeg

6 medium baking potatoes, peeled and sliced as thin as a potato chip
2 cloves garlic, chopped
Butter
1 cup grated Parmesan cheese
⅔ cup grated Swiss cheese

Preheat the oven to 350°. In a large, nonstick saucepan, bring the heavy cream and the milk to a simmer; add the salt, pepper, and nutmeg. Place the potatoes in the mixture and let simmer for 2 minutes.

Add the garlic to a buttered 9x13-inch baking dish. Layer half of the potatoes in the dish and cover with ⅓ of both the cheeses. Layer the remaining potatoes on top and cover with the remaining cheeses. Pour the remaining cream mixture over the potatoes.

Cover with foil and bake for 45 minutes. Uncover and allow to brown during the last 10 minutes.

Yield: 6 servings

*SIGN OF THE SORREL HORSE*

## Chipotle-and-Cheese Mashed Potatoes with Roasted Garlic

*Chipotles are dried jalapeños that impart a smoky, fiery flavor. Chipotles also come marinated.*

4 Idaho potatoes, peeled and cut into chunks
3 cloves garlic, roasted and chopped
1 cup grated white Cheddar cheese

½ cup cream cheese
5 dried chipotle chilies, crushed
2 tablespoons heavy cream
2 tablespoons butter
Salt and cayenne pepper

Boil the potatoes until they are tender. Drain well. In the bowl of an electric mixer, whip the potatoes with the remaining ingredients until the mixture is smooth. Season to taste with the salt and the pepper.

Yield: 6 servings

*INN OF THE ANASAZI*

## Creamed Potatoes and Cabbage

*Irish peasants devised potatoes Celcannon, a blend of cabbage and pota-*
*toes they called* Colcannon *in Gaelic, meaning "white-headed cabbage."*
*Here is a gourmet version. No doubt it was served at Victorian Villa when*
*it was a private home.*

| | |
|---|---|
| 5 pounds Irish red potatoes | 1 cup butter |
| 2 tablespoons salt | 1 pound clotted cream (or sub- |
| 1 head green cabbage, finely | stitute 1 pound cream cheese) |
| chopped | Paprika |

Peel, wash, quarter, and boil the potatoes in 2 quarts of water with the
salt. In a large saucepan, sauté the cabbage in half of the butter until
cooked *al dente,* a few minutes.

Preheat the oven to 375°. Place the potatoes, clotted cream, and
the remaining butter in the bowl of an electric mixer and whip until
the mixture is smooth. Blend the whipped potatoes with the cooked
cabbage and place the mixture in a 15x11-inch baking dish or lasagne
pan. Sprinkle with paprika and bake, uncovered, on the center rack of
the oven for 45 minutes or until lightly browned.

Yield: 10 servings

*VICTORIAN VILLA*

# Risotto Primavera

*Most of the vegetables for this risotto are more readily available during the summer months. However, the recipe works well with many other vegetables and the possibilities for success are endless.*

¼ cup olive oil
1 large onion, finely chopped
1 clove garlic, minced
1 pound Arborio rice
½ cup dry white wine
6 cups chicken stock
¼ pound mushrooms, thinly sliced
1 large red bell pepper, cut into 1-inch squares
¼ pound snow peas, cut in half diagonally
8 asparagus spears, cut diagonally into 1-inch pieces
4 plum tomatoes, peeled, seeded, and chopped
¼ cup finely chopped Italian parsley
Salt and freshly ground pepper
½ cup grated Parmesan cheese

Heat the oil in a large nonstick skillet. Add the onion and the garlic. Sauté over moderate heat, stirring until the onion is soft. Add the rice, and stir to coat with the oil. Add the wine, and stir until absorbed.

Meanwhile, bring the chicken stock to boil, lower the heat, and keep the stock to a simmer.

Begin adding the stock to the rice, ½ cup at a time. Stir until each addition is absorbed.

After 4 cups of the stock have been absorbed, add in the following order: the mushrooms, red bell pepper, snow peas, asparagus, and tomatoes, stirring constantly. Add more stock as needed. When all the liquid is absorbed, add the parsley, salt, and pepper.

Remove the skillet from the heat. Stir in the Parmesan cheese, and serve the risotto at once.

Yield: 8 servings

Note: Arborio rice is an Italian-grown, short-grain rice. It is traditionally used for risotto because its high-starch content gives the dish its characteristic creamy texture.

*NEWCASTLE INN*

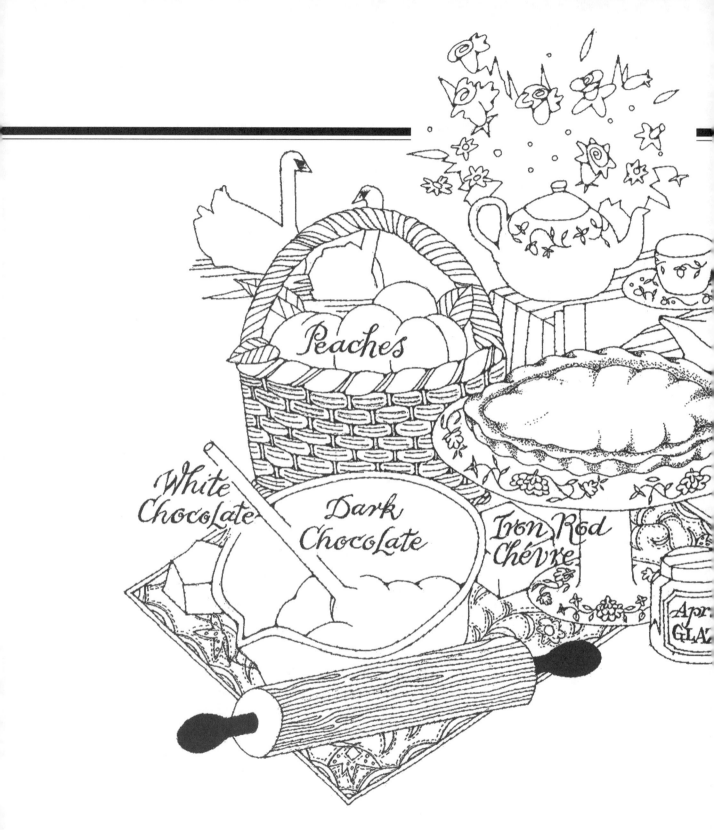

Peaches

White
Chocolate

Dark
Chocolate

Iron Red
Chèvre

Apr
GLA

# SWEETS

## Peaches and Chèvre in Puff Pastry with Apricot Glaze and Chocolate Sauce

1 package frozen puff pastry sheets

4 medium-to-large peaches, peeled

2 tablespoons sugar, plus more for sprinkling

4 ounces chèvre goat cheese

⅓ cup apricot preserves, melted

1 cup heavy cream

4 ounces quality dark chocolate

Roll out the puff pastry sheets to about ¼-inch thick. Cut the pastry out into the shape of a peach, about 4 inches in diameter. (Try to outline it so that you have a stem and a leaf coming on top of each peach.) Cut out 4 of these and reserve the rest of the pastry for another recipe.

Preheat the oven to 400°. Cut the peaches into ½-inch-thick slices. Set aside.

In a small bowl, mix together the sugar and the chèvre with a wooden spoon until combined. Scoop into a pastry bag, and pipe about 1 ounce of the cheese-and-sugar mixture into the center of each pastry peach. Arrange 1 peach in a fanlike or shingled fashion on top of the cheese, leaving a border of about ¼- to ½-inch of pastry surrounding the peaches. Sprinkle some sugar overtop. Bake the peaches in the oven for 15 minutes or until golden brown. While still warm, brush liberally with the apricot preserves.

Prepare the chocolate sauce by heating the heavy cream to a scald in a medium, nonstick saucepan. Remove from the heat; immediately add the chocolate and allow to melt, stirring until smooth. Serve over the top or on the side of the peaches.

Yield: 4 servings

*CLIFTON COUNTRY INN*

# Burnt Honey Ice Cream on a Fan of Citrus-Spiced Pears with Raspberry Sauce

*Start this recipe a day ahead of time to allow the ice cream time to freeze. If you choose not to make your own ice cream, go right to the pears preparation and just add your own ice cream flavor.*

### ICE CREAM
1½ cups quality honey
2½ cups whole milk
3½ cups heavy cream
 1 teaspoon pure vanilla extract
1½ cups sugar
12 egg yolks

### PEARS AND POACHING SYRUP
 2 cups white wine
 2 cups Burgundy wine
 2 cups water
½ cup crème de Cassis
 Zest of 1 orange
 Juice of 1½ oranges
½ teaspoon whole cloves
 1 stick cinnamon
½ teaspoon allspice
 Zest and juice of ½ lemon
 4 to 6 Asian pears, peeled, cored, and cut in half (or any pears will do)

### SAUCE
 1 pint fresh raspberries
1½ cups water
 1 cup sugar
¼ cup crème de Cassis
 Juice of 1 lemon
 1 tablespoon cornstarch

Heat the honey in a copper pan until it begins to caramelize and acquires a slight burned flavor. (Be careful when you taste the honey—it's very hot.) Set the honey aside, keeping it warm.

In a medium saucepan, scald the milk, 1½ cups of the cream, and the vanilla; then add 1 cup of the sugar to the milk mixture. Bring to a boil, stirring constantly and keeping the mixture warm.

Beat the egg yolks and remaining ½ cup of sugar until they are pale yellow and a slowly dissolving ribbon forms when the beaters are lifted. Gradually beat the hot milk mixture into the egg mixture. Return the combined mixture to the saucepan and stir over low heat until the custard thickens, but do not boil. Mix in the remaining 2 cups of cream and the warm caramelized honey. Cool the custard by setting it into a larger bowl of ice until chilled. Churn the mixture in

an electric ice cream churn. When finished, place the ice cream into a plastic container and freeze for several hours. About 30 minutes before ready, or next day, prepare the pears.

Combine all of the ingredients, except the pears, and bring the poaching syrup to a simmer. Add the pears and bring to just below a simmer. Poach for 20 to 30 minutes, checking periodically, until the pears are tender throughout. Let the pears cool in the syrup for 30 minutes to absorb the flavors. Remove the pears and save or freeze the syrup for another occasion. Slice the pears in slivers to fan out, and set aside.

Prepare the raspberry sauce. In a saucepan, combine the berries, water, and sugar. Simmer gently on low heat for several minutes to reduce, stirring occasionally. Process the raspberry mixture through a food mill or pass through a sieve to remove the seeds. Return the mixture to a low simmer. Combine the Cassis, lemon juice, and cornstarch, and add to the raspberry mixture. Cool the sauce.

To assemble, place a pool of raspberry sauce onto an individual serving plate. Fan half of a pear around the plate and add a scoop of ice cream. Drizzle extra sauce overtop if desired.

Yield: 8 to 12 servings

*HIGHLAND LAKE INN*

Burnt Honey Ice Cream

A Fan of Citrus Spiced Pears

## Baked-Hazelnut-Stuffed Pears

*These pears are wonderful for breakfast or dessert served with a scoop of vanilla ice cream.*

½ cup hazelnuts, shells removed
¼ cup dried sweet cherries
¼ cup Frangelico liqueur
6 pears, preferably Anjou or
   Bartlett, ripe but still firm

¾ cup confectioners' sugar
½ teaspoon vanilla extract

Preheat the over to 350°. Place the hazelnuts in a single layer on a baking sheet. Toast the nuts 15 minutes, or until they turn golden brown. Let them cool, then chop finely.

While the nuts are toasting, put the cherries into a small bowl and pour the liqueur over them. Let the cherries soak for 15 minutes. Drain the cherries, reserving the liqueur.

Turn the oven temperature up to 375°. Peel, halve, and core the pears. Arrange them in a single layer in a shallow baking dish. (Cut a small slice off the underside of each half, if needed, to keep them stable.)

In a bowl, combine the cherries, sugar, hazelnuts, and vanilla, and mix well. Fill the pear halves with this mixture. Pour the reserved liqueur over the pear halves.

Bake the pears for 15 minutes or until they are tender. Serve them hot or cold with some of the cooking liquid spooned overtop.

Yield: 6 servings

*NEWCASTLE INN*

172

## Pear Tarts with English Custard and Caramel Cream Sauce

**ALMOND CREAM**
¾ cup blanched almond slices
½ cup sugar
2 egg yolks
¼ cup unsalted butter, softened
2 teaspoons vanilla extract

**CUSTARD**
1 vanilla bean
2 cups milk
5 egg yolks
½ cup sugar

**CARAMEL SAUCE**
½ cup sugar
2 tablespoons water
½ cup heavy cream

**PEARS**
1 sheet puff pastry, thawed
2 small ripe pears, cut in half
1 tablespoon sugar
1 tablespoon pear brandy

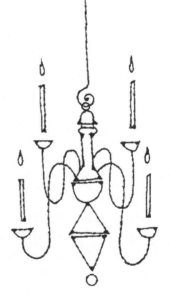

Begin by making the almond cream. Purée the almonds and sugar together in a blender or food processor. Add the egg yolks, butter, and vanilla and mix with a spoon until smooth. Set aside.

Prepare the custard. Split the vanilla bean in half and scrape away and discard the seeds. In a small, nonstick saucepan, bring the vanilla pod and the milk to a boil. Remove from the heat. In a medium-size mixing bowl, beat the egg yolks and sugar until white ribbons form. Slowly add the egg yolks into the milk. Return the custard sauce to the heat. Heat gently until it thickens and coats the back of a spoon. Cool in the refrigerator.

Prepare the sauce. In a small saucepan, over medium-high heat, cook the ½ cup sugar and the water to a medium dark caramel. Remove from the heat and whisk in the cream. (Be careful, the caramel may bubble up the sides of the pan.) Allow the sauce to cool to room temperature, then add to the custard to complete the sauce. Preheat the oven to 450°.

Cut the puff pastry into 4 4-inch circles, about ¼ inch larger in diameter than the pears. Spread ¼ of the almond cream over the center of each pastry circle. Thinly slice the pears. Fan out half a pear, placing it on a pastry circle. Sprinkle with sugar and brandy. Bake each pastry 10 to 12 minutes or until golden brown. Make 3 small circles of the custard and caramel sauce on each plate. Place the warm tart overtop and serve.

Yield: 4 servings

*OLD DROVERS INN*

# Plum and Lemon Clafouti

*Enhanced by the robust flavor of cognac, this cakelike pudding is a cinch to assemble, and I like the idea of being able to use fresh plums. Serve the clafouti with whipped cream if desired. Clafouti originated in Limousin, France, and today there are many different versions, but they all basically consist of a pancake-like batter with fruit.*

| | |
|---|---|
| 1 cup milk | 2 teaspoons lemon zest |
| ⅓ cup heavy cream | ¾ cup all-purpose flour |
| 3 eggs | ⅛ teaspoon salt |
| 2 teaspoons vanilla extract | 15 ripe Italian plums, quartered |
| 2 tablespoons cognac | and seeded |
| ⅓ cup sugar plus 4 tablespoons | Whipped cream, optional |

Preheat the over to 375° and butter a 10x1½-inch-deep tart, quiche, or pie pan. In a food processor, whirl together the milk, cream, eggs, vanilla, and cognac. In a small bowl, mix together ⅓ cup of the sugar, 1 teaspoon of the lemon zest, the flour, and the salt. Add to the food processor and whirl until a smooth batter forms (there should be about 3 cups of batter).

Pour 1½ cups of the batter into the prepared pan. Arrange the plums on top in a single layer. Sprinkle with the remaining lemon peel and gently pour the rest of the batter over the plums. Bake 15 minutes and remove from the oven. Sprinkle the remaining sugar overtop and return to the oven. Bake 45 minutes more, or until the center is set and the top is browned and puffed. (Note: If the top is not browned but the center is set, place the clafouti under the broiler for about 1 to 2 minutes.)

Allow the dessert to cool on a wire rack for 5 minutes. The clafouti falls as it cools, but that is the simple charm and simplicity of this dessert. Cut into wedges and serve warm with whipped cream.

Yield: 6 servings

*CHECKERBERRY INN*

# Lemon-Curd Blueberry Tart

*Used as a spread for toast and scones and as a filling for pastries, lemon curd is sweet and refreshing. Although this recipe contains many eggs, twenty-five, (wow!), I included it here because it is such a classic sweet condiment. Besides, you are not getting all of those eggs (and only the yolks) in any one serving-size piece of this tart. Lemon curd is available at gourmet food stores and supermarkets, if you wish to save time.*

*You may make twelve tart shells or two whole pies with this recipe.*

### PIE DOUGH
- 3 cups all-purpose flour, plus more for kneading
- 10 ounces unsalted butter, cut into ½-inch pieces
- ½ cup superfine sugar
- ¼ teaspoon salt
- 1 egg lightly beaten
- 1 egg yolk

### LEMON CURD
- 25 egg yolks
- 2½ cups sugar
- Juice and zest of 10 lemons
- ¾ pound butter

### ASSEMBLY
- 1½ quarts or more fresh blueberries
- 12 small mint bouquets, for garnish

Begin the recipe by making the pie dough. Preheat the oven to 400°. Place the flour in the middle of the work surface and make a well in the center. Add the butter, sugar, salt, egg and egg yolk. Mix with your hands to form a soft dough. Gather the dough into a ball. Knead until smooth and elastic, adding more flour to prevent it from being sticky. Roll the dough out to ¼ inch or less and cut to fit 12 (3- or 3½-inch tart pans. Refrigerate the pans for 20 minutes; then bake for 10 minutes or until golden brown. Remove from the oven and set aside to cool down to room temperature. Meanwhile make the lemon curd.

In a medium-sized mixing bowl, beat the egg yolks and sugar until the mixture forms ribbons. Mix in the juice and the lemon zest. Place the mixture in a pan over a double boiler and cook until thick and bubbling. Remove from the heat and beat in the butter, 1 spoonful at a time, until the mixture turns translucent, smooth, and gelatinous.

Cover the bottom of the cooled pie shells with the lemon curd, dividing it evenly among the 12 tarts or the 2 pie shells. Place a generous layer of fresh blueberries overtop the lemon curd and place a fresh mint sprig in the center of each tart.

Yield: 12 servings

*BEE & THISTLE INN*

*The air is scented with heavy perfume blossoms... daffodils have faded & Heaven's spring is rushing along in full flower.*

Erna Kubin-Clanin, Château du Sureau

# Tropical Fruit Napoleon with Passion Sauce and Toasted Papaya Seeds

## Guest-Room Pampering

• Fresh flowers are always welcome and make a guest feel special.

• Fruit or candy is a must. A guest who has been traveling for a while may need a sugar lift.

• A small basket of toiletries containing items guests might have forgotten will certainly take the pain away from their having to ask you for something. They may be a little shy about that.

• In that basket, there should be a bar of soap. I like to use a special scented or what I call gourmet soap. Tuck a small cellophane bag in the basket with a note: If you enjoyed this scent, please take home whatever is left. Guests are shy about taking home their soaps. But who better to make use of what you will discard than the original user?

• Travelers don't have it as easy as you think. Travel can do things to the body, such as dry it out because it is in a strange environment. One of the most satisfying

(Continued on page 177)

**CUSTARD**
4 egg yolks
½ cup sugar
1½ cups heavy cream
⅔ cup milk
2 vanilla beans, split and seeds scraped

**NAPOLEONS**
8 square spring-roll wrappers
¼ cup butter, melted
¼ cup sugar

**PAPAYA SEEDS**
Seeds reserved from a papaya
Sugar to taste

**SAUCE**
2 cups passion fruit concentrate (available in frozen food section of the supermarket) or any tropical mixed fruit concentrate
3 tablespoons sugar
3 tablespoons cream

**ASSEMBLY**
1 mango, peeled and diced
½ ripe papaya, peeled and diced (seeds reserved)
½ pineapple, peeled, cored, and diced
2 cups heavy cream, whipped and kept chilled
Fresh mint for garnish

Preheat the oven to 325°. Whisk the egg yolks and sugar together. Set aside. In a medium saucepan, mix the cream, milk, and vanilla beans, and heat over high heat just until it comes to a boil. Slowly whisk the cream mixture into the egg mixture. Generously coat 2 9x13-inch baking dishes with nonstick cooking spray and pour equal amounts of the custard into each pan. Bake the custard in a water bath for about 25 minutes or until set. Remove from the oven and let stand at room temperature to cool. Once the custard has cooled completely, place it in the freezer until firm enough to cut, about 30 minutes. Cut each pan into 20 2¼-inch squares. Refrigerate until needed.

To make the Napoleons, preheat the oven to 350°. Place the spring-roll wrappers on a sheet pan covered with parchment paper and brush each wrapper with melted butter. Sprinkle some sugar over each wrapper. Cut each into 4 equal pieces. Bake 8 to 10 minutes or until golden brown.

While the oven is on, toast the papaya seeds on a sheet pan for about 3 minutes or to just about dry. Remove the seeds from the oven and sprinkle with sugar. Return them to the oven until firm, about 15 to 20 minutes. Remove from the heat and let stand at room temperature.

Prepare the sauce. In a small saucepan, heat the passion fruit concentrate with the sugar. Bring to a boil and add the cream. Return to a boil. Remove from the heat and cool.

To assemble the Napoleon, lay 8 individual serving plates out onto the work space. In a bowl, mix together the mango, papaya, and pineapple. Place 1 tablespoon of the whipped cream onto each plate. Place a spring-roll square on top of the cream. Add 1 square of baked custard on top. Place 2 tablespoons of chopped mixed tropical fruit on the custard and add another spring-roll crisp. Add 2 tablespoons more of the whipped cream, followed by 2 tablespoons of the fruit. Add another crisp and another custard square. Add 2 tablespoons more of the tropical fruit and another crisp. Finish the Napoleon off with 1 tablespoon of the whipped cream, 1 tablespoon of the chopped fruit and a garnish of fresh mint. Drizzle a little passion fruit sauce around the Napoleon and sprinkle with toasted papaya seeds.

Yield: 8 servings

*SAN YSIDRO RANCH*

*Guest-Room Pampering*
*(continued)*

amenities I have ever enjoyed was found at an inn in Vermont. The innkeeper had a tiny compact of lip gloss by the side of the bed. I found it so useful at night as well as in the daytime. How thoughtful!

• A pincushion is one of those items we never think will have any use. But it can be handy, especially to a guest who is opening his new shirt bought for the trip and has nowhere to put those straight pins.

• No matter how little or how well you know your guests, try to place reading material they might enjoy in their room—magazines, newspapers, mail-order catalogs, books. You can always keep a poetry book in the room or some good-feeling book that they can more or less read at a glance.

• Opening the closet door and finding thick padded hangers is sheer pleasure for most guests. You can get a mixed set—feminine and frilly lace hangers and paisley or dark masculine ones.

(Continued on page 178)

## Guest-Room Pampering
(continued)

• A fluffy, terrycloth one-size-fits-all bathrobe is a handy addition to a guest room as well as a sweet amenity.

• I like to keep bookmarks by my guest's bed to be handy as well as a souvenir.

• This may sound a little offbeat for a private-home guest room, but it's really not all that off base. Keep a few postcards from your area in the room. Your guests may want to write home about their stay in your area. You may even want to make up personal postcards. Take a photo of your home. Then they can send their friends a picture-postcard of where they are staying.

• Many inns have guest books, such as those blank, fabric-covered notebooks, kept in individual guest rooms. That offers visitors more time to say what's on their minds and to peruse the thoughts of others who have stayed before.

# Brandied Berry Brûlée

*A pudding-like dessert, this sweet is easy to make and elegant to serve.*

2½ cups heavy cream
½ cup milk
¼ cup sugar
2 eggs
4 egg yolks
2 tablespoons Chambord (or substitute 1 teaspoon vanilla extract)

½ cup mixed fresh berries, chopped and soaked in Armagnac brandy
2 tablespoons granulated brown sugar

Preheat the oven to 325°. In a nonstick saucepan, heat the cream, milk, and sugar until just boiling. Remove the saucepan from the heat temporarily, and reset the heat to low. Meanwhile, in a separate bowl, whisk the eggs, egg yolks, and Chambord. Slowly add the egg mixture to the hot liquid, whisking constantly. Return the saucepan to the low heat and cook until the liquid thickens.

Fold the fruit into the sauce and, with a ladle, fill 6 4-ounce ceramic ramekins with the mixture. Place the cups in a shallow roasting pan and fill halfway up with warm water. Bake for 35 to 40 minutes. Sprinkle the tops with brown sugar. Place the cups under the broiler until the tops are caramelized. Let cool for 1 hour, then chill before serving.

Yield: 6 servings

*KEDRON VALLEY INN*

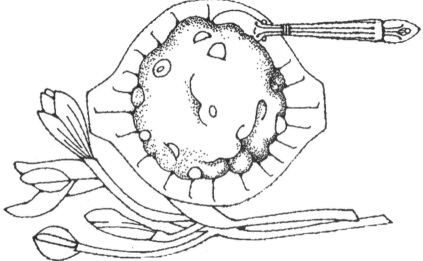

# Viennese Apple Strudel

## DOUGH
- 2 tablespoons butter, melted
- 2 tablespoons warm water
- 1 egg, beaten
- 1½ teaspoons sugar
- ⅛ teaspoon salt
- ½ teaspoon vanilla extract
- 1½ cups all-purpose flour

## FILLING
- 1 cup crushed corn flakes, moistened with 2 tablespoons melted butter
- ¾ cup fresh breadcrumbs
- 6 cups Granny Smith apples, cored, peeled, and diced
- ¾ cup raisins
- ¾ cup coarsely chopped walnuts
- 1 cup loosely packed dark brown sugar
- ½ teaspoon cinnamon
- ½ cup flaked coconut

## ASSEMBLY
- Egg wash or water
- 2 tablespoons butter, melted for brushing

## FROSTING
- ⅓ cup confectioners' sugar
- ⅓ cup whipping cream

Mix together all of the dough ingredients except the flour. Add the flour to make a soft, but not sticky, dough. Knead for about 150 strokes. Place in a greased and covered bowl in a warm place for 1 hour. Roll the dough out on a floured cloth, and stretch very thin, making an 18x24-inch rectangle.

Preheat the oven to 350°. To make the strudel, layer the filling ingredients over the dough in the order listed, making sure the ingredients are evenly distributed. Dampen the edge of the crust with egg wash or water. Roll the strudel up jellyroll style, beginning at the shorter end. Place the strudel on a greased baking sheet, seam-side down. Brush with melted butter. Bake 50 minutes or until golden brown.

Whip together the sugar and cream until glaze consistency. Frost the strudel immediately when removed from the oven. Cool well and slice.

Yield: 6 servings

*SCHUMACHER'S NEW PRAGUE HOTEL*

179

## Warm Caramelized-Apple Tart in a Brandied Cream Sauce

*TARTS*
2 medium Granny Smith apples
  (or other tart apples)
  Juice of 1 lemon
½ cup sugar
¼ cup butter
2 tablespoons Calvados brandy
1 egg
2 egg yolks
¾ cup heavy cream
6 ounces puff pastry

*SAUCE*
½ cup crème fraîche
2 tablespoons confectioners'
  sugar, plus more for dusting
1 tablespoon Calvados brandy
  Juice of ¼ lemon
  Vanilla ice cream

Prepare the filling. Pare, quarter, and core the apples, reserving the peels. Slice each apple into 12 equal wedges. Dice some of the peels into 2-inch strips, refrigerate in a covered dish and save for decoration later. Caramelize the fruit by combining the lemon juice with the sugar at a low boil until golden in color. Stir in the butter. Add the apple wedges and sauté about 2 minutes. Pour the brandy over the apples, cooking just until glazed over, about 1 minute. Drain the glazed apples through a sieve and collect the caramel in a bowl. Add the egg, the egg yolks, and the heavy cream to the caramel. Blend well.

Prepare the tarts. Preheat the oven to 400°. Roll out the puff pastry dough to about ⅛-inch thick. Line 4 4-inch tart forms with the dough. Fit each tart round with a piece of aluminum foil topped with some dried beans to weight the crust and keep it from bubbling when baked. Refrigerate for 20 minutes. Bake for about 15 minutes or until golden. Remove the beans and the foil, and let cool. Reduce heat to 300°. Place 6 of the prepared apple wedges into each tart shell and cover each with the caramel mixture. Return the tarts to the oven and bake for 15 minutes or until set.

Meanwhile, make the sauce. Mix the crème fraîche with the confectioners' sugar, brandy, and lemon juice until creamy. Spoon onto 4 plates. Place an apple tart in the center of each plate and add a scoop of vanilla ice cream. Sprinkle with the chopped apple peel strips and dust with more sugar.

Yield: 4 servings

*CHÂTEAU DU SUREAU*

## Chuckwagon Apple Cake

3 large cooking apples
2 teaspoons cinnamon
5 teaspoons plus 2 cups sugar, divided
3 cups all-purpose flour

1 tablespoon baking powder
¼ cup pineapple or apple juice
1 cup vegetable oil
2½ teaspoons vanilla extract
4 eggs

Preheat the oven to 350°. Pare, core, and slice the apples.

Mix the cinnamon and the 5 teaspoons of sugar in a small bowl and set aside.

In a large bowl, combine the 2 cups sugar, the flour, baking powder, pineapple juice, vegetable oil, vanilla, and eggs. Mix just to incorporate.

Grease and flour a bundt pan. Pour half the batter into the pan. Top with ½ the apples and ½ the cinnamon-sugar mixture. Add the remaining batter and top with the remaining apples and cinnamon mixture. Bake for 1 hour and 10 minutes or until a tester inserted in the center comes clean.

Yield: 10 to 12 servings

*Y. O. RANCH*

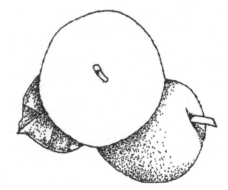

## Lazy Man's Peach Cobbler

3 29-ounce cans cling peaches
½ cup butter, melted
1 cup all-purpose flour
1½ cups sugar, divided
2 teaspoons baking powder

¼ teaspoon salt
1 cup milk
1 teaspoon cinnamon
½ teaspoon nutmeg

Preheat the oven to 350°. Grease a 9x13-inch baking pan.

Drain the peaches, reserving ½ of the juice, and set aside. Pour the melted butter into the bottom of the pan. In a mixing bowl, combine the flour and 1 cup of the sugar with the baking powder and salt. Whisk in the milk and the reserved peach juice. Pour the batter into the prepared pan, distributing it evenly.

Combine the remaining sugar, the cinnamon, and the nutmeg with the peaches. Spread the peaches over the batter and bake for 45 minutes to 1 hour or until the batter is cooked through and the cobbler is golden brown. Serve warm.

Yield: 12 servings

*Y. O. RANCH*

181

• A letter holder or (I use) an antique toast holder stores a pad and pencil next to the bed in case your guest has some eye-opening thought in the middle of the night.

• A small carafe and glass for water can be kept on the night-stand or atop a bureau. This prevents the guest from having to get up in the middle of the night for a glass of water.

• I will never understand why people do not have paper cups in their bathrooms for their guests. I guess because they don't use them in their own bathrooms. But a guest may not know where to find your drinking glasses. Have small cups on hand.

• Facial tissues are a must for every guest room.

• Guests are often unfamiliar with your home, and walking to a bathroom in the dark can create anxiety. If you do not have a night light on, or if that night light is a

(Continued on page 183)

# Caramel Apple Pandowdy

*It's an apple cake; it's an apple pie, it's both—applesauce cake baked atop yummy apple pie. Your guests will agree—apples never tasted so good.*

5 medium McIntosh, Rome, or Golden Delicious apples, peeled, cored, and thinly sliced (about 5 cups)
3 medium Granny Smith, Mutsu, or Pippin apples, peeled, cored, and thinly sliced (about 5 cups)
1½ cups lightly packed light brown sugar
1 cup butter, softened
2 cups all-purpose flour
1 tablespoon baking powder
¼ teaspoon salt
¼ teaspoon cinnamon
¼ teaspoon nutmeg
¼ teaspoon allspice
1 cup sugar
2 eggs
1 cup applesauce, fresh preferred
½ cup raisins
½ cup coarsely chopped pecans
Light cream, optional

Preheat the oven to 350°. Place the apples in a greased 9x13x2-inch baking dish, mounding the apples in the center. Spoon the brown sugar over the apples, then dot with ½ cup of the butter.

In a separate bowl, stir together the flour, baking powder, salt, cinnamon, nutmeg, and allspice. In a larger bowl of an electric mixer, beat the remaining ½ cup of butter on medium speed for about 1 minute. Add the sugar and beat until fluffy. Add the eggs, 1 at a time, beating well after each addition. Add the dry ingredients and the applesauce alternately to the mixture, beating well after each addition. Stir in the raisins and the chopped pecans.

Pour the batter over the apples. Bake on the bottom rack of the oven for 45 to 60 minutes or until the top is cooked. Let stand for 10 minutes. To serve, spoon into individual serving bowls. Top with light cream if desired.

Yield: 10 to 12 servings

*VICTORIAN VILLA*

# Bumbleberry Rhubarb Crisp

*The humble Bumbleberry can be found in Canadian pies and crisps. While the origin of its use is not known, Chef Yvonne Martin at the White Oak Inn has her own idea of what happened. "I like to think some harassed hostess who, when faced with unexpected guests, used her imagination and mixed up the various fruits she had on hand to create a delectable dessert." Any combination of fruits will do.*

FILLING
- 3 cups sliced rhubarb (fresh or frozen), about 1-inch pieces
- 1 cup raspberries, fresh or frozen
- 1 cup blueberries, fresh or frozen
- 2 cups strawberries, fresh or frozen, halved
- 1 cup sugar
- ⅓ cup all-purpose flour

TOPPING
- 1 cup margarine
- 1½ cups firmly packed brown sugar
- 1 cup quick oatmeal (not instant)
- 2 cups all-purpose flour
  Whipped cream or vanilla ice cream

Preheat the oven to 350°. Prepare the filling. In a large bowl, combine the filling ingredients. Mix well, then pour the mixture into a greased 9x13-inch baking pan.

Prepare the topping. Melt the margarine in a medium-size saucepan, then stir in the brown sugar, oatmeal, and flour and mix with a fork. The mixture should be crumbly. If not, add a little more flour. Spread the topping over the fruit mixture. Bake for about 45 minutes, or until the rhubarb tests soft with a fork. Serve warm with whipped cream or ice cream.

Yield: 8 servings

WHITE OAK INN

## Guest-Room Supplies (continued)

distance away, keep a flashlight by the bed so that your guests can navigate the way down the hall or down the stairs!

• A clock with an alarm is a must.

• A luggage rack is one of the most important supplies for the guest room. You don't want to be complaining about guests who put their suitcases on top of your beautifully made bed. They do that because there is no other place and the bed is the right height. In addition to a commercially available luggage rack, you can also use steamer trunks or tables.

• Even if your guests are just taking over someone's room in the house, provide them with a small space in the closet to hang their personal items.

• Be sure that there are ample lights—one for each side of the bed and one or two in the area of the foot of the bed.

## Strawberry-Rhubarb Pie

*When using fresh rhubarb, look for stalks that are blemish-free. Rhubarb and strawberries together form a traditional recipe used in early America.*

**PASTRY**
- 1 teaspoon salt
- 2 cups all-purpose flour
- ¾ cup shortening
- ¼ cup milk

**FILLING**
- 1¼ cups sugar, plus more for sprinkling
- ⅓ cup all-purpose flour
- ¼ teaspoon salt
- 2 cups strawberries (fresh or frozen), hulled and sliced
- 2 cups rhubarb (fresh or frozen), cut into 1-inch pieces
- 2 tablespoons butter
- Fruit juice (any type) for brushing

Preheat the oven to 425°. Prepare the pastry. In a mixing bowl, mix the salt with the flour. Cut the shortening into the flour mixture until it resembles coarse crumbs. Add the milk. Mix the ingredients together just until blended. Divide the dough in 2 and roll out each half on a board lightly dusted with flour. Press 1 of the halves into a 10-inch pie plate.

Prepare the filling. Combine the sugar, flour, and salt. Arrange half of the strawberries and rhubarb in the bottom of the pie shell. Sprinkle with half of the sugar mixture. Repeat layering with the fruit and the sugar mixture. Dot with the butter.

Place the remaining half of the dough on top of the fruit mixture, and crimp along the entire edge of the pie plate, sealing the fruit inside. Brush the top of the pie with juice and sprinkle up to 1 tablespoon of sugar overtop. Pierce the top of the pie with a fork to vent. Bake 40 to 50 minutes or until crust turns a golden brown.

Yield: 8 servings

*ROWELL'S INN*

# Cranberry-Raisin Pie

1½ cups sugar
1½ tablespoons all-purpose flour
1½ teaspoons vanilla extract
2 cups golden raisins

2 cups fresh cranberries, chopped
1 9-inch pie crust and top, uncooked

Preheat the oven to 350°. In a mixing bowl, combine all of the ingredients except the crusts.

Pierce the bottom of the crust with a fork, then spoon the filling mixture into the crust. Place the remaining pie crust dough on top and crimp the edges to seal in the filling. Pierce the top with a fork to allow steam to escape. Bake for 45 minutes or until the crust is golden.

Yield: 8 servings

*RANDALL'S ORDINARY*

# Buttermilk Mousse and Raspberries under a Lace of Almonds

### MOUSSE
½ cup sugar
1 cup buttermilk
  Juice of 1 medium lime
⅓ cup Grand Marnier
2 tablespoons unflavored powdered gelatin
1 teaspoon pure vanilla extract
1 cup heavy cream

### ALMOND LACE
¼ cup sugar
2 tablespoons very finely ground
  almonds
1 tablespoon all-purpose flour
1 tablespoon unsalted butter,
  melted
2 tablespoons orange juice

### RASPBERRY SAUCE
10 ounces frozen raspberries
3 tablespoons heavy cream
2 tablespoons Grand Marnier
2 ounces fresh raspberries for
  garnish
  Confectioners' sugar for garnish

Prepare the mousse. In a medium-size bowl, mix together the sugar and buttermilk until creamy. In a small saucepan, combine the lime juice, Grand Marnier, and gelatin powder, stirring until the powder is softened. Place the saucepan over low heat and keep stirring until the gelatin is dissolved. Add the vanilla. Set aside.

In the bowl of an electric mixer, beat the heavy cream until stiff. Stir the gelatin mixture into the buttermilk mixture, then gently fold in the whipped cream. Cover and chill in the refrigerator until firm, about 1 hour.

Prepare the almond lace. Mix all of the ingredients and set aside, at room temperature, for 30 minutes. Preheat the oven to 450°. Generously butter a baking sheet and, with the back of a spoon, spread thin circles (about 3½ inches) of the almond mixture (well spaced). Bake about 4 to 5 minutes or until they are a light golden color. Remove the baking sheet from the oven and quickly, but carefully, remove the almond lace with a spatula and place on a plate.

Prepare the raspberry sauce by puréeing the frozen raspberries in a blender. Strain the purée through a fine sieve and return the purée to a bowl. Whisk in the heavy cream and the Grand Marnier. This will lighten the color of the sauce and show off the color of the fresh raspberries when served.

For the presentation, divide the mousse into 3 equal portions. Place a pool of the raspberry sauce on a large plate. Carefully place each portion of mousse in the center of the plate and, using a tablespoon, shape each into a quenelle shape. Crown the trio of mousse dumplings with an almond lace and decorate with the fresh berries. Dust lightly with confectioners' sugar.

Yield: 3 servings

*CHÂTEAU DU SUREAU*

## Bird's Nest Pudding

*The unusual name for this delicious variation of baked stuffed apples in a custard refers to the raisins in the apples, or the bird eggs in a nest. So it was named that way in Colonial times, and so it is still today at this very special inn.*

6 to 8 small tart apples, cored
1½ cups golden raisins (or enough to fill the centers of all the apples)
½ cup sugar
1½ teaspoons all-purpose flour
1½ cups milk
3 eggs
Chopped walnuts
Grated nutmeg
Freshly whipped cream

Preheat the oven to 350°. Place the apples in a shallow baking dish and fill the centers with the raisins. In a bowl, mix together the sugar, flour, milk, and eggs, and pour the mixture into the dish, being certain to get some in the center of the apples. Sprinkle the walnuts and nutmeg overtop.

Bake for 1½ hours. (Test the apples and custard for doneness after an hour.) Serve topped with whipped cream.

Yield: 6 to 8 servings

*RANDALL'S ORDINARY*

# Individual Red Raspberry Trifles

*Trifles were very popular during Victorian times. They still are today because they are easy to make and set a stunning table. Picture one of these colorful desserts at each place setting.*

CUSTARD
¾ cup sugar
3 tablespoons cornstarch
¼ teaspoon salt
2¼ cups milk
6 egg yolks
3 tablespoons butter
2 teaspoons pure vanilla extract

TRIFLE
1 plain pound cake
8 to 10 coconut macaroons
½ cup cream sherry or
  amaretto liqueur
1 cup red raspberry preserves
½ cup pecan pieces
1 cup fresh red raspberries
  Fresh whipped cream

## Note:

If you prefer, you can make the custard with 2 (5.9-ounce) packages of instant vanilla pudding. Combine the pudding mix with 1 quart of whole milk and whisk until it is completely blended and thickened. Chill until ready to build the trifle.

Prepare the custard. In a heavy saucepan, combine the sugar, cornstarch, and salt. Stir in the milk and cook over medium heat, stirring constantly, until thick and bubbly. Cook and stir 2 minutes more and then remove from the heat. Gradually stir about 1 cup of the hot mixture into the egg yolks and mix well. Pour the egg yolk and pudding mixture back into the saucepan with the remaining hot mixture. Return the saucepan to the stove and cook 1 to 2 minutes more. Remove from the heat. Stir in the butter and vanilla until the butter just melts. Cover with clear plastic wrap and refrigerate.

Prepare and assemble the trifle ingredients. Cut the pound cake into ½-inch cubes. Crumble the macaroons and set aside. Set up 6 to 8 wide-mouth wine glasses and layer the trifle ingredients in each glass in the amount indicated as follows: for layer 1, place ½ cup of the cubed pound cake, with a splash of the sherry in the bottom of each glass. Next, spoon ⅓ cup of the custard over the cake, followed by a tablespoon of the red raspberry preserves. For layer 3, sprinkle 1 teaspoon of the pecan pieces and ¼ cup of the macaroon crumbles. Next, place ½ cup of the pound cake cubes, then ⅓ cup of the custard. For the last layer, place 1 tablespoon of the red raspberry preserves overtop and then a generous portion of whipped cream topped with fresh red raspberries. Chill for 1 hour.

Yield: 6 to 8 servings

*VICTORIAN VILLA*

188

# Baked Custard in Chocolate Phyllo Shells with Fresh Berries

*CUSTARD*
½ vanilla bean
4 cups heavy cream
½ cup sugar
7 egg yolks

*PHYLLO SHELLS*
½ cup sugar
½ cup cocoa

8 sheets phyllo dough
1 cup unsalted butter, melted

*ASSEMBLY*
1 pint assorted fresh berries of
   choice
Sugar

Preheat the oven to 350°. Scrape the seeds from the half of the vanilla bean into the heavy cream. Heat the cream and vanilla in a medium heavy-bottomed saucepan.

In a bowl, whisk together the sugar and the egg yolks. Slowly whisk the hot cream into the yolk-and-sugar mixture. Pour the mixture through a fine-meshed strainer and then into an 8- to 10-cup baking dish. Bake in a water bath for about 45 minutes or until barely set. Refrigerate until cool. Leave the oven on.

Prepare the phyllo shells. In a mixing bowl, sift together the sugar and cocoa. On a flat surface, brush 1 sheet of phyllo with the melted butter and sprinkle lightly with the cocoa sugar. Turn the phyllo over and repeat the process. Layer the second sheet over the first and press smoothly together so that they adhere to each other. Repeat the procedure until there are 4 sheets, making sure to brush and sprinkle the top of the last sheet. Using a pizza cutter, cut the phyllo into 4 squares. Fit each square carefully into tart rings that are 4 inches in diameter and 1½ inches high. Then place in the freezer for at least 30 minutes.

Fill the phyllo shells with foil or parchment and pie weights. Bake for 12 to 14 minutes or until slightly crisp. Let cool and remove the parchment, weights, and rings. Repeat the process to make 8 servings.

To assemble the dish, remove the skin off the top of the cooled custard. Place a few assorted berries into each phyllo and then scoop the custard into each, dividing the mixture evenly among the 8 shells. Sprinkle with sugar, and if desired, caramelize with a kitchen torch.

Yield: 8 servings

*SAN YSIDRO RANCH*

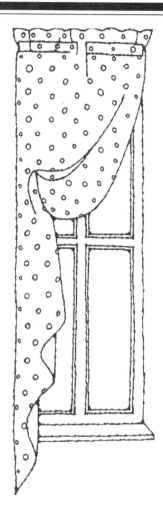

## Warm Cranberry Napoleons

*It is nice when a recipe comes along that is simple to assemble, makes use of not-so-common ingredients—such as the cranberries in this dish—and tastes and looks fabulous.*

1 orange (seeded)
12 ounces fresh or frozen cranberries (thawed if frozen)
½ cup dried currants
2 cups loosely packed dark
  brown sugar
1½ cups raspberry vinegar
1 teaspoon cinnamon

½ teaspoon ground cloves
½ teaspoon salt
⅛ teaspoon black pepper
6 puff pastry shells (3- to 3½-
  inch)
1 cup chopped walnuts, toasted
1 quart vanilla ice cream

Cut the orange into eighths and place the fruit (skin and all) in the food processor. Pulse the orange until finely chopped. Place the orange in a small saucepan along with the cranberries, currants, sugar, raspberry vinegar, cinnamon, cloves, and salt and pepper. Over low heat, simmer until the cranberries open up. The mixture will be chunky, almost like a chutney. Remove the saucepan from the heat, and stir in the walnuts.

Cut the puff pastry shells in half horizontally. Place the bottom half on a plate and top with 1 scoop of vanilla ice cream and 2 table-spoons of the hot cranberry mixture. Place the other half of the puff pastry overtop. Add a little more cranberry sauce. Top with chopped walnuts. Serve immediately. Repeat the process to complete 6 desserts.
  Yield: 6 servings

*ANTRIM 1844*

# White Chocolate Mousse in Pecan Lace Baskets

**MOUSSE**

12 ounces quality white chocolate
½ cup freshly squeezed orange
   juice
3 pounds unsalted butter
3 cups heavy cream
6 extra large eggs, separated
   (whites only)
5 tablespoons water
3 tablespoons light corn syrup

**BASKETS**

1 cup firmly packed light brown
   sugar
¾ cup light corn syrup
¾ cup unsalted butter
1½ cups finely chopped pecans
1 cup cake flour

**GARNISH**

1 pint fresh raspberries, puréed
1 medium mango, peeled, pitted, and puréed
1½ cups quality chocolate sauce
   Fresh mint

In a double boiler, melt the white chocolate with the orange juice and the
butter. Remove from the heat and let stand for 10 minutes. In a chilled
mixing bowl, whip the heavy cream until soft peaks form, then refrigerate.

Meanwhile, begin whipping the egg whites to soft peaks in the
bowl of an electric mixer. While the mixer is running, heat the water
and corn syrup in a small saucepan. Heat until 238° on a candy thermometer or just after it begins to boil. Slowly add this corn-syrup mixture to the egg whites and beat on high until cool, about 5 minutes.

Fold the white chocolate mixture and the chilled whipped cream
into the egg whites until blended evenly. Let this mixture cool in the
refrigerator for 1 hour or until assembling the baskets at serving time.

Meanwhile, make the pecan lace baskets. In a medium saucepan,
make the basket dough by bringing the sugar, corn syrup, and butter to
a boil, stirring constantly with a wooden spoon. When the mixture
reaches a boil, add the pecans and the flour. Allow the mixture to cool.

Preheat the oven to 325°. Coat a baking sheet with nonstick cooking spray. Once the dough has cooled, form into 1-ounce balls (2 tablespoons) and place on the baking sheet about 8 inches apart. Bake for
12 minutes or until golden brown. Allow to cool slightly and then
remove with a spatula. Immediately fold each piece over the top of a
soup can (10¾-ounce) to shape into baskets. Set aside and let cool.

When the baskets have cooled, about 30 minutes, pour the puréed
raspberries and mango onto each serving plate and add the chocolate sauce
in any fashion you wish. Add a basket to the center of each plate and scoop
the white chocolate mousse into the basket. Garnish with fresh mint.

Yield: 10 servings

*BEE & THISTLE INN*

# Stonehedge Inn's Silk Towers

*It is a lot of fun to make this dessert, and although it is most artistic, you do not have to be an artist to create this tower-like mousse.*

### MOUSSE
- 3 egg yolks
- ½ to ¾ cup sugar
- 2 cups heavy cream
- ¼ cup plus 2 tablespoons Grand Marnier

### CHOCOLATE
- 8 ounces quality white chocolate
- 16 ounces quality dark chocolate

### GARNISH
- Whipped cream
- Chocolate curls
- Fresh mint
- Berries of choice

Place the egg yolks in the top of a double boiler over medium heat. With an electric mixer, beat them, slowly adding the sugar until ribbons form. Beat the mixture over the heat until it reaches 160°. Take off the stove and continue beating until the mixture cools. Set aside.

In another bowl, whip the heavy cream until stiff peaks form. Stir in the Grand Mariner. Combine the 2 liquids. Using 7-ounce plastic cups as molds, fill each cup with the mixture and freeze the soufflé until frozen through, about 2 hours.

Using an upside down empty 7-ounce cup as a guide, cut pieces of parchment paper to fit around the outside of the cup so that it meets at the sides but does not overlap. The top of the paper should come above the cup as well. The parchment paper will resemble a cone, narrower at the top; wider at the bottom.

Lay the 6 pieces of cone-shaped paper on a flat surface. In a double boiler, melt both the white and dark chocolate separately. Fill 2 separate pastry bags with the chocolate when melted, fitting the bags with a number 3 or 4 round tip. Now, have some fun à la Picasso and make a design on the parchment papers. Using the white chocolate first, squiggle all over the parchment. Follow with the dark chocolate, so that very few holes are visible through the design. The chocolates should resemble an intertwined mixture of film or videotape that has dropped to the floor in curvaceous bundles.

Remove the mousse from the freezer, and with a paring knife, loosen the sides of the mousse from the cup. Cut off the bottom of the cup. Push out the mousse and place it on top of the chocolate design. Wrap the chocolate-covered paper around the mousse, being sure not to overlap the edges. When all are done, place them back in the freezer to set the chocolate and keep the mousse frozen, about 30 minutes.

Remove the mousse from the freezer and unwrap the paper. Place the frozen mousse, covered with the chocolate, onto a serving plate. Fill the remaining space at the top of the mousse with whipped cream and chocolate curls if desired. Place a bouquet of mint and a berry of choice at the foot of the dessert.

Yield: 6 servings

*PASTRY CHEF*
*BARBARA TANNENBAUM*

Step 1.

Parchment paper

Paper

Plastic cup

step 2.

White chocolate

Dark chocolate

Step 3.

# Fresh Berry and White Chocolate Mousse Miniterrines

*Easy to assemble, this terrine offers an elegant way to serve fresh berries in season. You actually will be layering a mousse with berries and letting it set (about one to two hours) before serving it with a trio of sauces: a dark and a white chocolate sauce and a raspberry sauce.*

TERRINE
1 pint each fresh strawberries
   (hulled and sliced),
   raspberries and blackberries
7 ounces white chocolate
3 sheets unflavored gelatin
2 eggs
1 egg yolk
¼ cup sugar
2 tablespoons Chambord liqueur
1 pint heavy cream

SAUCES
1½ cups heavy cream
8 ounces dark chocolate
8 ounces white chocolate
1 cup raspberries
½ cup sugar
1 tablespoon water

Combine the cleaned berries in a bowl and set aside.

Melt the white chocolate and keep warm.

In a medium bowl, soak the gelatin in enough cold water to cover.

In a stainless steel mixing bowl, over a bowl or pot of hot water, whip the eggs, egg yolk, sugar, and Chambord until the mixture doubles in volume and becomes silky. Set aside.

Squeeze the water out of the gelatin leaves and then melt the gelatin over warm heat. Whip the gelatin vigorously into the egg mixture. Fold the melted chocolate into the egg mixture until totally combined.

In the bowl of an electric mixer, whip the heavy cream to soft peaks. Fold the cream into the egg mixture. Place a layer of mousse in the bottom of a miniloaf pan. Add a layer of mixed berries, followed by another layer of berries, and then more mousse. Keep adding layers until you reach the top, ending with a layer of berries. Repeat the procedure in a second miniloaf pan. Place in the refrigerator until set, about 1 to 2 hours.

Meanwhile, prepare the sauces. To make the dark chocolate sauce, scald 1 cup of the heavy cream in a small saucepan. Add the dark chocolate and stir to incorporate. Remove from heat; allow to cool. To make the white chocolate sauce, repeat the procedure, but use only ½ cup of cream.

For the raspberry sauce, place the berries, sugar, and water in a small saucepan. Bring to a boil and then turn down to a simmer for 5 minutes. Purée the mixture in a food processor until smooth. Strain.

To serve, cut each terrine into 4 slices. Pool the dark chocolate sauce in the bottom of each individual serving plate. Top with some raspberry sauce and the white chocolate in the center. Pull the white chocolate out to the edges of the plate with a knife, to form a decorative garnish. Place a slice of the terrine in the center and serve.

Yield: 8 servings

Note: It is best to pour the finished sauces into squeeze bottles to make it easier to assemble the dessert later.

*CLIFTON COUNTRY INN*

# Spiced Apple-and-Nut Cake with Toffee Sauce

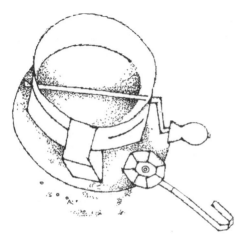

Cake

1½ cups sugar
⅓ cup butter, melted
⅓ cup vegetable oil
2 eggs
2½ cups all-purpose flour
1 teaspoon salt
½ teaspoon ground cloves
1 teaspoon freshly ground nutmeg
½ teaspoon allspice
1 teaspoon cinnamon
1 tablespoon plus 1 teaspoon
   baking soda
2 cups unsweetened applesauce
1 cup toasted walnuts, coarsely
   chopped
3 medium tart apples, washed,
   cored, and chopped

SAUCE

2 cups firmly packed light
   brown sugar
½ cup unsalted butter
1 cup cream
1 teaspoon apple brandy,
   optional

Preheat the oven to 350°. Make the cake. Lightly grease and flour two 8- or 9-inch round cake pans. In a large bowl, cream together the sugar, butter, and oil until light. Add the eggs and mix. In another bowl, sift the flour, salt, and spices together. Dissolve the baking soda in the applesauce and add it to the creamed mixture. Blend for about 1 minute. Add the flour mixture and mix until blended. Fold in the nuts and the apple pieces.

Pour the mixture into the prepared pans and bake for about 40 to 45 minutes or until a tester comes out clean. Serve with toffee sauce.

Make the sauce. Combine all the ingredients in a nonstick saucepan over medium heat. Bring to a boil, whisking as needed. Remove from the heat. Serve warm. The sauce can be stored in the refrigerator and reheated.

Yield: 8 servings

Note: If you like, you can top off the toffee sauce by placing a dollop of freshly whipped heavy cream on top.

*SETTLERS INN*

# Coffee Dacquoise

*A cake light in texture, this gâteau from the south of France is named after the people (the Dacquois) of Dax. It consists of meringue layers with nuts and is held together with whipped cream.*

**MERINGUE**
1½ cups hazelnuts, toasted and
    finely crushed
1 teaspoon cornstarch
6 egg whites
¼ teaspoon cream of tartar
¾ cup sugar

**FILLING**
6 egg yolks
1 teaspoon instant coffee gran-
    ules
2 teaspoons pure vanilla extract
½ cup sugar
¼ cup unsweetened cocoa pow-
    der
¾ cup butter softened
1 cup heavy cream
2 teaspoons powdered sugar

Preheat the oven to 275° degrees. Combine the nuts and the cornstarch, and set aside. Make the meringue layers. In a large mixer bowl, beat the egg whites with the cream of tartar until soft peaks form and tips curl. Gradually add the sugar until stiff peaks form. Fold in the nut mixture.

Cover 2 baking sheets with aluminum foil. Divide the meringue in half and spoon each half onto its own baking sheet. Then spread each half out into a 9-inch circle. Bake for 20 to 25 minutes. Cool.

Meanwhile, make the buttercream filling. In a large mixer bowl, stir the egg yolks, coffee, and vanilla together; let stand for 5 minutes to dissolve the coffee granules. Stir in the sugar and the cocoa. Beat at high speed for 4 minutes. Add the butter, 1 tablespoon at a time, beating until the mixture is fluffy. Chill. In a separate bowl, whip the heavy cream until stiff.

To assemble, pipe half of the buttercream in a border around the outside edge of 1 meringue layer. Fill the center with the whipped cream, then top with the other meringue. Sprinkle with confectioners' sugar, and pipe the remaining buttercream around the edge of the cake.

Yield: 8 to 10 servings

*SIGN OF THE SORREL HORSE*

*Making Your Own Gourmet Coffee*

Sprinkle spices or pour liqueur into your ground beans. Drip or perk as usual.

# Old Fashioned Chocolate Cake

*Sauerkraut in chocolate cake is an old way of keeping in the moisture. It is the secret ingredient that really makes this cake moist and delicious.*

CAKE
½ cup butter
1½ cups sugar
3 eggs
1 teaspoon vanilla extract
2 cups sifted all-purpose flour
1½ teaspoons baking soda
¾ teaspoon cream of tartar
¼ teaspoon salt
½ cup cocoa powder
1 cup water
2 cups, or 1 pound, sauerkraut,
    drained, rinsed, and chopped

FROSTING
6 ounces semisweet chocolate
¼ cup butter
½ cup sour cream
1 teaspoon vanilla extract
¼ teaspoon salt
2 cups confectioners'
    sugar, sifted

Preheat the oven to 350°. Prepare the cake. In a large mixing bowl, cream the butter and sugar until light. Beat in the eggs, 1 at a time. Add the vanilla. Sift together all of the dry ingredients. Add them to the creamed mixture alternately with the water. Stir the sauerkraut into the batter and mix well. Bake in a greased and floured 9x13x2-inch pan for 35 to 40 minutes. Cool.

Prepare the frosting. In the top of a double boiler, melt the chocolate and the butter over low heat. Remove from the heat and blend in the sour cream, vanilla, and salt. Gradually add the confectioners' sugar. Stir until smooth. Frost the top and the sides of the cooled cake.

Yield: 10 to 12 servings

*RANDALL'S ORDINARY*

# Chocolate Terrine with Espresso Sauce

*The terrine needs a day to chill in the refrigerator and the sauce is made just before serving. You will need a small piece of cheesecloth to envelope the espresso beans, plunging the package into the sauce to infuse the coffee.*

TERRINE
- 9 ounces bittersweet quality chocolate
- ½ cup plus 1 tablespoon unsalted butter at room temperature
- 5 eggs, separated
- ½ cup confectioners' sugar

SAUCE
- 1 vanilla bean
- 2 cups milk
- 4 egg yolks
- ½ cup sugar
- ¼ cup ground espresso beans
  Raspberries and fresh mint for garnish

Melt the chocolate in a double boiler. Stir in the butter. Add the 5 egg yolks, 1 at a time.

In the bowl of an electric mixer, beat the egg whites until medium-stiff peaks form. Add the confectioners' sugar and continue beating for 30 seconds at high speed. Fold ⅓ of the egg whites into the chocolate. Then fold in the rest. Pour the mixture into a parchment-paper-lined terrine or 8x5-inch loaf pan and refrigerate overnight.

Just before serving time, prepare the espresso sauce. Split the vanilla bean in half and scrape away the seeds. In a small nonstick saucepan, bring the seeds, the vanilla pod, and the milk to a boil. Remove from the heat.

Meanwhile, in a small bowl, mix together the yolks and the sugar to form thin ribbons. Slowly add the egg yolks to the milk. Return the sauce to the heat. Heat gently until the sauce coats the back of a spoon. Enclose the espresso beans in cheesecloth and tie with a kitchen string. Plunge the bean cloth into the sauce. Allow the sauce to cool. Squeeze the cloth to extract as much coffee flavor as possible and then discard. Stir the sauce to incorporate the coffee flavor.

Unmold the terrine. Cut the terrine with a hot knife. Arrange 2 slices on a chilled plate. Spoon the sauce all around. Garnish with raspberries and fresh mint.

Yield: 8 to 10 servings

*OLD DROVERS INN*

# Mocha Chocolate Mousse Cake

*Use a bakery-bought sponge cake and the recipe becomes a cinch to make with dramatic results. The final dessert will be about six inches high. It is impressive and delicious.*

1 10-inch round sponge cake
¼ to ½ cup Kahlua liqueur
1 4-ounce package instant chocolate pudding mix
1 cup cold espresso
1½ cups cold milk
1 teaspoon brandy flavoring or brandy

1½ cups nondairy whipping cream, beaten until stiff peaks form
1 teaspoon instant coffee or espresso powder
2 cups shaved semisweet chocolate

Cut the sponge cake in half and sprinkle each half with the Kahlua. Set aside.

To make the mousse, pour the chocolate pudding mix into a stainless steel mixing bowl. Add the cold espresso, milk, and brandy flavoring. Using an electric hand mixer, blend on medium speed for 2 minutes. Let stand for 10 minutes. Fold half of the whipped cream into the chocolate mixture.

Mix the remaining whipped cream with the instant coffee or espresso powder. Set aside for the topping.

To assemble, spread the bottom half of the sponge cake with half of the chocolate mousse. Sprinkle with half of the shaved chocolate. Place the remaining layer of the sponge cake on top of the chocolate mousse. Follow with the remaining mousse, spreading the chocolate all around the layer and adding more shaved chocolate, leaving a little for garnishing the whipped cream. Finish with a garnish of the coffee-flavored whipped cream and sprinkle the remaining chocolate shavings overtop. Chill in the refrigerator for at least 1 hour before serving.

Yield: 12 to 16 slices

*HERITAGE PARK B&B INN*

# Layered Almond Meringue Cake with Chocolate Filling

*The cake is easy to make but requires preparation a day ahead of serving time in order to set in the refrigerator.*

**MERINGUE**
- 4 egg whites
- 1½ cups sugar
- ⅓ cup blanched ground almonds

**FILLING**
- 2 egg whites
- ½ cup sugar
- 2 tablespoons sweetened cocoa powder
- 1 cup butter, softened
- 4 ounces semisweet chocolate, melted

Preheat the oven to 250°. Cut 4 rounds of aluminum foil, 8 inches in diameter. Lightly grease each round.

Whip the egg whites until stiff peaks form, gradually adding the sugar and the almonds as the eggs begin to hold their shape. Spread the meringue on the foil rounds with a rubber spatula. Transfer the rounds to a baking sheet and bake 15 minutes or until the meringue is dry. Carefully turn the meringues over and bake an additional 5 minutes or until dry.

Prepare the filling. In the top of a double boiler, over hot but not boiling water, beat the egg whites until foamy. Gradually whisk in the sugar, cocoa, butter, and melted chocolate. Beat the eggs until thick and creamy, then remove the mixture from the heat and cool in the refrigerator about 30 minutes.

To assemble the cake, reserve some of the chocolate filling for the icing. Place a meringue layer on the bottom of a cake plate and spread it with chocolate. Top with another meringue circle, pressing down lightly so that the meringue nestles gently into the chocolate. Spread the top of the layer with chocolate and repeat the layering process until all of the meringues are used. Carefully ice the top with the reserved cooled filling. Refrigerate the cake at least 24 hours.

Yield: 6 to 8 servings

*CHALET SUZANNE*

# Chocolate Tart with Wild Blackberry Sauce

PASTRY
½ cup unsalted butter
½ cup sugar
1 teaspoon pure vanilla extract
⅛ teaspoon salt
⅓ cup unsweetened cocoa powder, sifted
¾ cup all-purpose flour

FILLING
10 ounces semisweet chocolate, cut into small pieces
1¼ cups heavy cream
3 tablespoons cognac

SAUCE
2 cups wild blackberries
¼ cup sugar
1 tablespoon fresh lemon juice
3 tablespoons cognac
Confectioners' sugar for dusting

Prepare the pastry. In a food processor, combine the butter, sugar, vanilla, and salt and mix until creamy. Add the cocoa and continue to process until the mixture becomes dark and smooth. Add the flour. Using a pulsing method, continue mixing until the flour is incorporated and the mixture becomes doughy.

Spread the dough into a large, flat, disk shape on top of a large piece of plastic wrap. Enclose the dough in the plastic and refrigerate for at least 45 minutes. (The dough can be stored in this way for up to 3 days.)

When ready to use, remove the dough from the refrigerator. When the dough warms enough to be rollable, yet still firm, roll it out between the pieces of plastic wrap until it is about 1/8-inch thick and 10 to 12 inches in diameter. Slowly remove the top piece of plastic. Pick up the dough and turn it over into a 9-inch tart pan with removable bottom. Use the plastic wrap (now on the top side of the dough) to ease the dough carefully into the corners of the tart pan. Pinch off the dough at the upper rim of the pan. Peel away the plastic wrap very slowly, and inspect to see that the pan is evenly lined with the dough. Patch if necessary. Cover and refrigerate for at least 30 minutes before baking (can be much longer, if desired).

Preheat the oven to 350°. Pierce the bottom of the tart pastry with the points of a fork. Bake until the pastry is set around the edges, about 12 to 15 minutes (it may still look slightly wet or undone in the center). Remove the pastry from the oven and cool on a rack. Be certain that the pastry shell is completely cooled before using.

Prepare the filling. Set aside the chocolate pieces in a medium-size heatproof bowl. In a saucepan, bring the cream to a simmer over

medium heat. As soon as it begins to simmer, pour it over the chocolate pieces, and let stand briefly. Begin stirring gently until the chocolate and the cream have blended fully into a smooth mixture. Add the cognac, stirring gently until it is fully incorporated. Pour the mixture through a fine-mesh strainer directly into the cooled tart pastry shell, making sure that the chocolate fills the shell evenly. Refrigerate for 3 to 4 hours or until the filling has set. Remove the tart from the refrigerator at least 45 minutes before serving.

Make the sauce. Toss together all of the ingredients until well combined. Let marinate for 1 hour or more in the refrigerator. Remove the sauce from the refrigerator and allow it to warm to room temperature before serving.

To assemble, slice the tart and place pieces on individual serving plates. Ladle the blackberry sauce overtop. Dust with confectioners' sugar, if desired.

Yield: 8 servings

*CARTER HOUSE*

# Chocolate Mint Roulade with Fresh Raspberry Sauce

*ROULADE*
4 eggs, separated
⅔ cup sugar
1½ teaspoons pure vanilla extract
⅛ teaspoon salt
¼ teaspoon cream of tartar
½ cup all-purpose flour, sifted
¼ cup or more cocoa powder

*FILLING*
1 cup heavy cream
2 teaspoons pure mint extract
2 tablespoons white crème de menthe liqueur

*SAUCE*
3½ cups fresh raspberries (reserve a few for garnish)
¼ cup sugar
2 tablespoons freshly squeezed lemon juice

*GARNISH*
Fresh mint
Fresh whole raspberries

Prepare the roulade. Lightly grease and flour an 11x15-inch jellyroll pan. Line the bottom with parchment paper. Preheat the oven to 350°. In a large bowl, beat the egg yolks well. Add ⅓ cup of the sugar and continue to beat until the mixture is very well blended. Beat in the vanilla.

In a separate copper or stainless steel bowl, beat the egg whites until just foamy. Add the salt and cream of tartar and continue beating. When the mixture forms soft peaks, add the remaining sugar and beat until the peaks are stiff and shiny. Fold the flour into the yolk mixture gradually, then slowly add the egg white mixture, combining very gently, yet thoroughly.

Fill the prepared jellyroll pan with the batter and bake until the cake springs back when pressed gently with a finger, about 15 minutes. Cool the cake in the pan for a few minutes, then turn it out onto a towel covered with a sheet of parchment paper that has been dusted with cocoa powder. Remove the parchment paper from the bottom of the cake and trim off any crusts that may have formed during baking. Very carefully roll up the cake with the new parchment paper and secure with a towel. Let cool on a rack.

Prepare the filling. Whip all of the filling ingredients together until stiff peaks form. Set aside in a cool place.

Prepare the sauce. In a food processor, purée all of the sauce ingredients until well blended. Strain through a fine-mesh strainer and set aside.

When the cake is cool, gently unroll it. Spread the filling over the entire cake. (You will have excess cream filling; reserve it for garnish.) Roll up the cake again, discarding the parchment paper. Sift a heavy layer of cocoa powder over the entire roulade.

To make the raspberry sauce, purée raspberries in a blender with the sugar and lemon juice, just enough to make a smooth sauce. Pass through a sieve to remove seeds, if desired.

To serve, spread a pool of raspberry sauce on a plate and add a slice, about 1-inch thick, of roulade. Garnish with freshly chopped mints and fresh raspberries.

Yield: 6 to 8 servings

*CARTER HOUSE*

## Mexican Chocolate Cake with Pecan Frosting

*Since it is close to the border, Heritage Park B&B Inn utilizes many recipes with a Mexican influence. The use of buttermilk in this recipe gives it an ethnic twist, explains the inn's chef, Ralph Randau. This is an old-fashioned chocolate cake—moist and topped with a melt-in-your-mouth frosting.*

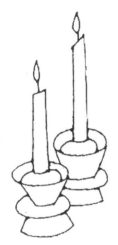

### CAKE
2 cups sifted all-purpose flour
2 cups sugar
1 teaspoon baking soda
1 teaspoon salt
1½ teaspoons cinnamon
½ teaspoon baking powder
¾ cup water
¾ cup buttermilk
½ cup shortening
2 eggs
4 ounces unsweetened chocolate, melted
1 teaspoon vanilla extract

### CHOCOLATE FROSTING
½ cup butter
2 ounces unsweetened chocolate
¼ cup whole milk
1 pound (about 3¾ cups) confectioners' sugar, sifted
1 teaspoon pure vanilla extract
1 cup finely chopped pecans

Preheat the oven to 350°. In the large bowl of an electric mixer, sift together the flour, sugar, baking soda, salt, cinnamon, and baking powder. Add the water, buttermilk, shortening, eggs, melted chocolate, and vanilla. Blend for 30 seconds at low speed, scraping the bowl occasionally. Spread the batter evenly in a greased and floured 9x13x2-inch pan or 2 9-inch round cake pans.

Bake for 40 to 45 minutes for a single large pan, or 30 to 35 minutes for 2 layer pans. Cool on wire racks.

Prepare the frosting. Combine the butter, the chocolate, and the milk in a medium saucepan. Heat until bubbles form around the edge of the pan, stirring occasionally. Remove from the heat. Add the confectioners' sugar, vanilla, and chopped pecans. Beat until the mixture becomes spreadable. (If necessary, add 1 to 2 tablespoons of milk.) Spread the frosting over the cooled cake.

Yield: 12 servings

*HERITAGE PARK B&B INN*

# White Chocolate Ravioli with Raspberry Sauce

*There's no need to cook these raviolis. They are all chocolate from the deli-
cious filling to the dough.*

FILLING
¼ cup heavy cream
6 ounces quality dark bittersweet chocolate
½ pint fresh raspberries

RAVIOLI
14 ounces quality white chocolate
½ cup light corn syrup
   Confectioners' sugar

SAUCE
2 pints fresh raspberries
¼ cup light corn syrup

Prepare the filling or ganache for the ravioli. In a small nonstick
saucepan, scald the cream. Add the dark chocolate to the cream. Mix
in the raspberries, blending until the chocolate is melted. Refrigerate
the mixture until cool but not hard.

Meanwhile, prepare the chocolate dough. Melt the white chocolate
over a double boiler. Remove it from the heat and mix it with the corn
syrup until combined. Dust with confectioners' sugar.

Use half of the dough to roll out through a pasta machine, making
it into a sheet about 1½ feet long. Dust with the powdered sugar and
repeat using the other half of the dough to form another sheet of the
same size. Lay one sheet out. Scoop out the ganache and place about
½ tablespoon at ½-inch intervals on the pasta sheet, making 2 rows.
Brush water around each mound of filling. Cover with the remaining
sheet and use your fingers to seal the 2 sheets. Use up any leftover
dough or ganache. Cut out the ravioli in squares or rounds.

In a blender or food processor, whirl until smooth the raspberries
and the corn syrup to make the sauce. Garnish the raviolis with the
fresh raspberry sauce and serve.

Yield: 24 raviolis

CHECKERBERRY INN

## Chocolate Cheesecake Muffins

**CREAM CHEESE FILLING**
3 ounces cream cheese, softened
2 tablespoons sugar

**MUFFINS**
1½ cups all-purpose flour
4½ tablespoons unsweetened
　cocoa powder
½ cup sugar

1 tablespoon baking powder
½ teaspoon salt
2 eggs, beaten
1 cup milk
½ cup oil
1 cup confectioners' sugar, for
　dusting

Grease a 12-cup muffin tin. Preheat the oven to 375°. Prepare the filling. In a small bowl, blend the cream cheese and the sugar until fluffy. Set aside.

Prepare the muffins. In a large bowl, mix well the flour, cocoa, sugar, baking powder, and salt. Create a well in the center of the dry mixture. In a separate bowl, combine the eggs, milk, and oil. Add this liquid mixture all at once to the dry mixture, stirring until very moist (the batter should be quite lumpy).

Spoon about 1 tablespoon of the muffin batter into each muffin cup. Drop 1 teaspoon of the cream cheese filling on top of each half-filled muffin cup. Then fill with more batter until each cup is ¾ full. Bake the muffins for 20 minutes. Let cool. Dust with confectioners' sugar before serving.

Yield: 1 dozen

*CARTER HOUSE*

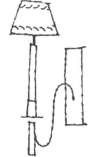

## Cream Cheese and Nut Chocolate Surprise Squares

*Chef Bertie Varner gets rave reviews when she serves this at the ranch after a tasty Texas meal. The recipe is a cinch and the taste simply divine.*

4 eggs, divided
1 18¼-ounce box German
　chocolate cake mix
½ cup margarine, cut into pieces

½ cup chopped nuts of choice
8 ounces cream cheese
1 teaspoon vanilla extract
1 pound confectioners' sugar

Preheat the oven to 350°. Beat 2 of the eggs in a large bowl. Add the cake mix, margarine, and nuts. (The mixture will be thick.)

Grease a nonstick or regular 9-inch cake pan. In another bowl, beat the remaining eggs. Add the cream cheese and vanilla and beat to

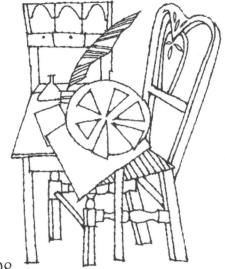

incorporate. Add the confectioners' sugar and beat by hand until smooth. Bake for 35 minutes or until a tester inserted in the center comes out clean. Do not overbake.

Yield: 8 to 10 servings

*Y. O. RANCH*

## Chocolate-Glazed Biscotti

*Biscotti are hard Italian biscuits great for dunking in a mug full of coffee, and it's perfectly acceptable.*

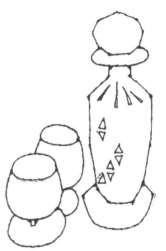

| | |
|---|---|
| 3 cups all-purpose flour | ⅓ cup olive oil |
| ¾ cup sugar | 2 tablespoons orange juice |
| ½ cup firmly packed brown sugar | 2 tablespoons light or dark rum |
| 1 tablespoon baking powder | 1 tablespoon grated orange peel |
| ¾ teaspoon salt | 1 teaspoon vanilla extract |
| 3 ounces unsweetened baking chocolate, melted and cooled | 1 cup semisweet chocolate chips |
| | 1 cup chopped almonds |
| 3 large eggs | 12 ounces white chocolate |

In a large bowl, combine the flour, sugars, baking powder, and salt. Add the unsweetened chocolate, eggs, oil, juice, rum, orange peel, and vanilla. Stir to combine. Add the chocolate chips and the almonds. Mix until the dough is well blended.

Preheat the oven to 350°. Shape the dough into a ball. Then divide the ball into 4 equal portions, shaping each section into a log about 2 inches wide by 12 to 14 inches long. Place 2 logs on each of 2 lightly greased baking sheets, and flatten the logs gently. Bake for 20 minutes. Remove from the oven and cool for 1 minute. Then cut diagonally into ½-inch-wide slices. Place the slices, cut-side down on the baking sheets and return them to the oven to bake for an additional 15 minutes or until crisp. Cool on wire racks.

Meanwhile, melt the white chocolate in a double boiler over medium heat, stirring until smooth. (Vegetable oil may be added to the chocolate 1 teaspoon at a time if the chocolate is too thick for dipping.) Dip the tip of each cookie about 1 inch into the melted chocolate to coat. Lay on a wire rack until cool and set. Store in an airtight container.

Yield: 6 dozen cookies

*GINGERBREAD MANSION INN*

# Tea-Time Petit Fours

*These bite-size confections date to the eighteenth century, to accommodate the nuances of brick ovens. After large cakes had been baked and the temperature had dropped, small items were cooked at lower temperatures or à petit four. Allow a lead time of six hours before serving to make the petit fours, as the cake base must be frozen. This recipe makes several dozen that may be frozen for later use.*

CAKE
1½ cups butter, softened
2½ cups sugar
5 eggs
1 teaspoon pure vanilla extract
1 teaspoon almond extract
2½ cups unbleached flour
½ teaspoon salt
½ teaspoon baking soda
1 cup sour cream

FROSTING
1 cup semisweet chocolate
    chips, plus 1 cup for topping
¼ cup butter
3 cups confectioners' sugar
½ cup milk

FILLING
1 12- to 14-ounce jar preserves,
    such as raspberry or apricot

Preheat the oven to 300°. Line 2 11x15-inch jellyroll pans with parchment paper. In the bowl of an electric mixer, cream the butter until fluffy. Gradually add the sugar, ½ cup at a time, and mix until very light and fluffy; add the eggs, 1 at a time, then add the vanilla and almond extracts.

In a separate bowl, sift together the flour, salt, and baking soda. Add the flour mixture to the butter mixture alternately with the sour cream. Pour equal amounts of the batter into the jellyroll pans. Bake for 25 to 30 minutes or until a tester inserted comes out clean.

Meanwhile, prepare the frosting. Melt the 1 cup of chocolate and butter in the top of a double boiler over hot, but not boiling, water. When melted and smooth, add the sugar and the milk. Stir to incorporate. Remove from the heat and beat until smooth. When the frosting is completely cooled and thickened, spread a thin layer on 1 of the cooled cakes. Follow with a thin layer of the preserves. Invert the unfrosted cake layer on top of the frosted cake, forming a sandwich. Press the 2 layers gently together. Cover with foil and freeze for 4 to 5 hours so that the cake can be cut and frosted without breaking. When cake is just frozen, melt the remaining 1 cup of chocolate. Set aside and keep warm.

Cut the frozen cake into 1-inch squares and, using a fork as a lift, dip into the melted chocolate. Transfer to a wire rack to set.

Yield: 14 dozen

Note: Additional tinted white chocolate may be piped on top of each petit four with a fanciful design of stripes or flowers.

*GINGERBREAD MANSION INN*

## Nanaimo Bars

*These are Canadian bars served at major family celebrations as a sweet tradition that unites everyone.*

BOTTOM LAYER
½ cup butter
¼ cup sugar
5 tablespoons unsweetened cocoa
1 egg, lightly beaten
1½ cups graham cracker crumbs
¾ cup coconut flakes
½ cup chopped walnuts

MIDDLE LAYER
½ cup butter
3 tablespoons milk
2 tablespoons custard powder (see note)
2 to 3 cups confectioners' sugar

TOP LAYER
4 ounces semisweet chocolate
2 tablespoons butter

Prepare the bottom layer. Melt the butter in the top of a double boiler. Add the sugar and the cocoa. Add the egg and stir until the mixture thickens slightly. Remove from the heat and add the remaining bottom-layer ingredients. Press the mixture firmly into the bottom of an 8-inch square pan. Refrigerate.

Prepare the middle layer. In a medium-size bowl, cream together well the butter, milk, custard powder, and confectioners' sugar. (This should result in a firm, not runny, frosting.) Remove bottom layer from the refrigerator, and spread the frosting over it.

Prepare the top layer. In the top of a double boiler, melt the chocolate and butter together. Spread the mixture over the second layer. Before it is completely firm, score with a knife into 24 squares. Chill completely, then cut with a sharp knife.

Yield: 24 servings

*WHITE OAK INN*

*Note:*

A product called Bird's Custard Powder is sold at some specialty food shops and supermarkets. If unavailable, mix together these ingredients to make the middle layer: 2 cups confectioners' sugar, 8 tablespoons milk, ¼ cup melted unsalted butter, and ½ teaspoon vanilla.

## Rowell's Inn Old Molasses Cookies

¾ cup shortening, softened
1 cup sugar, plus more for
  rolling
¼ cup dark molasses
1 egg
2 cups all-purpose flour

½ teaspoon salt
2 teaspoons baking soda
½ teaspoon cloves
½ teaspoon ginger
1 teaspoon cinnamon

Preheat the oven to 325°. In a large bowl, cream together the shortening and sugar. Add the molasses and the egg, beating until well mixed. In a separate bowl, sift together the dry ingredients. Blend the dry ingredients into the molasses mixture, just until flour and spices are incorporated.

Roll the dough into balls, using about 1 teaspoon of dough per ball. Drop each ball into the sugar, rolling until the ball is covered.

Place the sugared balls onto a greased, nonstick cookie sheet. Bake for about 15 minutes or until lightly browned.

Yield: 4 dozen

*ROWELL'S INN*

## Mocha Chocolate Chip Cookies

*Chef Patrick Runkel cooks all kinds of exotic cuisine at the inn, including fabulous desserts and unusual breads. These are his favorite cookies, which he said everyone must try, because inn guests insist consistently that they are the best they've ever had.*

3 cups semisweet chocolate
  chips
½ cup butter
4 ounces unsweetened chocolate
4 eggs, room temperature
1½ cups sugar

1½ tablespoons instant
  coffee granules
2 teaspoons vanilla extract
½ cup all-purpose flour
½ teaspoon baking powder
½ teaspoon salt
2 cups chopped pecans

Preheat the oven to 350°. In the top of a double boiler, melt 1½ cups of the chocolate chips, the butter, and the unsweetened chocolate. Stir until smooth. Remove from the water.

In the bowl of an electric mixer, beat the eggs, sugar, coffee granules, and vanilla extract at high speed for 2 minutes. Add the melted chocolate mixture and stir, combining well.

In a separate bowl, combine the flour, baking powder, and salt; stir into the batter. Fold in the remaining 1½ cups chocolate chips and the pecans. Drop by the tablespoonful about ½ inch apart onto baking sheets lined with parchment (or use nonstick cookie sheets). Bake 8 minutes until crackled and shiny on the outside and still soft inside. Don't overbake. Cool before removing from the baking sheets.

Yield: 3 to 4 dozen

*OCTOBER COUNTRY INN*

## Danish Pretzel Cookies

*The Danish people settled heavily in the Ferndale area where Gingerbread Mansion chef Larry Martin was raised by Danish parents. The kringle, or butter cookie shaped like a pretzel, is a traditional sweet made by the Danes and served to this day at the bed and breakfast as a salute to the area's heritage.*

|  |  |
|---|---|
| 1 pound butter, softened | ¾ cup heavy cream |
| 5½ cups all-purpose flour | 3 egg whites, slightly beaten |
| 3 egg yolks, slightly beaten | 1 cup sugar |

In a large bowl, cream together the butter and the flour. In a separate bowl, mix the egg yolks with the cream, then incorporate this mixture into the butter mixture, blending well. Form the dough into a ball, wrap, and chill for 1 hour.

Preheat the oven to 375°. Divide the dough into thirds. Roll each section into a 9x14-inch rectangle, ⅛-inch thick. Brush the tops of each rectangle with the egg whites. Using a crinkle-cut pastry roller or pizza cutter, cut each rectangle into ½x9-inch strips. Twist each strip into a pretzel shape and turn eggwhite-side down onto a plate filled with the sugar. Turn the pretzel right-side up and place on an ungreased baking sheet. Bake 8 to 10 minutes or until lightly browned. Cool on a wire rack and store in an airtight container.

Yield: 9 dozen cookies

*GINGERBREAD MANSION INN*

# The Mansion's Gingerbread Scones

### DOUGH
4 cups all-purpose flour
3 tablespoons firmly packed
  brown sugar
4 teaspoons baking powder
½ teaspoon salt
½ teaspoon cream of tartar
2 teaspoons ground ginger
1 teaspoon cinnamon
¾ cup butter
1 large egg, separated
⅓ cup dark molassses
½ cup pumpkin purée
¾ cup half-and-half

### TOPPING
½ cup chopped pecans or more
  or less for spreading
½ cup brown sugar, or more or
  less for sprinkling

Preheat the oven to 400°. Grease 2 baking sheets or use nonstick pans. In a large bowl, combine the flour, brown sugar, baking powder, salt, cream of tartar, and spices. Using a pastry blender, cut in the butter until the mixture resembles coarse crumbs.

In a small bowl, beat the egg white slightly and set aside for use later.

In a medium bowl, beat the egg yolk with a fork. Stir in the molasses, pumpkin, and the half-and-half. Add the yolk mixture to the dry ingredients and mix lightly with a fork until the mixture clings together and forms a soft dough.

Turn the dough out onto a lightly floured board and knead gently several times. Divide the dough in half. Pat each half out into an 8-inch circle. In a small bowl, mix together the topping ingredients. Brush the dough circles with the egg white and then sprinkle them with the topping mixture. Cut each circle into 8 wedges. Place the wedges on the baking sheets and bake for 15 to 18 minutes or until golden brown.

Yield: 16 scones

*GINGERBREAD MANSION INN*

## Tavern Sticky Buns

½ cup sugar
1½ teaspoons salt
½ cup butter
1 cup mashed potatoes (reserve
   1½ cups of potato water and
   keep warm)
1 package active dry yeast
2 eggs
7 cups all-purpose flour

3 cups firmly packed brown
   sugar
6 tablespoons pure maple syrup
½ cup finely chopped walnuts
¼ cup butter, melted
2 cups cinnamon-sugar mixture
   (1½ cups sugar and ½ cup cinnamon)

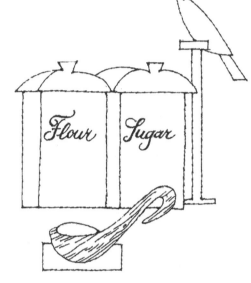

Add the sugar, salt, and butter to the hot potatoes. When the mixture is lukewarm, add the yeast, eggs, and the 1½ cups reserved potato water. Stir in the flour to make a stiff dough. Knead well. Put the dough in a greased bowl and let it rise until it doubles in bulk (about 45 minutes to 1 hour). Punch down the dough and refrigerate. (This will keep several days.)

When ready to use, preheat the oven to 350°. Butter three 8-inch nonstick cake pans. Cover the bottom of each pan with 1 cup brown sugar. Drizzle each with the maple syrup. Sprinkle each with walnuts. Roll out the dough into a rectangle about ⅓-inch thick. Brush the dough with melted butter. Sprinkle with the sugar and cinnamon mixture. Roll the dough, like a jellyroll, and slice it into 24 ½-inch round slices. Place the circles side by side in the pans. Let them rise until they double in bulk. Bake for 25 to 30 minutes or until a toothpick inserted comes out clean. Invert on a plate while the buns are still hot.

Yield: 24

*ROWELL'S INN*

# Maple Ice Cream

*The philosophy of Settlers Inn is to use almost all organic products and ingredients made locally. Chef/Owner Grant Geinzlinger advises us to take the time out to search for small farms and cottage food industries in our own areas. The maple syrup in this recipe came from Journey's End Farm, not far from the inn.*

1½ pounds cream cheese (3 8-
    ounce blocks), softened
 4 cups sour cream (2 pounds)
1¾ cups loosely packed light
    brown sugar
 ½ teaspoon salt

2 cups pure maple syrup
   (grade B dark)
1½ teaspoons vanilla extract
1½ teaspoons maple extract
1 cup milk
3 cups heavy cream

In a large bowl, blend the cream cheese, sour cream, and brown sugar until smooth. Add the salt, syrup, vanilla, and maple flavoring, and blend. Add the milk and the heavy cream and stir until mixture is well blended. Transfer the mixture to an ice cream maker; then chill and freeze it according to the ice cream machine instructions.

Yield: 1 gallon

Note: It is best to make the mix the day before serving to let the flavors incorporate. Or, complete the recipe, and make the ice cream the day before, too.

*SETTLERS INN*

# Strawberry Yogurt Sherbet

*Chef Barrie Aycock has created a winner with this unusual sherbet made with—of all things—yogurt!*

2½ pints fresh strawberries
1¾ cups sugar
1½ tablespoons fresh lemon juice
 1  cup plain nonfat yogurt

Wash and slice the strawberries. Toss with the sugar and lemon juice and allow to sit at room temperature for about 1 hour.

Purée the strawberry mixture in a blender or food processor; add the yogurt and blend until smooth. Freeze in an ice cream churn or in shallow trays until firm.

Remove from the freezer and thaw slightly. Transfer to the bowl of an electric mixer and beat until smooth. Refreeze until ready to use.

Yield: 2 quarts

*GLEN-ELLA SPRINGS INN*

# INN THE CUPBOARD

## Roasted Tomatoes

*The delicious flavor of roasted tomatoes may enhance a number of your recipes or you may enjoy them as a side dish as I demonstrated on the show. I turn the tomatoes into a sandwich, between two pieces of crusty bread, and add a sprinkling of oregano and garlic. These may also be served as an appetizer by spreading on slices of French bread, crostini-style. Use your outdoor grill to roast the tomatoes.*

6 whole medium tomatoes
⅓ cup olive oil

1 teaspoon red pepper flakes

With skins on, roast the tomatoes on the grill until the skins start to sag. (Do not blacken as you do with bell peppers.) Purée the roasted tomatoes with a fork. Add the olive oil and the pepper flakes. Add to your favorite recipe or spread onto bread.

Yield: 3 to 4 cups.

## Nasturtium Butter

*Edible flowers are not just for garnish, as Chef/owner Christi Carter's recipe proves. Serve this with crackers or bread, or for morning meals. The flowers add great color.*

1 quart nasturtium blossoms
(reserve 1 flower for garnish)
1 teaspoon freshly squeezed
lemon juice

1 pound unsalted butter, softened

In a food processor, combine the flowers and lemon juice and purée thoroughly. Add the butter and continue to process until the mixture is well combined and smooth. Place in a serving dish and garnish with a nasturtium blossom. Keep refrigerated until use.

Yield: 2 cups

*CARTER HOUSE*

## Clarified Butter

Heat the butter in a small saucepan until it is completely melted. Remove all of the foam that rises to the top of the liquid. Remove from the heat, and let stand until all of the milk solids settle to the bottom of the pan. Remove the clear or clarified (drawn) butter from the pan.

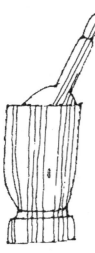

## Crème Fraîche

*In France, crème fraîche enhances many savory as well as sweet recipes, adding a tangy, nutty flavor to a dish. Crème fraîche can be added to cooking soups and sauces because it can boil without curdling. For sweets, the crème is great over warm pies and tarts or puddings and cakes. The cream is very thick, sometimes even as thick as a stick of margarine. It is unpasteurized and therefore contains the bacteria necessary to thicken it naturally. You may find an American pasteurized version of crème fraîche in some supermarkets and gourmet shops but it is expensive. Here is an easy recipe for making your own.*

1 cup heavy cream              2 tablespoons buttermilk

Combine the heavy cream and the buttermilk in a glass container. Cover and let stand at room temperature for 8 to 24 hours, or until very thick. Stir well. Cover and refrigerate for up to 10 days.

## Pesto Sauce

1 pound fresh basil leaves            ¼ cup grated Parmesan cheese
10 cloves garlic, roasted             1 cup olive oil
¼ cup roasted pine nuts               Salt and pepper

Combine all of the ingredients in a blender and purée, being careful not to overblend, thus dulling the color. Refrigerate, covered until ready to use. The sauce may be frozen.
   Yield: 2 cups

   *BEE & THISTLE INN*

## Jalapeño Dressing

*This dressing is nice served over a salad of soft lettuces and great as an aside to the Black Bean Chili (page 34).*

3 to 5 pickled jalapeño chilies, seeded
¼ cup white wine vinegar
½ teaspoon salt
½ cup packed fresh cilantro
⅔ cup olive oil

Combine all of the ingredients in a food processor except the olive oil. While whirling, slowly drizzle in the oil.

Yield: 4 to 6 servings

*OCTOBER COUNTRY INN*

## Savory Pie Crust

3 cups all-purpose flour
1 teaspoon salt
1¼ cups shortening
1 egg
1 teaspoon vinegar, any type
5 tablespoons water

Mix together the flour and salt. Cut the flour mixture into the shortening until it resembles coarse crumbs. Beat the egg with the vinegar and water; add to the shortening-and-flour mixture, just until blended. Divide the dough into 3 equal parts. (This dough keeps in the refrigerator 3 days or may be frozen indefinitely. If you freeze the dough, double wrap it in plastic and then aluminum foil. Thaw completely at room temperature before rolling out.)

Preheat the oven to 425°. Roll out the dough to a ⅛-inch thickness and place into an 8- or 9-inch pie baking dish. Be careful not to stretch the dough. Flute the edges. Bake for 8 to 10 minutes or until lightly browned. Cool.

Yield: 3 crusts

*CANYON VILLA*

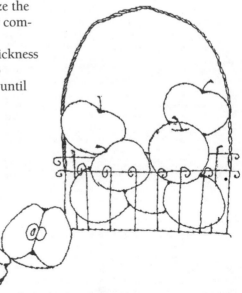

## Country Inn Quick Brown Sauce

*Be sure to check your requirements when making this for a specific recipe. You may have to increase the ingredients.*

2 tablespoons butter
1 clove garlic, finely minced
2 tablespoons all-purpose flour
1 cup beef broth or bouillon
1 teaspoon dry sherry
1 teaspoon Worcestershire sauce

1 teaspoon lemon juice
1 tablespoon mixture of dried
herbs: rosemary, thyme,
sage, basil
Salt and pepper

Melt the butter in a small saucepan over medium-high heat. Sauté the garlic but do not brown. Stir in the flour until blended. Pour in the broth and bring to a boil. Add the sherry, Worcestershire, lemon juice, and herbs. Season with salt and pepper. Cook for 2 minutes more and adjust seasonings as desired.

Yield: 1 cup

## Schumacher's Thousand Island Dressing

*John Schumacher's version of this classic salad dressing may also be used on the Reuben Strudel on page 28.*

1 cup sour cream
2 cups mayonnaise
2 eggs, hard-boiled and diced
¼-inch thick
¾ cup chili sauce
¼ cup ketchup
¼ cup red bell peppers, diced to
¼ inch

¼ cup green bell peppers, diced
to ¼ inch
1½ tablespoons chopped
parsley leaves
1 teaspoon lemon juice
1 teaspoon Worcestershire sauce
½ teaspoon black pepper
1 teaspoon salt

Combine all of the above ingredients, mixing well, gently and thoroughly. Keep refrigerated in a covered container.

Yield: 1 quart

*SCHUMACHER'S NEW PRAGUE HOTEL*

## Cranberry Conserve

*Such a dish as this was a staple in the early American pantry. It is a nice condiment to turkey and other poultry, and the thick mixture of fruits and nuts is also suitable to breads, biscuits, and scones.*

3 cups peeled, diced red apples of choice
1 navel orange, peeled and diced
2 12-ounce bags whole fresh cranberries
1½ cups diced celery
½ cup sugar
½ cup firmly packed brown sugar
1 teaspoon ground ginger
¾ cup chopped walnuts

Finely chop the fruit and celery in a food processor. Add the sugars, ginger, and walnuts. Mix well. Refrigerate.

Yield: 2 quarts

*RANDALL'S ORDINARY*

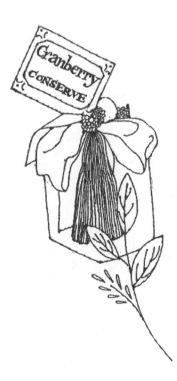

# CULINARY CRAFTS

## Candied Edible Flowers

*When we were visiting the Heritage Park B&B Inn in San Diego, California, we stopped by the Green House in Encinitas, a company that specializes in growing edible flowers and herbs which are shipped throughout the United States.*

*Edible flowers are not only a popular way to garnish a plate but are also being used in the cooking itself. In this book, we have a recipe for Nasturtium Butter (page 219) and for cooking crêpes made with edible pansies, violas, and scarlet bees (page 104). There is also a recipe that includes stuffed squash blossoms (page 53).*

*We learned from the people at The Green House just how to increase the effect and longevity of the flowers by candying or crystallizing them. There are several ways to do this. Here is one.*

| | |
|---|---|
| Edible flowers | Soft small paintbrush |
| 2 egg whites | Tweezers |
| ½ cup or more granulated sugar | Baking sheet |

Wash and dry the flowers thoroughly. Beat the eggs until frothy. Use the paintbrush to paint each flower, leaf, or petal—back and front—with the egg white. Use the tweezers to dip each coated flower into the sugar, making sure that they are completely coated. Place the flowers on a baking sheet or tray. Dry in a warm oven with the door ajar. Place the dried flowers between sheets of waxed paper or greaseproof paper in clean boxes or tins. Garnish everything from cereals to French toast, salads, desserts, and everything in-between. And, of course, encourage your guests to eat them! The flowers will keep for about 2 days.

To keep flowers for several months, dissolve a teaspoon of gum arabic (available at pharmacies) in 2 tablespoons of water. Paint the flowers with the mixture and then coat with granulated sugar. Dry on a rack in a warm place until crisp.

# How to Make Herbal Vinegars

Herbal vinegars liven up salads, stir-fry dishes, marinades, dressings, and sauces at The White Oak Inn in Danville, Ohio. In fact, they often substitute an herbal vinegar in place of any vinegar called for in a recipe. "When fresh herbs are not available through the winter, the fresh taste of the herbal vinegar brings back the sunshine of summer, and it makes wonderful gifts," explained the folks at the inn. So, we thought it would be fun to learn how they are made from the cottage-industry supplier where innkeeper Yvonne Martin buys her vinegars. Making the vinegars is really easy. "There's really no recipe per se," vinegar-maker Laura Wedemeyer told us. The best ingredients, she explained, are fresh herbs from the garden, flavorful spices, and any good quality vinegar.

## CHOOSING A VINEGAR BASE

In choosing a vinegar base, here are some of the do's and don'ts Laura told us about:

- Wine vinegar affords the most versatile base for an herbal vinegar because it is made from grapes.

- Distilled vinegar, on the other hand, is not a good choice because it is made from fermented grains and has a harsh, sour taste.

- Other bases for excellent herb vinegars include apple cider vinegar, rice wine vinegar, and champagne vinegar.

- Some specialty stores carry fruit vinegars, such as apricot, plum, and peach, which are also great bases for herbal vinegar.

## PUTTING A BASE WITH THE HERBS

The base depends on the herbs you are going to use. For example, Mediterranean herbs go well with red wine vinegar and sage with apple cider vinegar.

Try fun combinations such as lemon with chives and rosemary, or blueberries with basil. Edible flowers such as chive blossoms and nasturtiums give wonderful flavor and a beautiful tint to the vinegar.

## CHOOSING THE BOTTLES

Laura prefers making herbal vinegar in glass containers with a wide mouth, such as glass pickle jars. But the vinegar will corrode metal tops, so use plastic tops, plastic wrap, or waxed paper between the bottle and the metal top to prevent the vinegar from being tainted. The traditional thin, neat, fancy jars will also do well here.

*PUTTING IT ALL TOGETHER*

Laura prefers aging the vinegar naturally, so she advises pouring the base vinegar into the bottle to approximately three inches below the top. Rip, crush, and bend the herbs to release their oils. Then, stuff them into the bottle until the bottle is full. If you are going to add spices to the vinegar, release their flavors by heating the spices first. Place a few tablespoons of the base vinegar in a nonreactive saucepan, add the spices, and simmer for a few minutes. Add to the herbal vinegar. The only rule of thumb here is that spices are generally stronger than herbs, so you want to use a smaller proportion of spice to vinegar than herb to vinegar.

Stir the vinegar a few times, place the cap on top and set in a cool spot away from sunlight. Laura told us that this method allows the vinegar to better retain more vitamins and natural flavor.

*WHEN THE VINEGAR IS READY*

The amount of time before the vinegar will be ready depends on the particular herb(s) and how strong you want the flavor to be. Every few days, stir the vinegar and check the strength by sniffing and tasting. Once the vinegar has reached a desired pungency, strain out the herbs and/or spices.

If giving the vinegar as a gift, wrap a pretty ribbon around the neck and you might even tuck a tiny salad-dressing whisk into the ribbon.

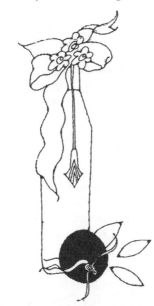

## Making Flavored Oils

Vinegar is not the only dressing that may be flavored. Nearly any type of quality oil, from olive to truffle and walnut oils, may be enhanced with a little help from some herbs and spices. This in turn enlives the flavor of salads or just about whatever you are cooking that requires the use of oil. At Kedron Valley Inn, we learned how to enrich several oils.

Chef Tom Hopewell showed us how to work with four oils that are used quite frequently in the Kedron Valley kitchen. Tom suggests using a 750-milliliter bottle that has a cork. An empty wine bottle is a good choice, for example. Allow the oils to marinate to your desired taste or serve right away.

## Truffle Oil

4 cups cold-pressed extra virgin olive oil

1 ounce truffle peeling (available in a can in gourmet shops)

Combine the oil and truffles into a 750-milliliter bottle and add the cork.

## Rosemary and Lavender Walnut Oil

*Look for an oil mixture that contains such oils as canola, corn, or soybean, and only 10 percent olive oil. It is actually called 10 percent olive oil. Or, substitute the oil mixture with 100 percent olive oil.*

2 cups oil that contains 10 percent olive oil
3 3-inch sprigs fresh rosemary

1 3-inch sprig fresh lavender
2 cups walnut oil
24 whole black peppercorns

Place the 2 cups of oil containing 10 percent olive oil into a medium saucepan over medium heat. Add the rosemary and lavender and heat for 2 minutes. Remove the pan from the heat and allow to cool. Remove the rosemary and lavender and stuff the sprigs and peppercorns into a 750-milliliter bottle. Add the cooled oil and then the walnut oil. Add the cork.

## Chili Garlic Oil

6 dried chilies of choice
4 cloves garlic

4 cups 10 percent olive oil

Preheat the oven to 350°. Split the chilies lengthwise. Peel and slice the garlic into halves.

Pour 2 tablespoons of the oil into a pie tin. Add the garlic and the chilies and roast in the oven for 20 minutes, turning the chilies and garlic every 5 minutes. Remove the pie tin from the oven and allow the roasted vegetables to cool. Stuff the chilies, garlic, and the oil into a 750-milliliter bottle. Add the remaining oil. Cork.

Note: Once the bottle is ¾ empty, you may add more oil to the roasted garlic and chilies for 1 more infusion.

## Oriental Oil

1 2-ounce piece ginger root
2 6-inch shoots lemon grass

3 cups 10 percent olive oil
1 cup sesame oil

Peel and quarter the ginger root. Peel the outer layer of the lemon grass and split the bulb end. Stuff the ginger and lemon grass into a 750-milliliter bottle. Add the oils and the cork.

## Natural Table Centerpiece: Herbal Wreath

Made the size of a large front-door wreath, this circle of herbs, tied together with wire, adds not only an attractive look to the table, but it also enhances your dinner party with its flavorful scents. The fragrant whisps of herbs of your choice permeate the air, increasing the sensuality of the dining experience. An herbal wreath for the table is a perfect companion to any table where food is present.

We learned how to make this decorative accessory at Clifton Country Inn in Charlottesville, Virginia, where garden naturalist Judy Johnson used herbs from the inn's gardens as she does for most of the greenery and living plant arrangements at Clifton.

One reason I prefer this type of centerpiece to most is that it is only a few inches high, allowing you to see your guests across the table. Judy embellished the wreath by placing a small, clear-glass container of fresh, low-cut flowers in the center. You can also consider a candle for the center of the wreath, or even make it the condiment tray for the salt and pepper, butter, etc.

I also have made this wreath much smaller, making several small wreaths around the table, near each place setting, where dinner guests can inhale the herbal perfumery more directly. I then encourage the guests to take the wreaths home and dry them. My instructions for that are simple: just place the wreath in a dry place on a wire baking rack until dried, then hang or use as desired.

The best time to make the wreath is the day of the party or dinner. Gather the herbs in the morning and put the wreath together:

1 wire coat hanger, more thick than thin
1 spool dark green florist wire
Bounteous assortment of fresh herbs such as thyme, purple basil, cinnamon and lemon basils, rue, tarragon, rosemary, sage, and dill. (Choose an assortment of colors, if possible.)
Assortment of tiny-bud flowers such as scarlet bee balm, lemon and tangerine marigolds, and tansies

The wire coat hanger forms the base of the wreath on which the herbs are fastened. Shape the hanger into a circle. It does not have to be a perfect circle as the herbs will fill it in.

Using strips of dark green wire, tie the green herbs into small bundles and then wire them to the hanger, completely encircling the hanger. Fill in with more herbs if you have gaps. Gather small bundles of purple basil and attach them to the inner circle, all around the

wreath. (The variety of the purple shading from this variety of basil gives the wreath definition.)

Tie the flowers into small bundles and add to the top of the wreath, fastening with wire. You can add as many bundles as desired.

Sprinkle some water overtop the wreath and store in the refrigerator, covered very lightly with plastic wrap. Place on the table just before guests arrive. Fluff up carefully with your fingers to release the herbal oils a bit, just before your guests sit down to the table.

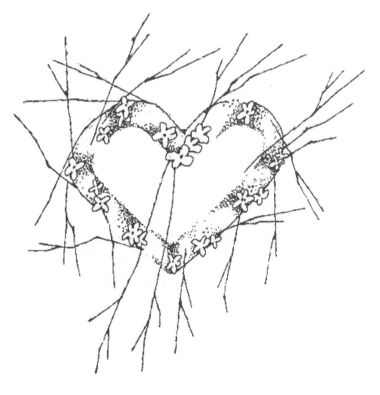

## Bean-and-Vegetable Soup Mix in Gift Jars

*While at Canyon Villa in Sedona, Arizona, I peeked in the inn's pantry and found Marion Yadon's bean soup gift jars. We showed them on camera and here is how to make them.*

*The recipe will make four gift jars (each jar makes eight cups of soup) and each jar includes a surprise packet of bundled spices. I have provided Marion's recipe for making the soup as well, so that you may pass it along with the jar if you give it as a gift.*

| | |
|---|---|
| 4 cups thinly sliced celery | 2 teaspoons ground nutmeg |
| 1 pound carrots, very thinly sliced | 2 teaspoons salt |
| 1 cup dried onion flakes, toasted | 4 cups dried white navy beans |
| ½ cup dried parsley flakes | 1⅓ cups dried lentils |
| 2 tablespoons dried whole basil | 1⅓ cups dried yellow split peas |
| 1 teaspoon garlic powder | 1⅓ cups dried small red pinto beans |
| 2 teaspoons mustard seeds | 4 spice bags (cheesecloth) |
| 2 teaspoons cracked black pepper | |

Preheat the oven to 200°. Spread the celery and carrots on baking sheets lined with parchment paper. Bake for 1 hour. Turn off the oven and cool the vegetables in the oven for 2 hours or until they are dry and crisp. Set aside.

Cut 4 8-inch squares of a double-layer cheesecloth. Spoon ¼ cup of onion flakes, 2 tablespoons of the parsley, 1½ teaspoons of the basil, ¼ teaspoon of the garlic powder and ½ teaspoon each of the mustard seeds, pepper, nutmeg, and salt into the center of each square. Bring the edges of the cheesecloth together at the top. Tie securely with a piece of burlap string or thin paper ribbon; set aside.

Sort the navy beans. Spoon ½ cup into a 1-quart jar, followed by ⅓ cup each of the lentils and split peas. Add ½ cup more navy beans and ⅓ cup of the pinto beans. Repeat the procedure with the remaining beans into 3 additional jars. Add 1 spice bag to each jar. Divide the carrots and celery evenly among the jars. Cover with metal lids and screw bands tightly.

Yield: 4 gift jars

# Bean-and-Vegetable Soup Recipe

*Either carefully print this recipe, do it in calligraphy, or type it onto a recipe card and attach it to the jars. With pinking shears, cut decorative edges around the recipe card. Punch a hole in the left-hand corner and tie around the jar with a ribbon.*

To make the soup, carefully remove the dried vegetables and spice bag from the jar. Set aside.

Wash the beans. Combine the beans and 6 cups of water in a large saucepan. Bring to a boil. Remove from the heat and let stand for 30 minutes. Drain.

Return the beans to the saucepan. Add 8 cups water, the dried vegetables, and spices from the spice bag. Discard the cheesecloth. Bring the bean mixture to a boil. Cover and reduce the heat. Simmer 1 to 1½ hours or until the beans are tender. Serve the soup with Tabasco, if desired, for flavor. (Add 2 drops Tabasco per 1 cup of soup.)

Yield: 8 cups

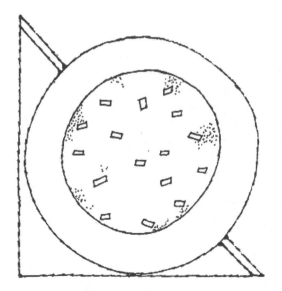

## Old Fashioned Cornucopia

*This makes a great decorative centerpiece any time of year as it symbolizes prosperity. The cornucopia is easy to do, basically involving shaping a foil frame and baking bread dough overtop the frame. You will need quite a bit of flour to make the cornucopia. When done, decorate the horn as desired, such as topping it with a ribbon, flowers, or just some greenery. Fill its cavity with colorful fruits or flowers, or use the cornucopia as a server to hold crackers with a favorite wheel of cheese beside it. I thank Randall's Ordinary for showing us how to do this.*

*DOUGH*
  Heavy-duty aluminum foil
4 cups warm water
½ cup sugar
2 tablespoons yeast
5 pounds (10½ cups flour) or more (there will be leftover dough)

2 tablespoons salt
  Nonstick cooking spray
1 egg

Crumple the foil to create an 18-inch-long cone that is about 5 inches in diameter at the widest end (mouth of the cone). Slightly curve up the tail portion.

Prepare the dough. In a large mixing bowl, combine the warm water, sugar, and yeast. Allow the yeast to proof. Then add half of the flour and all of the salt. Add as much of the remaining flour as needed to get a smooth, nonsticky dough. Knead for 8 to 10 minutes. Cover the dough with a tea towel and let rise until doubled in size.

Punch the dough down. Divide the dough into 20 equal pieces. (Cut the dough in half and cut each half into 10 pieces (each piece just a little larger than a golf ball).

These pieces will be wrapped around the foil frame. Roll 17 of the pieces out to 18- to 20-inch strips that are just slightly more than ¼-inch thick.

Roll out the remaining 3 pieces of dough to 24-inch lengths and ½-inch thickness. These pieces will be braided and used to cover the mouth of the cornucopia. Set all of the strips aside, covered with a towel to keep moist.

Preheat the oven to 350°. Generously coat the foil mold with nonstick cooking spray. Taking 1 strip at a time, begin covering the aluminum-foil frame, working your way from the pointed end to the mouth. The best way to do this is to fold the strip in half to find its center. Drape the center over the top, letting the ends fall over the

sides and tucking them under the frame, pinching the ends together. Cut away any excess dough. Continue with the strips, making sure that you overlap, slightly, if necessary, so that there is no foil showing. When you get to within 2 inches of the mouth of the horn, pick up the 3 24-inch strips and braid them together. Wrap this braid around the mouth of the horn, tucking underneath.

Place the cornucopia onto a nonstick baking sheet. Mix the egg with 2 tablespoons of water for an egg wash. Coat the entire horn with the egg wash. Bake for 45 to 55 minutes or until a light golden brown. Remove to a rack and let cool.

When cool, remove the inside aluminum foil frame. Place the horn back in the oven for 15 to 20 minutes, just enough to dry out the interior dough. Remove from oven; cool completely before use.

## Bread Bowls

*Serving more bread or soup, or even chips and undressed salads, from edible bowls is a lot of fun and a surprise for your guests. I'm holding one of Settlers Inn's bread bowls in my hands in the picture that appears on the back inside flap of the book. There I have filled it with fruit as an individual serving bowl, while avocado soup in a plastic-lined bowl appears in the center of the table spread in front of me.*

To make a bread bowl, you will need 1 recipe of the inn's Birdseed Bread on page 21 of the bread and soups section of this book. You will also need a 10-ounce ovenproof bowl to use as a mold.

Take ⅓ of the amount of 1 loaf of bread dough and roll it into a circle about 10 inches in diameter and about ¼-inch thick. Invert the ovenproof bowl on a work surface and coat well with a nonstick spray. Place the inverted bowl on a nonstick baking sheet. Place the circle of dough over the bowl. Pinch or cut the base to make a decorative rim.

Preheat the oven to 350°. Let the dough rest for 15 minutes. (You do not want this dough to rise or you will lose the shape of the bowl.) Bake the bowl in the oven and cook through, about 20 minutes or until browned. Let the bowl cool for about 10 minutes and invert. Gently pry the bowl mold from the bread bowl, using a paring knife to loosen the edges.

Yield: 3 bread bowls

# Sunflower Bread

*On the show, you saw the making of unusual breads at The Settlers Inn in Hawley, Pennsylvania. Here are their instructions on how you may do it, too.*

*Use this recipe for a basic loaf bread or for making a variety of unusually shaped breads (two of the breads appear on the back inside flap of this book) including the three that follow, for shaping into large sunflowers, serving bowls, or wreaths. When done, serve these fanciful breads, or coat with a clear varnish to preserve and use them as decorations. The sunflower bread is very large and makes a fabulous centerpiece. Have your guests cut or pull from the loaf as desired throughout the meal.*

| | |
|---|---|
| 2¾ cups water | ¼ cup sunflower seed oil |
| ⅓ cup sugar | 1¼ tablespoons fast-acting yeast |
| 1½ teaspoons salt | 8 cups all-purpose flour or more |
| 3 egg yolks | 1 cup toasted sunflower seeds |

In a large bowl, combine all of the ingredients except for the flour and the sunflower seeds. Mix in the flour and knead to form a soft, satiny dough. Allow the dough to rest 10 minutes and knead in sunflower seeds, adding any flour necessary to form a nonsticky dough. Turn the dough into a lightly greased bowl and allow to rise until double in bulk, about 1 hour.

At this point, you may make 3 loaves of regular bread instead of going on to make the art-formed breads. If making the loaves, proceed, or if not, skip the next few steps and go on to the sunflower-making section that follows.

Preheat the oven to 350°. Punch the dough down and divide into 3 equal parts, forming the pieces into loaves. Place each loaf into a 9x5-inch greased bread pan and cover each with a tea towel. Allow to rise until almost doubled. Bake in the oven for about 35 to 40 minutes or until the loaves sound hollow when tapped.

## Sunflower-Making

| | |
|---|---|
| 2 egg yolks | ¼ cup or more flax seed or |
| 2 tablespoons water | poppy seeds |
| ½ teaspoon turmeric | |

Use the entire recipe above, rolling the dough out into a 14-inch circle, instead of dividing it into 3 equal parts. In the center of the

dough, make an 8-inch round impression with a cake pan or bowl to form the center of the flower. Brush the center with an egg-yolk glaze made from a mixture of the yolks, water, and turmeric. Cover the entire center with flax seed (available at health-food stores), using more or less to achieve desired look.

To create the petals of the bread, make cuts with a sharp knife from the edge of the inner circle to the outer rim of the dough at ¾-inch intervals. Bring up some of the petals and overlap them for a more natural look. Brush the petals with more of the egg glaze. Preheat the oven to 350°. Allow the dough to rise for about 15 minutes. Place the bread in the oven and bake for 30 to 40 minutes or until the petals are golden.

Yield: 1 large sunflower bread or 3 loaf-size breads

## Bread Wreath

*The bread wreath is an all-purpose decorative accessory for any table. See it pictured on the back inside flap, resting on its side, just below the chocolate mint roulade to my right. Make a few of these loaves and have them sitting on the table as bases for a candleholder and candle, or just set them out in a pretty basket.*

| | |
|---|---|
| 1 recipe Birdseed Bread (page 21) | 2 egg yolks |
| | 2 tablespoons water |

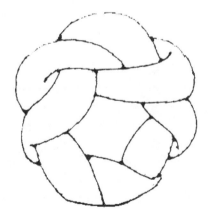

To make this wreath, use the Birdseed Bread recipe from The Settlers Inn on page 21. Take the full recipe and roll the dough out into a cylinder about 18 inches long. On a nonstick baking sheet, form the roll into a circle, pinching the ends together. With a pair of kitchen scissors, make V-shaped cuts into the top of the circle at a 45° angle—about 3 inches apart. (The cut should go quite deep, up to ½ inch before hitting the pan.) Spread the points out in alternating directions, 1 pointing away from the center of the circle. Do this around the entire circle.

Glaze the loaf with a mixture of the egg yolks and water. Sprinkle the points with the seed mixture from the Birdseed Bread. Preheat the oven to 350°. Let the bread rise about 20 minutes and bake until browned, about 25 to 35 minutes.

## Preserves Southern Style

*At Glen-Ella Springs we learned how to make preserves from fruits that are particularly abundant in Georgia. Chef Barrie Aycock told us that flexibility is the secret to making good jams and preserves. "Making preserves is not an exact science," she said. "Fruit varies in sweetness and taste, so you have to keep tasting and adjusting seasonings and cook until the batch reaches the consistency you want." She offered us these recipes to use as guides, adjusting seasonings and consistencies to individual preferences.*

## Spiced Blueberry-Peach Jam

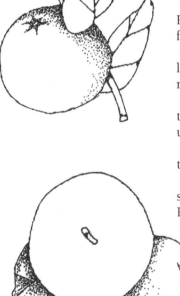

4 pounds fresh fully ripened peaches
1 quart fresh blueberries, stems removed
2 tablespoons lemon juice
½ cup water
4 cups or more (up to 5⅓ cups) sugar
½ teaspoon salt
1 teaspoon cinnamon
¼ teaspoon ground cloves
¼ teaspoon allspice

Peel the peaches, remove and discard the pits, and coarsely chop the fruit. Set aside.

In a heavy saucepan, bring to a boil the peaches, blueberries, lemon juice, and the water. Cover and turn down to a simmer for 10 minutes, stirring occasionally.

Add the 4 cups of sugar, the salt, and the spices. Return the mixture to a boil and cook rapidly, stirring constantly. After about 10 minutes, taste the mixture, adding more sugar and spices as desired.

Continue boiling the mixture vigorously, stirring until it reaches the soft-ball stage or 209° on a candy thermometer.

Test the mixture for doneness by placing a spoonful of the preserves on a chilled metal pan. When ready, it will congeal quickly. Place into sterilized jars and seal. Store in the refrigerator.

Yield: 4 pints

## Glen-Ella Springs Fig Preserves

2 pounds fresh figs
3 cups sugar
1 cup water

1 lemon, very thinly sliced,
    seeds removed

Rinse the figs and remove the stems.

Place the sugar and water in a heavy saucepan and bring the mixture to a boil over high heat. Boil for about 10 minutes until the mixture is clear and slightly thickened. Add the figs and the lemon. Bring the mixture to a boil for about 1 minute, then reduce the heat to a simmer. Simmer for about 30 minutes, stirring occasionally until the figs are tender and the syrup is thick. Taste and add more sugar or lemon juice, if desired. Pack the mixture into sterilized jars (do not remove the lemon slices). Seal in sterilized jars and store in the refrigerator.

Yield: 1½ pints

## Brandied Peaches

*Pour these over ice cream, pound cake, or just serve as the dessert itself. At Glen-Ella Springs they use locally grown freestone peaches for this recipe. It is best to store the peaches for about one month before serving.*

8 fully ripe, unblemished
    peaches
2½ cups sugar
2 cups water

1-2 cups brandy
1 quart canning jar and ring, or
    2 1-pint jars with lids

Blanch the peaches by placing the fruit into a pot of boiling water. Remove the peaches and let them cool just enough to handle. Rub off the skins. Prick the peaches all over with a sterile needle. (This will allow the flavors to soak through.) Cut the peaches in half and remove and discard the pits.

In a medium saucepan, combine the sugar and water and boil for 10 minutes. Cook the peaches a few at a time in the sugar syrup until tender when pierced with a fork, about 5 minutes.

Transfer the peaches into a sterilized 1-quart canning jar. Pour syrup ½ to ¾ of the way up the jar and fill the rest with brandy. Close the jar and process in a simmering water bath at 185° for 10 to 15 minutes. Store for 1 month before using.

Yield: 1 quart

# Cooking in Your Fireplace at Home

Taping a show at historic Randall's Ordinary in North Stonington, Connecticut, was anything but ordinary. The word *ordinary* was colloquial for a tavern of the day where meals could be had and politics debated. And life has not changed much in more than two hundred years at Randall's. The inn was originally the home of military Colonel William Randall, who helped stave off the British invasion of Stonington. The hearth is still the heart of this home.

Randall's is probably the only inn in America where you can eat a breakfast, lunch, and dinner of food prepared over an open hearth.

Chef and former Randall's owner Cindy Clark told us how we can do this in our own fireplaces at home. "The main ingredient you need," she said, "is confidence." Cindy, who started open-hearth cooking in her own home, had even more courage to rehabilitate the old Randall's homestead (the oldest part of the house dates to 1650) and serve meals over the hearth to overnight guests.

If you have a fireplace at home, Cindy encourages you to cook in it for the smoky flavor and for the sheer pleasure of it with friends.

Here are a few basic tips.

• Use hardwoods such as red or white oak or fruit woods such as apple. These tend not to coat the chimney with creosote.

• Most newer homes do not have rumford fireplaces, which have narrow hearths and create a fabulous draft. So stack the logs campfire style, which creates a better draft.

• The fire should be roaring hot before starting any cooking.

• Although you can use heavy pottery, the best kitchenware to use comes in the form of cast-iron antiques or reproductions. You can find them at antiques shops and in country catalogs. Mainly you will need:

  • Dutch oven for baking casseroles and some things like baked macaroni and cheese. The pot is filled with the food and placed over hot embers. The lid is put in place and hot coals are placed on top, smothering the lid.

  • Whirling broiler for broiling steaks, seafood, chops, and such. It is a small circular grill that you place over hot embers, away from the main fire. You whirl the grill around to cook evenly.

  • Reflector oven that resembles half of a steel drum whose open side faces the fire. A spit is placed inside for roasting large cuts of beef, lamb, and poultry.

- An iron trivet is always needed for resting hot utensils, such as forks and spatulas.
- Griddles are flat and hang above the fire for sautéing vegetables and meats or making flapjacks.
- Soups are made in black kettles or caldrons that also hang over the fire.
- A spider pan is a round small skillet-like pan with higher sides and three legs to sit in front of the fire and bake cornbreads.
- An iron crane or long heavy bracket attached to the inside walls of your fireplace serves as the holder for the kettles and griddles. Cranes can be found at antiques stores or be made by a blacksmith to fit your own hearth.

Cook over an open fire

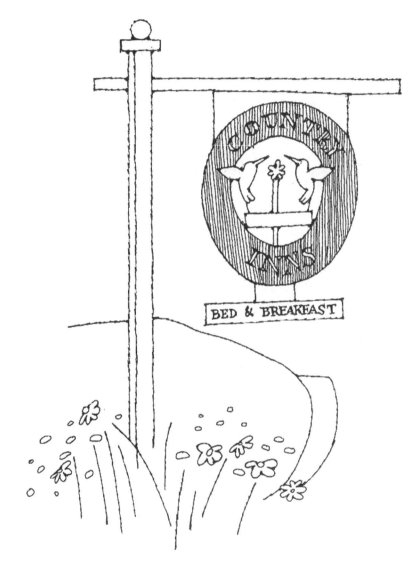

# INN DIRECTORY

### ANTRIM 1844

Chef Sharon Ashburn
Innkeepers Richard
& Dort Mollet
30 Trevanion Road
Taneytown, MD 21787
Phone: 410-756-6812
Rooms: 13
Meals Served: Breakfast, Dinner
Recipes: Pages 39, 48, 55, 62, 64, 72, 73, 88, 191

A sprawling plantation-style inn with guest cottages and dining in an elegantly restored old brick smokehouse. European antiques mix well with the bright and cheerfully decorated guest rooms and the personality of the zany innkeepers, Richard and Dort Mollet.

### BEE & THISTLE INN

Chef Francis Brooke-Smith
Innkeepers Bob & Penny,
Lori & Jeff Nelson
100 Lyme Street
Old Lyme, CT 06371
Phone: 203-434-1667
Rooms: 11 plus 1 cottage
Meals Served: Breakfast, Lunch, Afternoon Tea, Dinner
Recipes: Pages 60, 76, 84, 98, 105, 139, 175, 190, 220

The banks of the winding Lieutenant River scallop the backyard of this gracious and traditional country inn where afternoon tea is served several times a week in the parlor in true English form. Canopy beds, ladderback chairs, and an English garden are the backdrop to an award-winning kitchen.

### CANYON VILLA

Chef Marion Yadon
Innkeepers Chuck
& Marion Yadon
125 Canyon Circle Drive
Sedona, AZ 86351
Phone: 520-284-1226
Rooms: 11
Meals Served: Breakfast, Snacks
Recipes: Pages 2, 7, 14, 18, 54, 57, 63, 221

Huge red rock formations peer through the sprawling windows at this Southwestern-style bed-and-breakfast. Gourmet morning meals set the tone for an elegant but comfortable stay in rooms that are named after regional wild flowers such as: Spanish Bayonet, Mariposa Suite, Evening Primrose, and Strawberry Cactus. Every detail has been attended to in this award-winning inn.

243

## CARTER HOUSE

Chef Christi Carter
Innkeepers Mark
& Christi Carter
301 L Street
Eureka, CA 95501
Phone: 707-444-8062
Rooms: 23
Meals Served: Breakfast, Dinner
Recipes: Pages 10, 11, 15, 66, 105, 148, 202, 204, 208, 219

Innkeepers Christi and Mark Carter have worked hard to build their property into a national centerpiece. The food is California style—very inventive, very inviting, very delicious. Mark created a Bon Bonière or old-style ice cream parlor for to display Christi's talent for creating show-stopping confections.

## CHALET SUZANNE

Chef John Taylor
Innkeepers Carl & Vita Hinshaw
3800 Chalet Suzanne Drive
Lake Wales, FL 33853
Phone: 813-676-6011
Rooms: 30
Meals Served: Breakfast, Lunch, Dinner
Recipes: Pages 1, 12, 45, 59, 63, 130, 134, 161, 201

In a fairytale atmosphere, this is a personal country inn where even the antique china and crystal at the dinner table comes from the private collection of the inn's owners. The Hinshaws can their own soups on the premises— soups that are sold at fine guest shops and gourmet stores. This is one of Florida's few country inns.

## CHÂTEAU DU SUREAU

Chef Kimberly D. Schor
Innkeeper Erna Kubin-Clanin
48688 Victoria Lane
Oakhurst, CA 93644
Phone: 209-683-6800
Rooms: 10
Meals Served: Breakfast, Lunch, Dinner
Recipes: Pages 94, 95, 140, 180, 186

Closer than the French countryside, that same European spirit awaits the guests of Erna Kubin-Clanin, the innkeeper whose dream it was to build her own castle someday. Furnished to perfection but very inviting, the inn also hosts magnificent gardens— one with a live chessboard. A gem of an inn, Château du Sureau is visited by many culinary celebrities who say they don't want to leave.

## CHECKERBERRY INN

Chef Gregory Lutes
Innkeepers John & Susan Graff
62644 C.R. 37
Goshen, IN 46526
Phone: 219-642-4445
Rooms: 11
Meals Served: Breakfast, Snacks,
Dinner
Recipes: Pages 40, 80, 116, 162,
174, 207

In the midst of Indiana Amish country, this modern farmhouse-style inn is a mélange of Asian, country, Victorian, romantic, and other styles rolled into one. The dining room sports pressed linens, flowers and the eclectic touch of elegant, woven rush-and-bark chairs. A rare find in the middle of the country.

## CLIFTON COUNTRY INN

Chef Craig Hartman
Innkeepers Craig
& Donna Hartman
Route 13, Box 26
Charlottesville, VA 22901
Phone: 804-971-1800
Rooms: 14
Meals Served: Breakfast,
Afternoon Snacks and Tea,
Dinner
Recipes: Pages 5, 43, 58, 74, 106,
142, 169, 194

They toast Thomas Jefferson here frequently, as the inn was once the home of the third president's daughter, Martha. Every night in the parlor, just before dinner, the chef invites diners to gather around the fire so that he can tell what is on the menu and pour all a sampling from the evening's suggested wine list.

## GINGERBREAD MANSION INN

Chef Larry Martin
Innkeeper Ken Torbert
P.O. Box 40
Ferndale, CA 95536
Phone: 707-786-9667
Rooms: 11
Meals Served: Breakfast,
Afternoon Tea
Recipes: Pages 6, 9, 13, 17, 25,
209, 210, 213, 214

In the Victorian village of Ferndale, Gingerbread Mansion Inn is one of America's best-known bed-and-breakfast inns. Built in 1899, the house still sports spacious clawfoot tubs in highly decorated guest rooms. The gingerbread trim is everywhere. Gourmet breakfasts and lush afternoon teas delight the guests.

## GLEN-ELLA SPRINGS INN

Chef Barrie Aycock
Innkeepers Bobby
& Barrie Aycock
Bear Gap Road
Clarkesville, GA 30523
Phone: 706-754-7295
Rooms: 16
Meals Served: Breakfast, Dinner
Recipes: Pages 51, 52, 120, 152, 155, 217

Off the beaten path in the Georgia mountains, Glen-Ella Springs is a warm, rustic, and welcoming, kick-off-your-shoes kind of place where guests gather on porch rockers or in front of the living room's stone fireplace. Delicious, comfortable American and New Southern cuisines—with a bent toward the gourmet—lead the bill of fare.

## HERITAGE PARK B&B INN

Chef Ralph Randau
Innkeepers Charles
& Nancy Helsper
2470 Heritage Park Row
San Diego, CA 92110
Phone: 619-295-7088
Rooms: 9
Meals Served: Breakfast, Dinner
by reservation
Recipes: Pages 44, 46, 109, 131, 152, 200, 206

Antiques abound at this traditional Victorian inn where decor and amenities are all updated and done in exquisite taste. Guest chambers have themes, and while most B&Bs don't serve dinner, they do at Heritage Park, making it a romantic, candlelit occasion—by reservation only.

## HIGHLAND LAKE INN

Chef Larc Lindsey
Innkeepers Kerry & Larc Lindsey
Highland Lake Drive
Flat Rock, NC 28731
Phone: 704-693-6812
Rooms: 20 plus 10 cabins and 5 cottages
Meals Served: Breakfast, Dinner
Recipes: Pages 8, 17, 19, 50, 51, 112, 124, 126, 130, 154, 170

The Lindsey family started this inn after they bought it as a summer camp. Although a bit larger than most country inns, the family attention to guest service is everywhere, especially on the table. The chef gathers most of the ingredients right from the family's own organic greenhouse and spacious produce garden. The atmosphere here is relaxed and perfect for families and outdoor-minded romantics.

## INN OF THE ANASAZI

Chef Peter Zimmer
Innkeeper Merry Stephen
113 Washington Avenue
Santa Fe, NM 87501
Phone: 505-988-3030
Rooms: 59
Meals Served: Breakfast, Lunch,
Dinner
Recipes: Pages 16, 29, 33, 91,
147, 156, 165

The mood is happy but mystical and very Santa Fe, and the food matches the atmosphere with modern Southwestern gourmet dishes created by a vivacious young staff. Although the Anasazi is a little larger than most country inns, the staff here is most attentive and the rooms have everything you need—including individuality.

## KEDRON VALLEY INN

Chef Tom Hopewell
Innkeepers Max
& Merrily Comins
Route 106, P. O. Box 145
South Woodstock, VT 05071
Phone: 802-457-1473
Rooms: 27
Meals Served: Breakfast, Dinner
Recipes: Pages 123, 157, 163, 178

Museum-quality family quilts are throughout this award-winning inn. In horse country, Kedron Valley brings back the romance of horse-drawn sleighs through hills of snow in winter, and guests take in the sun by a spring-fed pond on the inn's grounds in summer. Guest chambers are modern with antiques. The food here is so memorable, it's hard to leave it behind.

## NEWCASTLE INN

Chef Chris Sprague
Innkeepers Ted & Chris Sprague
River Road
Newcastle, ME 04553
Phone: 207-563-5685
Rooms: 15
Meals Served: Breakfast, Dinner
Recipes: Pages 42, 69, 77, 99,
115, 167, 172

Chris Sprague creates meals that critics love to write about. This small inn is filled with the flavors of the region and the heart of the innkeeper, which is very big.

## OCTOBER COUNTRY INN

Chef Patrick Runkel
Innkeepers Richard Sims &
Patrick Runkel
P.O. Box 66
Bridgewater Corners, VT 05035
Phone: 802-672-3412
Rooms: 10
Meals Served: Breakfast, Dinner
Recipes: Pages 24, 30, 34, 36, 37, 82, 89, 101, 120, 135, 151, 159, 160, 212, 221

Come down in the morning and choose from a large collection of ceramic mugs given to the innkeepers by former guests. This is a very informal inn where the heart of the home is Chef Patrick Runkel's kitchen, which takes you around the world in eighty days. Each weekend, Patrick creates a menu from a different country. It's scrumptious and what a culinary education.

## OLD DROVERS INN

Chef François de Melogue
Innkeepers Alice Pitcher
& Kemper Peacock
Old Route 22
Dover Plains, NY 12522
Phone: 914-832-9311
Rooms: 4
Meals Served: Breakfast, Dinner
Recipes: Pages 61, 114, 127, 137, 173, 199

A member of the prestigious Relais & Chateau, this exciting restored inn hosts a classically trained chef who knows his wines and loves talking about them to his guests. Seasonal game and seafood are specialities of the house that originated in the 1750s as a hangout for cowboys or drovers. The candlelight against the rustic wood and stone sets a soft, romantic mood in the Taproom or Library where dinner is served.

## RANDALL'S ORDINARY

Chef Cindy Clark
General Manager Bill Foakes
P.O. Box 243
North Stonington, CT 06359
Phone: 203-599-4540
Rooms: 15
Meals Served: Breakfast, Lunch, Dinner
Recipes: Pages 26, 31, 35, 90, 150, 185, 187, 198, 223

Randall's Ordinary is about as primitive as you can get in this country when it comes to a country inn. The dining rooms are warm and romantic, left the way they were in the 1600s. Something from every meal of the day is cooked here on an open hearth. The flavor is almost unmatched.

## ROWELL'S INN

Chef Beth Davis
Innkeepers Lee & Beth Davis
RR #1 Box 267-D
Simonsville, VT 05143
Phone: 802-875-3658
Rooms: 6
Meals Served: Breakfast, Dinner
Recipes: Pages 71, 92, 128, 158, 162, 184, 212, 215

When you think of a traditional country inn, a place like Rowell's comes to mind. This small, former stagecoach stop is warm, friendly, beautifully decorated, and seats only twelve for dinner. There are plenty of common rooms, including one with a small pool table and adjoining bar.

## SAN YSIDRO RANCH

Chef Gerard Thompson
General Manager Janis Clapoff
900 San Ysidro Lane
Montecito, CA 93108
Phone: 805-969-5046
Rooms: 43 rooms plus 21 cottages
Meals served: Breakfast, Lunch, Dinner
Recipes: Pages 68, 86, 97, 110, 150, 176, 189

Nestled behind the hills of Santa Barbara, this special place boasts an ocean view and lots of active sports. A relaxing spa treatment may be the order of the day, just before sitting down in The Stonehouse Restaurant.

## SCHUMACHER'S NEW PRAGUE HOTEL

Chef John Schumacher
Innkeepers John
& Kathleen Schumacher
212 W. Main Street
New Prague, MN 56071
Phone: 612-758-2133
Rooms: 11
Meals Served: Breakfast, Lunch,
Dinner
Recipes: Pages 28, 49, 87, 132,
144, 154, 179, 222

A touch of Old Bavaria earmarks this inn. Rooms are decorated with great taste and charm. The inn is the pride of Chef/owner John Schumacher and his wife, Kathleen. The food is scrumptious.

## SETTLERS INN

Chef Grant Genzlinger
Innkeepers Grant
& Jeanne Genzlinger
Four Main Avenue
Hawley, PA 18428
Phone: 717-226-2993
Rooms: 18
Meals Served: Breakfast, Lunch,
Dinner
Recipes: Pages 3, 5, 21, 38, 41,
53, 81, 104, 127, 196, 216

Regional cooking is the hallmark of this quaint inn. The inn prides itself on organic ingredients supplied by area farmers and other purveyors. An English-style tavern offers a libation and social gathering around the fireplace. Bread-making is a specialty here.

## SIGN OF THE SORREL HORSE

Chef Jon Atkin
Innkeeper Monique
Gaumont-Lanvin
4424 Old Easton Road
Doylestown, PA 18901
Phone: 215-230-9999
Rooms: 5
Meals Served: Breakfast, Lunch,
Dinner
Recipes: Pages 39, 122, 124, 144,
145, 165, 197

Chef Jon Atkin's crisp British accent is only part of the atmosphere here. Jon's enthusiasm for cooking comes across in the dining room, where he serves modern and French cuisine without a British accent.

## STONEHEDGE INN

Chef David Blessing
General Manager Levent Bozkurt
160 Pawtucket Boulevard
Tyngsboro, MA 01879
Phone: 508-649-4400
Rooms: 30
Meals served: Breakfast, Lunch,
Dinner
Recipes: Pages 70, 96, 100, 102,
133, 192

An elegant country inn with a spa/resort atmosphere and facilities. High teas served daily and an award-winning wine cellar are just some of the inviting reasons to visit this inn. Dining here is considered an art, combining French and Mediterranean styles with a New England flair.

## VICTORIAN VILLA

Chef/Owner Ron Gibson
Innkeeper Cindy Coats
601 North Broadway Street
Union City, MI 49094
Phone: 517-741-7383
Rooms: 10
Meals Served: Breakfast,
Afternoon Tea, Dinner
Recipes: Pages 47, 119, 134, 149,
166, 182, 188

When you meet Ron Gibson, you will think surely he is a left-over from the Victorian era. Everything suggests Victorian days—from ice cream socials to old-fashioned dinner theatre and readings beside a filigreed gazebo. Rooms are decorated in high Victorian with quilts made by the Amish. The inn once served only breakfast, but thanks to great demand for Ron's special Victorian suppers it is now a country inn, serving dinner regularly. A visit here is truly a step back in time that you don't mind at all.

## WHITE OAK INN

Chef Yvonne Martin
Innkeepers Ian & Yvonne Martin
29683 Walhonding Road
Danville, OH 43014
Phone: 614-599-6107
Rooms: 10
Meals Served: Breakfast, Dinner
Recipes: Pages 27, 32, 79, 118, 136, 143, 183, 211

Gracious gourmet dining in a country setting best describes Yvonne Martin's oasis in the middle of nowhere. A former Canadian resident, Yvonne and her husband, Ian, are true hosts who know how to pamper.

## Y. O. RANCH

Chef Bertie Varner
Mountain Home, Texas 78058
Phone: 210-640-3222
Rooms: 9
Recipes: Pages 22, 23, 67, 117, 136, 138, 148, 181, 208

Historic Texas log homes flank the Y.O. Ranch and serve as guest quarters. Only two hours from San Antonio, the ranch has the rustic beauty of Texas lore—from the brushed tumbleweeds to the Longhorn cattle roaming wild. The Schreiner family welcomes guests to a unique experience, including real cowboys and original artifacts from the Wild West.

Note: Not all of the meals listed for each inn are served every day of the week, and meal service is subject to change. Call the inn in advance to verify specific meal service on any given day.

# INNDEX

*Special Thanks To:*

DuPont

No-Stick Systems®

Meyer Permaglide and Permaglide Pro

Le Creuset's Haute Cuisine

Hestia International

Chicago Metallic, The Baking Company

Berndes SignoCast

Budget Rent a Car

Progressions of Rockville, Maryland

G Street Fabrics

Nicholas Mosse Pottery

Cloth & Clay

Toscana Imports

Char Designs of Santa Fe

Looking West of Sedona

Shepherds of Australia

Schieffelin & Somerset Co.

# About the Author

Gail Greco is the co-executive producer and the host of *Country Inn Cooking with Gail Greco*, a Public Television series presented by Maryland Public TV.

"Gail is a sort of Martha Stewart of country inns," describes Chef Craig Hartman of Clifton Country Inn. She has been a chronicler of country inn cooking and travel for more than a dozen years. She was the first to author a series of books showing readers how to bring the ideas found at the inns into their own homes.

"My suitcase would be bulging with new ways to decorate, new recipes to try, and new plants to grow in my garden," says the author. "This propelled me to write it all up for the folks at home."

Gail wrote *Secrets of Entertaining from America's Best Innkeepers; Tea-Time at the Inn,* a Better Homes and Gardens Book Club selection; *Great Cooking with Country Inn Chefs,* selected by *USA Today* as one of the top ten cookbooks of 1992; *The Romance of Country Inns: A Decorating Book for Your Home; A Country Inn Breakfast; Breakfast and Brunches;* and three *World Class Cuisine* TV companion books.

In addition to her work with American inns, Gail is a food editor for *World Class Cuisine,* a popular television show on the Discovery channel, highlighting chefs of restaurants, hotels, and small inns in Europe. She is a member of the advisory board of the Professional Association of Innkeepers International and is a member of the International Association of Culinary Professionals.